T0301256

Financial Constraints and Market Failures

Financial Constraints and Market Failures
The Microfoundations of New Keynesian Macroeconomics

Edited by

Marcello Messori
Professor of Economics, University of Rome, Italy

Edward Elgar
Cheltenham, UK • Northampton, MA, US

© Marcello Messori 1999

Published by
Edward Elgar Publishing Limited
Glensanda House
Montpellier Parade
Cheltenham
Glos GL50 1UA
UK

Edward Elgar Publishing, Inc.
136 West Street
Suite 202
Northampton
Massachusetts 01060
USA

A catalogue record for this book
is available from the British Library

Library of Congress Cataloguing in Publication Data
Financial constraints and market failures : the microfoundations of
    the new Keynesian macroeconomics / edited by Marcello Messori.
        1. Keynesian economics. 2. Neoclassical school of economics.
    3. Macroeconomics. I. Messori, Marcello.
    HB99.7.F54   1999
    330.15'6—dc21   98–42882
                                                                                    CIP

ISBN 1 85898 625 7

Printed and bound in Great Britain by Biddles Ltd, Guildford and King's Lynn

Contents

List of Contributors

Pier Giorgio Ardeni, University of Bologna, Italy

Andrea Boitani, Catholic University of Milan

Mirella Damiani, University of Perugia, Italy

Domenico Delli Gatti, Catholic University of Milan

Mauro Gallegati, University of Teramo, Italy

Marcello Messori, University of Rome II "Tor Vergata", Italy

Roberto Tamborini, University ot Trento, Italy

Preface

This book synthetizes the main results reached by the research activity of an Italian study group on the "New Keynesian economics", formed at the beginning of the Nineties and supported by the Italian Research National Council. The book is divided into two parts. The first part, which includes three papers, analyzes the theoretical set-up of the new Keynesian approaches, compares their results to those reached by the New classical economics, and grafts a number of new Keynesian concepts into a sequence framework. The second part of the book which also includes three papers, analyzes the working of two markets which play a crucial role in the new Keynesian models, that is, the credit and the labor markets; moreover, it analyzes the impact of financial constraints on the 'real' side of the economic system.

In chapter 1, Ardeni, Boitani, Delli Gatti and Gallegati start from the unsolved problems of Keynes' theory and from the related criticisms raised by the orthodox approaches to come to the theoretical solutions suggested by the two main streams of the new Keynesian economics: the stream centred on nominal and real rigidities in markets with imperfect competition, and that centred on asymmetric information, could be strengthened by their mutual integration. In chapter 2, Tamborini investigates the New Keynesian macroeconomics of imperfect capital markets in a general-equilibrium framework. In particular he finds that the New Keynesian claim that supplyside effects of monetary variables alter output and employment in rational-expectations equilibrium has not general validity, but depends on the behaviour of labour supply. This result suggests that research should be extended beyond financial constraints on aggregate supply. In chapter 3, Messori runs again through Keynes' shortcomings and through a critical reconstruction of the two new Keynesian streams analyzed in chapter 1, in order to show that the models based on information asymmetries offer more stimulating results than those based on markets with imperfect competition. The former stream too has, however, unsolved analytical problems which become clearer if embedded in a sequence analysis.

This shows that (i) the three chapters included in the first part of the book offer an overview of the new Keynesian approaches and a comparison between these approaches and other orthodox and heterodox views, but that (ii) they differ from each other in their analytical and explanatory point of view. In particular, chapter 1 and chapter 3 have a number of overlapping topics but work out different interpretations; moreover, while chapters 1 and 3 are mainly critical surveys, chapter 2 compares the new Keynesian and the new classical economics by altering few variables of a unitary basic model. These differences do not prevent the three chapters from sharing a general statement: the new Keynesian approaches open promising ways of research, but leave unsolved a number of analytical problems. As a consequence, the second part of the book aims at elaborating solutions for some of these problems. The possible solutions are based on the analysis of specific markets, in particular the labour and the capital markets, and are developed by three original papers.

A first problem concerns the explanation of credit rationing, which makes one of the most binding constraints in the capital market. The new Keynesian models based on asymmetric information, prove the possibility of credit rationing by assuming that all the projects financed are indivisible, that is of fixed size; however, new Keynesians apply these analytical results to the general case of divisible projects. In chapter 4, Ardeni and Messori obtain robust under-financing and rationing results with projects of variable size. In their model firms' quality is unobservable by banks, and this information asymmetry raises persistent adverse selection effects. A second problem concerns the determination of unemployment equilibria. The new Keynesian models reach these Keynesian equilibria by focussing on a separate labour market affected by various imperfections. In chapter 5, Boitani and Damiani extend the analysis to a goods market with imperfect competition. They show that (i) the various market imperfections reinforce each other in generating inefficient equilibria, and that (ii) an increase in these imperfections, combined with nominal rigidities, reduces the anti-cyclical effectiveness of monetary policy. This last result leads to a third problem. Several new Keynesian models maintain that monetary policy affects real output since the bankruptcy risk sets a limit to production decisions, and hence aggregate supply is an increasing function of the net worth firms'. However, these models do not analyze the aggregate demand side. In chapter 6, Delli Gatti and Gallegati fill this gap, and determine macroeconomic equilibria under alternative monetary regimes. In particular, they show that monetary policy can be effective even with rational expectations.

This book can have various utilizations. Its first part offers to undergraduate students a synthetic but careful survey of the most important new Keynesian approaches, and locate them in the current debate. Compared to other surveys, it has the advantage of putting together the models with nominal and real rigidities and those with information asymmetries, and of comparing these two types of models from different perspectives. In this respect, the overlaps between chapters 1 and 3 could represent a strength point instead of a redundancy of the book. This first part of the book can also be a useful reference for graduate students and professional economists. It does not only allow a brushing up of the specific new Keynesian topics, but it also points out a number of unsolved analytical problems. And the second part of the book offers to graduate students and professional economists possible analytical solutions to these problems. In this respect, the heterogeneity of the different papers which form the book could become a way to get original results.

As stated above, this book is the result of a long research activity developed by an Italian study group. It is thus impossible to acknowledge here the contribution of all the people who have provided us with helpful comments and criticism through time. Besides the colleagues who read single papers, we are particularly indebted to those who shared specific stages of our research activity: Elettra Agliardi, Mario Amendola, Claudio De Vincenti, Massimo Egidi, Axel Leijonhufvud, Fabrizio Mattesini, Hyman Minsky, Enrico Saltari, Giorgio Rodano, Piero Tedeschi, Teodoro Togati, Gerd Weinrich. We are also indebted to an anonymous referee who carefully read the whole typescript and made stimulating remarks. Finally, we thank the board of Società Italiana degli Economisti who gave us the permission to publish chapters 1 and 3 which are slightly revised English versions of two Italian papers already published in *La nuova economia keynesiana*, edited by Marcello Messori, il Mulino: Bologna.

Marcello Messori

1. The New Keynesian Economics: A Survey[*]

Pier Giorgio Ardeni

Andrea Boitani

Domenico Delli Gatti

Mauro Gallegati

1. FROM THE DECLINE OF THE NEOCLASSICAL SYNTHESIS TO THE RISE OF NEW KEYNESIAN ECONOMICS

Names often contain a fragment of history. This also applies to *New Keynesian Economics* (NKE),[1] whose theoretical frame of reference — and this should be pointed out immediately — is not Keynes' *General Theory* but the neoclassical synthesis in the Hicks-Modigliani-Klein formulation. In the 1970s, the crisis of the Phillips curve led to a revision of the IS-LM model which proceeded on at least two levels: the microeconomic foundations of aggregate relations and the reformulation of an aggregate supply curve which replaced the one more or less directly derived from the Phillips curve.[2] NKE therefore sets out to construct a sort of sub-system of aggregate supply to be integrated with the sub-system of aggregate demand largely taken from the IS-LM apparatus, the aim being to develop a macroeconomic model with solid micro-foundations. In so doing, however, NKE ends up by going well beyond the neoclassical synthesis.

In the course of this introduction we shall seek to identify the most direct

---

[*] We wish to acknowledge M. Amendola, M. Damiani, C. De Vincenti, M. Messori, G. Rodano, E. Saltari, R. Tamborini and G. Weinrich for helpful comments on an earlier draft of this paper.

[1] The origin of the term 'New Keynesian Economics' is a matter of some debate in the literature. Phelps (1990) attributes the neologism 'New Keynesian' to Parkin (1984). Reference to a well-established paradigm is made by Rotemberg (1987) and Greenwald and Stiglitz (1987: 308).

[2] Topics addressed, and already contained in the title, of the manifesto for a research programme, *Microeconomic Foundations of Employment and Inflation Theory*, Phelps (1970).

1

antecedents of NKE by following the linking theme of the construction of an aggregate supply curve alternative to that derived from the Phillips curve, and of its micro-foundations.

1.1. Neoclassical criticisms

According to NKE, Keynes' main contribution to macroeconomics can be summed up in two propositions: (a) contrary to the claims of New Classical Macroeconomics (NCM), changes in the nominal quantity of money produce real effects (that is money is not neutral); (b) it is likely that coordination failures are endemic — that is, they are due to the allocative inefficiency of the price system. The most striking large-scale manifestations of such inefficiency are mass involuntary *unemployment* and *fluctuations* in income (the alternating pattern of booms and slumps is none other than the manifestation of the failure of the market).[3]

The IS-LM model of the neoclassical synthesis is able to give effective specification to these propositions by adopting the hypothesis of rigid nominal prices and wages. If, in fact, workers fix a reservation wage, then prices too (because of the Lipsey relation) are rigid. Increases in the quantity of money therefore have real effects, and involuntary unemployment and disequilibrium fluctuations may ensue. However, in this model the rigidity of nominal wages is simply assumed. It thus becomes possible to argue that the entire old-style Keynesian edifice, unlike that of Keynes himself, is based on an *ad hoc* and consequently unreliable assumption. Once rigidity is removed, and taking appropriate account of the wealth effect, it is possible to maintain that the Keynesian model is a special case within the more general neoclassical approach.[4]

Furthermore, in the 1970s, the Phillips curve — on which was based the practically universal 'convergence without consensus' (Gordon, 1976: 53) of the previous decade — became unstable, while stagflation highlighted the crisis of that 'fact in search of a theory'. The crisis in the empirical evidence for the trade-off between inflation and unemployment also affected the model of the neoclassical synthesis, for which such a trade-off was fundamental.

---

[3]   This summary of Keynes' contribution closely reflects the research themes pursued by the Marshallian school of Cambridge (whose leading members, besides Marshall, were Pigou, Robertson, Hawtrey, Lavington and the younger Keynes); themes which centred on short-period fluctuations in income and employment and on the long-period neutrality of money.
[4]   Modigliani (1963) points out other conditions, besides the wealth effect, for the flexibility of wages to have neoclassical effects — including the hypothesis, subsequently ignored by both NCM and NKE, of perfect information.

At the end of the 1960s, Friedman (1968) and Phelps (1967) showed that nominal rigidity and rational behaviour are incompatible, and that the Phillips curve therefore had to be reformulated in order to incorporate expectations of inflation. The central thesis of this criticism was a powerful one, and it went beyond the controversy on the stability of the Phillips relation and on the effectiveness of economic policy: no theory can be constructed without postulating a maximising behaviour which — as Samuelson had argued years before — constitutes the indispensable foundation of economic analysis. The time was ripe for the neoclassical counter-revolution.

There still remained, of course, the problem of justifying a positive rate of unemployment in a Walrasian environment, but on the occasion of his presidential address to the *American Economic Association*, Friedman provided a definition of the *natural rate of unemployment* (Friedman, 1968: 8). Thanks to the hypothesis of the natural rate unemployment, monetarism appeared able to explain the persistence of a positive rate of unemployment and to deny a trade-off between unemployment and inflation in the long run.

The revision of the Phillips curve was not restricted, of course, to disputing the validity of the fine tuning of Keynesian economic policies. Since, to all effects, the Phillips curve in the IS-LM model represented an aggregate supply curve, the puzzle that the macroeconomist had to solve in the 1970s was how to derive some aggregate supply curve from first principles. In the first half of the decade, stagflation due to a series of supply shocks disproved the hypothesis of the trade-off, so that the empirical evidence further emphasised the importance of aggregate supply.

1.2. Keynesian criticisms

Almost simultaneously with the monetarist revision of the IS-LM model, Leijonhufvud (1967, 1968) published a series of works in which he distinguished 'Keynesian economics from the economics of Keynes' (see also Clower, 1965). In Keynesian economics, characterized by perfect information, the existence of nominal rigidities inhibits the allocative function of the price system, which consists of 'coordinating' individual decisions by means of the market. In this approach, Keynes is a 'classical' economist who, by emphasising the short-term rigidity of nominal wages, views involuntary unemployment as resulting from market failures.

Conversely, 'the economics of Keynes' blames coordination failures not on the inability of agents — as embodied in price stickiness — to seize the opportunities offered by the system, but on the presence of imperfect information, from which, moreover, nominal rigidities may derive as a side-effect.

Leijonhufvud warns that only in the case of *ad hoc* nominal rigidities —

3

that is, rigidities which do not derive from imperfect information — can the tools-box employed by the orthodox economist be rescued; otherwise, the introduction of incomplete information has devastating effects on static theory *à la* Walras, and frustrates the construction itself of the demand and supply curves.

From the early 1970s onwards, the hypothesis of nominal rigidities was adopted in non-Walrasian models (Barro and Grossman, 1971; Benassy, 1975) which, following the formulations of Leijonhufvud, and of Hicks (1965) based on the fixed price method, postulated the possibility of exchanges at 'false' prices and of adjustment through changes in quantities. The limited success of non-Walrasian models was due, besides their assumption of nominal rigidities not derived from first principles, on their inability to generate the Keynesian reverse of Say's law; namely the result that aggregate demand creates its own supply (on the inability of these models to account for effective demand failures, see Leijonhufvud, 1992: 300). In fixed-price non-Walrasian models, in fact, the equilibrium quantity equals the minimum between aggregate supply and demand (the short-side rule).

Therefore if supply is greater than demand, an increase in the latter will produce an increase in production; conversely, if demand is greater than supply, its contraction will have no effect. The assumption of non-competitive markets whereby it is possible to have changes in output of the same sign as changes in demand has become one of the principal areas of inquiry of NKE.[5]

1.3. From New Classical Macroeconomics...

At the beginning of the 1970s, economic theory was or ready to tackle the issue of the 'micro-foundations of macroeconomics'; the question, that is, of the compatibility of individual rational processes with not necessarily optimal aggregate outcomes. As we have seen, the hypothesis of a natural rate of unemployment required the incorporation of some form of imperfection into the Walrasian model.

In this regard Phelps (1970) urged the refounding of macroeconomic theory on an alternative basis (Frydman and Phelps, 1983).

As a matter of fact, the introduction of informational problems into the Walrasian model was only apparently innocuous (indeed, it entailed the abandonment of this line of inquiry) because the externalities and *non-convexities* that derived from it rendered the equilibrium indeterminate. The 'Trojan horse' of limited information, however, only revealed the model's inner contradiction to a limited extent; and, not coincidentally, it was scholars

---

[5] Note, moreover, that in the 1980s the proponents themselves of non-Walrasian models adopted the hypothesis of non-competitive markets. See Benassy (1987, 1990).

of information economics who launched, but not until a decade later, the counter-offensive of NKE.[6]

Lucas (1972, 1973) initiated a further line of inquiry (which subsequently developed into NCM) by introducing incomplete information into the Arrow-Debreu model[7] and the hypothesis of rational expectations, which was intended to replace the complete ordering of markets. In the presence of limited information, even rational agents may mistakenly interpret price signals. The confusion between temporary and permanent movements of relative prices on the one hand, and between relative and absolute prices on the other, gives rise to equilibrium fluctuations[8] in the presence of a positive rate of unemployment.

Friedman's model adapted by NCM with the hypothesis of rational expectations in Muth's sense (1961), in a stochastic environment and with limited information, optimizing agents and markets in constant equilibrium, should have been able to sustain the neutrality of money even in the short period and the complete ineffectiveness of systematic policies — thereby definitively reasserting the primacy of the neoclassical account. The aggregate supply curve becomes vertical even in the short period, and all shifts in the curve are due to forecasting errors by agents. However, given that expectations are rational, on average such errors cancel each other out.

The rapid rise of NCM, in years in which it was difficult to find an economist under the age of forty declaring himself a Keynesian (Blinder, 1988: 298), was followed by its equally rapid decline, both because it found scant confirmation in the empirical evidence and because it was internally incoherent; an incoherence due to the irreconcilability between imperfect information and the Walrasian model demonstrated in the mid-1970s by the *information economics* of Grossman (1975) and Stiglitz (1971, 1974; also Grossman and Stiglitz, 1976, 1980).

According to these authors, although the point of departure of NCM was Walrasian equilibrium theory supplemented with the hypothesis of imperfect

---

[6] Since information is limited for all agents, there is no logical distinction among them, and the Walrasian allocative mechanism can, in principle, be preserved. Only with NKE does the specification of information sets change from limited to asymmetric: there consequently exist information differences among subjects which entail the abandonment of the Walrasian model.

[7] From a logical point of view, the possibility of having, in the Walrasian scheme, competitive markets, incomplete information and, in general, incomplete market arrangements is highly dubious. Chamberlin (1933) distinguished between *pure* and *perfect* competition, attributing full and complete information to the former. More than a hundred years ago, Marshall (1890) already stressed that only pure competition could guarantee the existence and uniqueness of equilibrium; conversely, in the case of information limitations a plurality of equilibria might arise which could be called, using contemporary terminology, path-dependent (Appendix XIX of the *Principles*).

[8] This methodology draws on von Hayek's analysis of the generation of equilibrium fluctuations in a Walrasian environment.

information, it had to be acknowledged that it 'is not robust' (Stiglitz, 1985: 21). Specifically, if prices yield information about quality, a competitive equilibrium may not exist (Grossman and Stiglitz, 1976).

Faced with this impasse, which prompted Ando (1983) to announce the failure of the NCM's research programme, macroeconomics once again lost the consensus created by the neo-monetarist account, and its practitioners went their separate ways. Those working in the neoclassical tradition shifted their attention to an old paradigm: the theory of the Real Business Cycle (RBC), which shared with NCM the hypotheses of behaviour based on first principles and of markets in constant equilibrium, although it abandoned the attempt, by now demonstrably fruitless, of conciliating Walrasian intertemporal optimization with limited information, and altered the stochastic origins of fluctuations from monetary to technological. The neoclassical school's only option was to re-exhume Friedman's (1953) 'positive' methodology and its assumption that the capitalist economy behaved *as if* it obeyed the rules of competitive markets.

In RBC theory, given its Walrasian background, the neutrality of money proposition is true by definition. Without rigidities or imperfections, unemployment can only be voluntary and stems from a marked preference for free time (a hypothesis not corroborated by the empirical evidence, like that which posited a sectoral diffusion of disturbances). It is difficult to believe, however, that during the Great Depression, or in the 1980s, workers voluntarily opted for unemployment because of low wages.

1.4. ...to New Keynesian Economics

The decline of the NCM left the field open for the NKE account, which shared the methodological premise of NCM relative to the micro-foundation of macro-relations and the need to reformulate the aggregate supply function, but not its conviction that markets are always efficient. As Stiglitz points out, whereas the New Classical Economists maintained that 'all that one needs to understand macroeconomic activity is the neoclassical model', the New Keynesians seek to 'change microeconomics to make it possible to derive from 'correct' microeconomic principles commonly observed macroeconomic phenomena' (Stiglitz, 1992b: 3-4). Microeconomic principles that inevitably differ from Walrasian ones.

The New Keynesians, moreover, are distinguished from the 'classically' inspired school by their methodological approach based on a rejection of the *positivist* methodology of Friedman and Cassel, which they dismiss as 'pseduo-scientific' Stiglitz, 1992a: 276). Consequently, they also reject the hypothesis of perfect markets as the *normal* point of departure of economic models and justify the adoption of the hypothesis of imperfect markets on the basis of its greater realism. Again in Stiglitz's words: 'We count it a virtue, not a vice, if the assumptions of the model are themselves plausible; if the microfoundations underlying the theory are themselves testable — and tested' (Stiglitz, 1992b: 40).[9]

Apart from these common features, it is possible to distinguish two distinct strands of inquiry within NKE. The first — which for brevity's sake we shall call NKEmi (market imperfections) — sets out to escape from the Walrasian paradigm by exploring the macroeconomic implications of imperfect competition in the goods and labour markets. The second strand — henceforth NKEai (asymmetric information) — seeks instead to construct a macroeconomic theory alternative to NCM by examining the coordination difficulties caused by asymmetric information in the financial and labour markets.

The point of departure for NKEmi analysis is the endeavour to give explanation from first principles for the nominal rigidities taking the form of the asynchronically fixed wages proposed by Fischer (1977) and Taylor (1979, 1980), in order to obtain the non-neutrality of money in models incorporating the hypothesis of rational expectations. And, in effect, imperfection in the goods and labour markets makes it possible to analyse the problem of price and wage adjustments in a manner that would be impossible in the perfect markets context of Walrasian economics (something which was already realized by Arrow in 1959).

At first sight, the aim of NKEmi is apparently limited to providing a more solid micro-foundation for the neoclassical synthesis. However, its explicit consideration of imperfections of the goods and labour markets extends the scope of the inquiry beyond the neoclassical synthesis, whose Walrasian methodology implies that constant (or almost constant) prices and wages are to be regarded as 'rigidities'.

In imperfect markets, prices and wages (nominal and real) are set optimally from the individual point of view; but because the 'invisible hand' does not operate, the individual optimum does not coincide with the collective one. Reciprocal externalities among agents give rise to macroeconomic externalities. If prices and wages maintain themselves constant despite demand shocks this choice is evidently the most convenient from the individual point of view (although not from the collective one), but it does not stem from some unreasonable nominal 'rigidity'. Likewise, if real wages higher than Walrasian ones are the result of rational choices and of contractual agreements freely arrived at by rational subjects, the consequent unemployment will be involuntary because it results from the mismatch between the individual optimum and the collective optimum, and does not result from the real 'rigidity'. The problem, though, is whether the explanations of rigidities — especially nominal ones — provided by NKEmi are satisfactory; and this, as we shall see, has been

---

[9]   For a similar position see Mankiw and Romer (1991: 2).

seriously and cogently questioned.

NKEai provides a more complex and detailed account of the financial markets and of firms' behaviour than that typical of the neoclassical synthesis and of NKEmi. The origins of the NKEai strand of inquiry lie in the information economics first developed in the 1970s. Its genetic code is therefore freed from the 'imperative' of finding justifications for rigidities. In the NKEai account, as indeed in Keynes (*General Theory*, chap. XIX), price flexibility is the necessary — although not sufficient — condition for the non-neutrality of money.

With asymmetric information, the ability of firms to acquire funds on both the credit and the stock markets is severely hampered by the effects of adverse selection and adverse incentive. If managers are faced by possible bankruptcy, their production decisions are constrained both by the technology and by the financial resources available, which have costs and risks differentiated according to their origin. The Modigliani-Millet theorem cannot be applied in this context, and the borrowing capacity of firms becomes crucial, as well as the financial fragility of the economy.

The aggregate supply curve constructed by NKEai differs from both the Lucas and the NKEmi curves in that output is an increasing function of the internal financial resources of firms. Thus nominal shocks may have real effects to the extent that their impact on the firm's internal financial resources or on credit influences production decisions and aggregate supply. Moreover, the changes in the financial position of firms brought about by a shock influence investment and therefore also aggregate demand. Fluctuations are the result of the transmission of impulses through both the 'demand side' and the 'supply side'. Unfortunately, this wealth of interpretative insights is still constricted, in the NKE literature, by models which leave some of their most important components to intuition rather than giving them rigorous formulation.

In the rest of this essay we shall focus on each of the themes outlined above and, without any claim to chronological order, describe the essential features of the models used by NKEmi (section 2) and by NKEai (section 3). The fourth section is devoted to an assessment of both NKE as a whole and, separately, its two principal strands of inquiry.

2. NEW KEYNESIAN ECONOMICS: IMPERFECT COMPETITION AND NOMINAL RIGIDITIES

2.1. Introduction

It is not easy to find a common denominator to the many contributions of NKEmi. However, we can perhaps identify a common nucleus in its exploration of the macroeconomic implications of market imperfections (the goods and labour markets in particular) — that is, its exploration of *imperfect competition* in the broad sense. The imperfection at the centre of NKEmi inquiry is, to use Silvestre's (1993) terminology, the presence of market power, which can manifest itself to various extents (monopolistic competition, oligopoly, monopoly) and in various forms according to the type of market and to the positions of agents in each market.[10]

The Keynesian revival of NKEmi therefore assumes imperfect competition as the market background and generates the two fundamental Keynesian results: the presence of involuntary unemployment and the effectiveness of aggregate demand policy through rigidities, respectively real and nominal, derived from the hypothesis of rational (or at least 'quasi-rational') behaviour. As a first approximation, we may say that real rigidities are superfluous because in the presence of nominal rigidities both results would be obtained. However, in a deeper and more indirect sense real rigidities are necessary because they justify and bolster nominal rigidities.

Market power may also be associated with multiple Pareto-ranked Nash equilibria. In these cases the notion of 'coordination failure' acquires a much more stringent meaning because it is defined in the canonical terms of non-cooperative game theory. The possibility of multiple equilibria, too, is somehow tied to the question of rigidities, both real and nominal, although certain NKEmi authors have tried to keep the approach based on multiple equilibria sharply distinct from the approach based on real and nominal rigidities.

Table 1.1, which is freely adapted from Silvestre (1993), marks out the

---

[10] The New Keynesian literature does not deal with the problem of the origins of market power (which is treated, as a primitive concept). In the absence of information asymmetries, the hypothesis of increasing returns to scale — examined with polemical vigour by M. Weitzman (1982) (and before him N. Kaldor, 1978; 1983) — allows refutation of Say's law, logically grounded on the hypothesis of constant returns (constant returns and perfect competition make in- voluntary unemployment impossible because each potential unemployed worker may employ him/herself and sell everything that s/he produces at a given price), but it is not sufficient to explain the emergence of market power — as has been shown by the literature on contestable markets — unless sunk costs are introduced. We shall later meet the hypothesis of increasing returns again as one of the possible sources of multiple equilibria. Market power seems to be based on rent-seeking behaviour, the origins and consequences of which, however, is still a matter of debate.

field of inquiry and the principal findings of NKEmi with respect to the other contemporary schools of macroeconomics.

Table 1.1

	Nominal rigidities	*Wage and price flexibility*
Imperfect competition	NKEmi: Non neutrality of money	NKEmi: Neutrality of money; inefficiency
Perfect competition	Neoclassical synthesis; disequilibrium theory; monetarism	NCM

In the pages that follow we first present, in broad outline, the principal conclusions of a simple NKEmi model with imperfection in the goods market and perfect flexibility of prices and nominal wages (sections 2.2 and 2.3). We then examine the result of the non-neutrality of money in the presence of nominal rigidities, paying particular attention to those generated by 'small menu costs of adjusting prices' (2.4). The inability of small menu costs to impede price adjustment, when shocks are substantial, obliges us to analyse the role of real rigidities — and in particular those deriving from labour market imperfections — in supporting nominal rigidities. Labour market imperfections, moreover, enable us rigorously to derive the result of equilibrium with involuntary unemployment (2.5). Sections 2.6 briefly examines the characteristics of models displaying multiple equilibria and shows the connections between these and nominal rigidities.

2.2. Macroeconomic inefficiency and the neutrality of money

In the presence of imperfect competition, if nominal wages and prices are flexible,

(a) macroeconomic equilibrium does not envisage involuntary unemployment, only ineffective low employment;

(b) monetary policy is inefficient; that is, a monetary shock has no real effects.

Just as an example, consider the extreme case of a goods market in which one single firm produces a single good using labour according to a technology with decreasing returns and faces an isoelastic demand curve of which money is a

10

shift parameter.[11] In order to maximise profit, the firm equalizes cost and revenues at the margin and derives a *price setting rule* which states that the latter is obtained by applying to the marginal cost a mark-up which depends on the elasticity of demand. The marginal cost is the ratio between the nominal wage and the marginal product of labour, which depends negatively on employment. This price rule therefore translates into a monopolist's labour demand curve (N^d_m) which lies — in the plane (w,N) — entirely below the perfect competition labour demand curve (N^d_c) in which it is the price which equalizes the marginal cost (Figure 1.1a).

Assuming that the labour supply function (N^s),[12] is well behaved — that is with a positive slope in the same plane — we obtain an intersection between demand and supply which determines the equilibrium real wage and employment for the labour market. Obviously, the real wage and employment under monopoly (that is the coordinates of point M) will be lower than those obtained under perfect competition (coordinates of point C). The employment level Nm therefore helps to define a *'natural' unemployment rate under imperfect competition* which is obviously higher than that of perfect competition. Imperfect competition entails an inefficiency at the macroeconomic level which is measured by the fall in employment with respect to the perfect competition regime. Once the level of employment has been fixed, the production function determines output (Y_m) which when incorporated into the demand function (D) determines price (P_m) (see Figure 1.1b).[13]

Such a price is derived from a profit maximization assumption. Put otherwise, the equilibrium output is represented by the abscissa of the intersection of the monopolist's marginal cost curve (CMg) and marginal revenues curve (RMg), since the labour demand curve is only an algebraic transformation of the monopolist's price rule. In other words, the model is recursive: equilibrium employment and the real wage are determined in the labour market, the production function determines aggregate supply, and the goods market determines price.

A nominal shock in this context can only have the effect of a variation of the same sign in the price level: money is neutral. For example, the impact effect of an increase in the quantity of money is the greater availability of real

---

[11] By 'money' in this context is meant — following the practice customary in the NKEmi literature — any non-produced good which appears in the utility function of the representative consumer.

[12] The labour supply curve can be interpreted as a wage setting rule operating in conditions of competition among workers.

[13] In order to render the graphic representation as uncluttered as possible, we have omitted the production function. For this purpose, the unit of measurement of output — represented by the horizontal axis in Figure 1.1b — has been normalized in order to make it equivalent to the unit of measurement of labour represented by the horizontal axis of Figure 1.1a. In other words, the same distance measures a certain amount of labour on the horizontal axis of Figure 1.1b and the output obtained with this same amount of labour on the horizontal axis of Figure 1.1a. The reader is reminded that we have assumed decreasing returns.

money balances and therefore an increase in the demand for goods (that is, there is an upwards shift of the demand curve from D' to D which also entails an upwards shift of the marginal revenue curve from RMg' to RMg).[14] Nominal wage remaining equal, there should ensue an increase in both price and output. However, the monetary wage does not remain unchanged but adjusts to the price (the real wage has not varied from the labour market equilibrium level). Consequently the marginal cost curve shifts upwards (from CMg' to CMg). The intersection between the new marginal cost curve and the new marginal revenue curve can only occur at the abscissa point Y_m, given that equilibrium on the labour market has not changed. Thus the nominal shock is entirely absorbed by a price response.

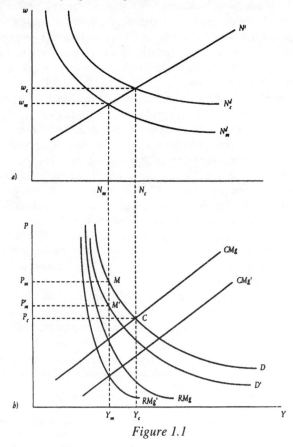

Figure 1.1

---

[14] As is usual in NKEmi, the only mechanism transmitting monetary shocks in this model is the Pigou effect.

2.3. Strategic interaction and macroeconomic externalities

Figure 1. clearly represents an extreme case, one useful for focusing on problems but undoubtedly with no correspondence in reality. Let us now imagine a goods market under monopolistic competition and therefore composed of n technologically identical firms producing n not perfectly substitutable goods. If there is no *specialization of consumption* — that is if, the employees of each firm do not restrict themselves to consuming only the good produced by themselves but also purchase the products of other firms — we have spillovers of demand which — when markets are imperfectly competitive — generate a strategic interdependence among the producers.

In Blanchard and Kiyotaki's model (1987) — perhaps the best known and the most widely used in NKEmi literature[15] — strategic interaction gives rise to a non-cooperative game in which the strategic variable is price. Each firm has a demand curve whose arguments are the relative price of the good with respect to other goods and the overall income, which in its turn is a function of real money balances.[16] The optimum response function of each firm is therefore an (increasing) relation between the individual price and the average level of prices charged by competitors, given the real wage and income.

Price competition generates a positive *reciprocal externality*: one firm's decision to raise its price leads, *ceteris paribus*, to an increase in its competitors' profits. In equilibrium, moreover, a *macroeconomic externality* appears[17] which can be illustrated by the following example. Assume an initial symmetrical Bertrand-Nash equilibrium in which all firms charge the same price so that the relative price of any two goods is always equal to one. An *identical and coordinated* price reduction by all firms boosts their real profit because — although it does not affect relative price — it stimulates an increase in aggregate demand through the increase in real money balances. However, no individual producer has an incentive to reduce its price because it would suffer a second-order loss of profits.

The presence of an externality under Nash equilibrium entails, of course, that equilibrium is Pareto inefficient. Referring again to the above example and assuming initial equilibrium, all the price configurations in which — relative price remaining the same — the absolute price charged by each and

---

[15] Macroeconomic modelling based on monopolistic competition was inaugurated by the pioneering work of Weitzman (1982), followed by Akerlof and Yellen (1985), Benassy (1987), Rotemberg (1987), Pagano (1990), Startz (1989) and, of course, Blanchard and Kiyotaki (1987). Boitani (1991) compares the role of imperfect competition in Post Keynesian and New Keynesian macro-models. See also Boitani and Salanti (1994) for a methodological assessment of Post Keynesian and new Keinesian Macroeconomics.

[16] The demand curve is derived from the maximization of the utility of the representative household (whose arguments are a basket of consumption goods, real money balances and leisure) subject to an income constraint and an initial endowment of money.

[17] Or 'aggregate demand externality' as Blanchard (1990) calls it.

all of the firms is lower than the present one are preferable to the actual configuration. If the Pareto-superior situations are not Nash equilibria, however, they cannot be realized.

Let us return to Blanchard and Kiyotaki's model. In order to determine symmetrical equilibrium on the goods market, in the reaction function of the individual firm equality is imposed between the individual price and the average price of its competitors. By so doing, a price setting rule is established whose algebraic transformation gives rise to an inverse relation between the real wage and employment; that is, it gives rise to the labour demand function in monopolistic competition. This function — in the plane (w,N) — lies entirely below the labour demand curve of perfect competition. In fact, in monopolistic competition, at the point of individual optimum a gap opens between real wage and marginal labour productivity on account, ultimately, of the imperfect substitutability among goods in the utility function.

If the labour supply is normal, in monopolistic competition labour market equilibrium displays features entirely analogous to those represented in Figure 1.1a which regards monopoly. Employment and the equilibrium real wage are lower than those obtainable under perfect competition.[18] Once the real wage has been set, in symmetrical equilibrium the reaction function determines the output of each firm, and when incorporated into the demand function it determines the individual price. Point M in Figure 1.1b can be reinterpreted as the optimal point of each individual firm in symmetrical equilibrium of monopolistic competition.

Money is neutral in this context too. An increase in the quantity of money pushes up the demand for goods, one of which is produced by the firm in question. The nominal wage and the price charged by other firms remaining equal, an increase in both price and output will ensue. However, at this point the relative price has also increased. Substitutability entails a shift of demand from the firm in question to other firms, which in turn raise their price. Symmetrical equilibrium is restored when the price charged by each firm is equal to that charged by all the others. Simultaneously, the monetary wage does not remain unchanged but adjusts to the price (the real wage has remained invariant at the equilibrium level for the labour market). The sequence proceeds as in the simple monopoly model described above.[19]

---

[18] In fact, Blanchard and Kiyotaki's model assumes that each firm uses different types of not perfectly substitutable labour. The labour supply curve must therefore be replaced by a wage setting rule which lies wholly above it.

[19] Given the previous considerations one intuitively concludes that the results of macroeconomic inefficiency and the neutrality of money are robust with respect to market structure. In the context of a market in an intermediate position between monopoly and monopolistic competition — oligopoly — the above results do not change. The first macroeconomic model based on oligopoly was developed by Hart (1982), who was followed by Madden (1983), Heller et al. (1986), Cooper and John (1988) and Roberts (1989). The substantial equivalence of the results — other assumptions remaining equal — obtained from models based on imperfect competition and models based on oligopoly is discussed in Boitani, Delli Gatti and Mezzomo (1992).

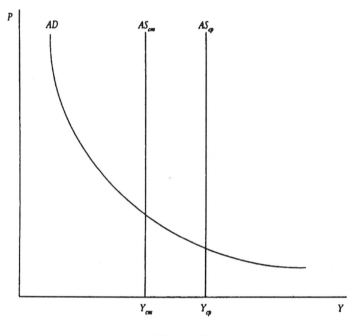

Figure 1.2

A vertical aggregate supply schedule can be drawn in the (P,Y) plane starting either from the monopoly model or from the monopolistic competition model (under symmetric equilibrium). The intercept of such a schedule with the Y-axis depends on the (inefficient) equilibrium on the labour market and it will be more to the left than the corresponding intercept under perfect competition. The aggregate demand schedule will be represented by the standard hyperbola derived from the quantity theory of money. The neutrality result is apparent.

2.4. Nominal rigidities and the non-neutrality of money

Abandoning the paradigm of perfect competition, still does not explain the real impact of the nominal variables; nor does it invalidate the assertion of the ineffectiveness of economic policy.[20] How can a role be restored for aggregate demand? The answer provided by the NKEmi approach is based on introducing

---

[20] Fiscal policy, in fact, is able to influence equilibrium employment through suitable supply policies. See Dixon and Rankin (1994).

15

nominal rigidities which, in the presence of a shock, compel adjustment through quantities.

The first form of nominal rigidity to appear in contemporary macroeconomic debate was long-term wage contracts (Fischer, 1977; Taylor, 1979, 1980). In Fischer, nominal wages are established at the beginning of the period on the basis of available information, the aim being to maintain real wage expectations constant. Nominal shocks influence output if they are unexpected (as in NCM), but they do so, not through the neoclassical mechanism based on misperception but through the Keynesian mechanism: a nominal shock increases prices and — given the nominal wage — reduces the real wage and increases employment.

In our simple graphical representation, a nominal shock (for example, an expansion of the money supply) shifts the demand curve upwards from D' to D (Figure 1.1b) and the marginal revenue curve from RMg' to RMg. Contrary to what happens with perfect wage flexibility, in the presence of staggered wage contracts — and therefore of a delay in the adjustment of wages to prices — there is no shift in the marginal cost curve. The marginal cost curve and the new marginal revenue curve intersect at a point corresponding to a higher level of prices and output.

This, of course, entails a fall in the real wage. Assuming the initial situation represented by point M' in Figure 1.3b, the nominal shock induces a shift along the labour demand curve (from M' to M): the combination of real wage and employment that prevails after the shock lies outside the labour supply curve. Hence, the nominal shock triggers a price response, but it is precisely this price response that also induces a quantity response because, with a given nominal wage (in the short period), the increase in prices reduces the real wage and makes it possible to hire new workers.

We now turn to price rigidities. Prices, in fact, are not necessarily less volatile under imperfect competition than under perfect competition, unless differences in technology between the two regimes are introduced. Although imperfectly competitive firms have more capital available than perfectly competitive ones, marginal costs may be flat across a broader interval of output. Excess capacity may be justified by the need to deter the entry of new firms (Fudenberg and Tirole, 1983).

With constant marginal costs, if the demand curve is isoelastic (so that the mark-up on the marginal cost is constant), prices are rigid and a nominal shock induces only quantity responses. Bils (1987), however, argues on the basis of detailed empirical inquiry that marginal costs increase (regardless of market structure). In the presence of increasing marginal costs, price rigidity can be explained by the variability of mark-ups. In this context, a demand shock leaves the price unaltered only if the mark-up is counter-cyclical (Rotemberg and Woodford, 1991). The counter-cyclicity of the mark-up may be determined by the pro-cyclicity of the elasticity of demand so that the degree of monopoly

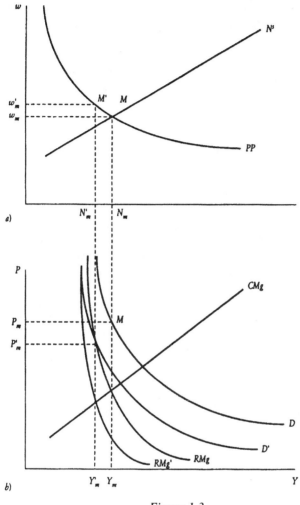

Figure 1.3

is lower during booms (Stiglitz, 1984). Alternatively, one may surmise that during booms the degree of sustainable collusion is lower (Rotemberg and Saloner, 1986).

The explanation of nominal rigidities which has rapidly moved to the forefront in NKEmi is based on small menu costs (Mankiw, 1985). This notion can be set out very simply within the framework of the optimum problem of our monopolist. The Taylor expansion of the profit function around the optimum price can be written as follows:

17

Financial Constraints and Market Failures

$$\Pi(P) = \Pi(P^*) + \Pi'(P^*)(P-P^*) + [\Pi''(P^*)/2](P-P^*)^2$$

At the optimum point $\Pi'(P^*)=0$,[21] so that the profit loss associated with price non-adjustment due to a shock which changes the optimal price from P to P* is:

$$\Pi(P) - \Pi(P^*) = [\Pi''(P^*)/2](P-P^*)^2$$

that is, a second-order loss of profit. It therefore only requires relatively small price adjustment costs for it to be no longer convenient for the monopolist to adjust its price after a nominal shock.

The profit loss is given graphic representation in Figure 1.4. The initial situation is represented by point $Y°$. The new optimum point after the negative nominal shock is represented by Y^*. The failure of prices to adjust implies that the firm chooses point Y' and entails a profit loss represented by the triangular area ABC lying between the marginal cost curve and the marginal revenue curve at the level of output associated with Y'. In the labour market, point Y' corresponds to a disequilibrium situation.

The small menu costs explanation of nominal rigidities has been criticised on various grounds. Caplin and Spulber (1987), for example, argue that small nominal frictions at the level of the individual firm do not necessarily translate into a nominal rigidity at the macroeconomic level if one considers a dynamic context with shocks. However, Caplin and Spulber's result is unable to withstand minor changes of hypothesis. They assume, in fact, that firms change their prices if they diverge 'too much' from the desired values according to a state-dependent rule (s,S),[22] that shocks are only ever aggregate in character and that they are never negative — that is money supply never diminishes. But it is sufficient for the adjustment rule to be time-dependent (if information is costly) — as in the case of staggered labour contracts — or for there also to be firm-specific shocks, or for the money supply to both increase and decrease, and doubt is cast on the neutrality obtained by Caplin and Spulber and small frictions at the microeconomic level translate once again into aggregate level rigidities.[23]

Secondly, the small menu costs hypothesis has been criticised on the ground that it is not the case that only price adjustment costs exist; quantity adjustment costs do as well, and they may even be higher (Greenwald, Stiglitz, 1989). However it has also been pointed out that when competitors are not

---

[21] Note that this happens only if the firm is a price-maker. The hypothesis of small menu costs is therefore based on imperfect competition.
[22] See Barro (1972); Sheshinski and Weiss (1977).
[23] See Blanchard (1990); Blanchard and Fischer (1989, chapter 6).

18

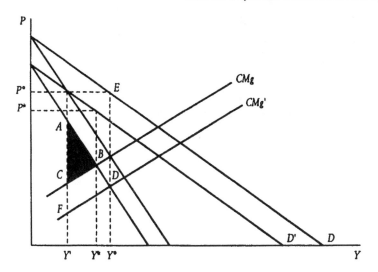

Figure 1.4

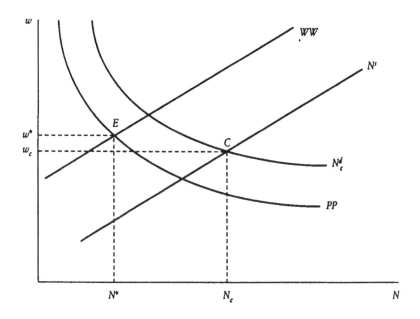

Figure 1.5

expected to adjust their price, a nominal shock is perceived as a real shock (Hargreaves Heap, 1991), in reaction to which the firm adjusts quantities and does not alter its long-run equilibrium price. If this is so, then price adjustment is an unnecessary source of extra costs, whereas a change, even a minor one, in quantities would be an anticipation of a rationally inevitable behaviour. In this context, menu costs are not compared with quantity adjustment costs; instead, one asserts that only the former matter because the latter are inevitable.

An interesting device to give greater robustness to the explanation of price rigidities has been proposed by Lindbeck and Snower (1992), taking up a suggestion by Gordon (1990). If production takes place by means of intermediate inputs, as well as labour, then serious consideration should be made of input-output chains within a natural sequence of decisions. There exists at least one lag between input acquisition and output production. Consequently, firms — assumed as operating in some form of oligopolistic market — set the prices for their products before observing their demand. Therefore a negative nominal shock at time t=0 will leave the prices of the intermediate inputs unaffected, because they were set in the previous period, in which the shock was not foreseen. As a consequence prices of the outputs will not diminish in proportion to the quantity of money either. And since the outputs are also the inputs to the productive process which yields products saleable in period t=1, the price level will continue to fall less than proportionally to the initial shock.[24] This conclusion applies to not perfectly predictable shocks but 'it is worth noting that fully anticipated demand changes are practically inconceivable when final output prices depend on intermediate input prices, which in turn depend on nominal wages, which depend on final output prices and so on' (Lindbeck and Snower 1992: 2).

This technology-based explanation of price stickiness does not require the presence of menu costs, although these may amplify the inertia effects inherent in input-output chains with time lags. The input-output approach, moreover, can justify the existence of price staggering in that if technological lags are not perfectly synchronised among sectors, one can plausibly expect price decisions not to be synchronised either. It therefore seems that the various explanations of nominal rigidities are not incompatible; they instead mutually reinforce each other and thus provide a more complex and convincing explanation. An effort at producing such a synthesis, though, has yet to be made.

There still, however, remains a fundamental question to deal with. The presence of nominal rigidities — whatever the explanation for them — only

---

[24] It is worth noting that Lindbeck and Snower's result depends crucially on the hypothesis that firms operate in a context of imperfect competition. If the demand curve of each firm were infinitely elastic, a nominal shock would only have the effect of shifting these curves vertically, inducing a complete adjustment of product prices independently of the temporary rigidity of the cost of intermediate goods.

justifies the assertion of the *temporary* effect of nominal shocks on real variables. It does not justify the claim that real effects are permanent, since in the absence of other obstacles the adjustment mechanism will restore the economy to the 'natural' — albeit inefficient — equilibrium discussed earlier. The crucial point, obviously, lies in this 'absence of other obstacles'. Obstacles which may take the form of the path dependence whereby the economy, once it has shifted from its 'natural' equilibrium, follows a path different from the one that it would have followed in the absence of an initial shock. Research in this area is still in its early stages, but what is certain is that the models examined in the previous sections have too 'poor' a dynamic structure to provide the basis for thoroughgoing discussion of the permanence of real effects.

2.5. Labour market imperfections and involuntary unemployment

On its own, imperfect competition in the goods market is able to generate macroeconomic equilibria with inefficiently low levels of employment, but it is certainly unable to generate involuntary unemployment. The fact that the equilibrium (M) of Figure 1.1 lies on the labour supply curve implies, in fact, that all unemployment is voluntary. Involuntary unemployment would only come about if the small menu costs inhibited the reduction of the price level in reaction to a negative nominal shock, allowing the quantities produced, and therefore employment, to adjust to the new level of effective demand.

On the other hand, the presence of small menu costs, in a context of imperfect competition, is not enough to compensate for the loss of profit, and therefore to generate nominal rigidities, when the nominal shock is of substantial size. This therefore creates the paradox that non-neutrality and involuntary unemployment only arise when negative shocks are small. And this is a result that is hardly encouraging for a theory which claims to be Keynesian.

However, it is not difficult to find a way out of the paradox by extending the imperfection hypothesis to the labour market as well. By so doing, in fact, one obtains real rigidities in the wage formation mechanism. The consequences of this are important, because an imperfect labour market entails that the perfect competition labour supply curve must be replaced by a wage setting rule (WW in Figure 1.5) which lies entirely above the former (Ns).[25] Point (E),

---

[25] As we shall see, not all models of an imperfect labour market generate a positively sloped WW. However, this is considered in the literature to be the most 'normal' case (see Lindbeck, 1992, p. 213).

at which the price rule (PP) and the wage rule (WW) intersect, is characterised by a level of employment certainly lower than that which would be obtained with a perfectly competitive labour market.[26]

Equilibrium unemployment, moreover, is involuntary, since the workers concerned would be willing to supply a greater quantity of labour at the present wage. It is involuntary, but not Keynesian because it is not unemployment caused by a lack of effective demand. A reduction in the quantity of money in the stylized model of Figure 1.4 only generates deflation, which once again increases real money balances until they return to their initial level — unless a negative nominal shock (even a large one) induces a change in real aggregate demand which forces firms to reduce employment.

It is at this point that the second important consequence of labour market imperfections arises. The reduced sensitivity of real wages to the business cycle[27] reduces the incentives for each firm to adjust its relative price (and therefore its absolute price) in response to a nominal shock. In other words, real rigidity makes the marginal cost of firms, and therefore also the optimal price charged by them, less pro-cyclical. Hence, it follows that the inhibiting capacity of small menu costs is greater the greater the rigidities of the real wage: even with large nominal shocks firms find it economically convenient to react by adjusting quantities (and therefore employment) and not prices.[28]

From the discussion so far one may conclude that labour market imperfection — by generating real rigidities which reinforce small menu costs in producing major nominal rigidities — indirectly raises the possibility of Keynesian involuntary unemployment. Of course, other sources of real rigidities can be cited — for example, the existence of customer markets (Woglom, 1982), the already-mentioned counter-cyclicity of the degree of collusion among firms (Rotemberg and Saloner, 1986), and so on — yet none of them enables one to obtain, at once, a reinforcement of nominal rigidities and an explanation of involuntary unemployment.

The introduction of imperfections in the labour market is therefore a

---

[26] Comparison between the real equilibrium wage in the two cases (w* and wc respectively) is imprecise because it depends on the relative degrees of imperfection of the labour and goods markets. The diagram based on the price and wage rules is immediately reminiscent of the labour market analysis conducted by Layard and Nickell (1986), in which the price and wage rules determine a level of employment corresponding to the NAIRU, that is the rate of unemployment which renders the competing claims of workers and firms regarding output compatible.

[27] An important stylized fact which every theory should help to explain.

[28] The question can be formulated in the following manner, following and simplifying the approach used by Ball and Romer (1990). Assume that the profit function of the i-th firm under monopolistic competition is:

$$\Pi_i = \Pi\ (M/P,\ P_i/P) - z D_i$$

$\Pi_2 = 0$, $\Pi_{22} < 0$, $\Pi_{12} > 0$, at the maximum point, where M/P is the quantity of money in real

22

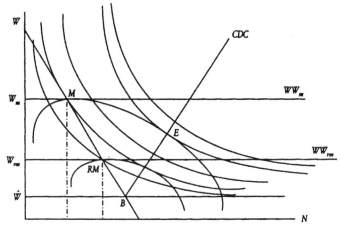

Figure 1.6

terms, P_i/P is the ratio between the firm's price and the price level, whereas D_i is a dummy which denotes whether or not the firm adjusts its nominal price. By implicitly differentiating the first-order condition ($\Pi_2 = 0$), one obtains

$$\frac{d(P_i \, / \, P)}{d(M \, / \, P)} = -\frac{\Pi_{12}}{\Pi_{22}} = \phi > 0$$

where a high ϕ denotes low real rigidity, and a low ϕ denotes high real rigidity.

The nominal rigidity is measured by the range of variations of M for which the non-adjustment of all prices is a Nash equilibrium: $(1+x^*, 1-x^*)$.

If the i-th firm does *not* adjust and the others do *not* adjust, one has: $D_i=0$, $M/P=M$, $P_i/P=1$, therefore $\Pi_i = \Pi (M, 1)$. If the firm adjusts and the others do *not* adjust $D_i=1$, $P_i/P=P_i^*/P$, $M/P=M$ (because the individual firm does not influence P).

Hence it follows that $\Pi_i=\Pi (M, P_i^*/P)-z$.

Should it happen that the non-adjustment loss is lower that the cost of adjustment $L_N = \Pi (M, P_i^*/P) - \Pi (M, 1) < z$, the firm gains no advantage from adjusting. Using a Taylor approximation of the second order of the loss function around M=1, one obtains:

$$L_N \approx -\frac{(\Pi_{12})^2}{2\Pi_{22}} = x^2 \qquad \text{where } x = M - 1$$

from which one deduces that the rigidity is an equilibrium if M lies within the range $(1+x_N, 1-x_N)$, where x_N is defined as:

$$x_N \sqrt{\frac{2\Pi_{22}z}{(\Pi_{12})^2}} = \sqrt{\frac{2z}{\phi\Pi_{12}}}$$

which confirms that increasing real rigidity increases nominal rigidity as well, because it increases the magnitude of the monetary shock to which the equilibrium response is not to adjust.

One can straightforwardly show that ϕ depends on the elasticity of the labour supply: the more inelastic the labour supply, the greater is ϕ. By increasing the elasticity of the WW with respect to the wage, labour market imperfections increase real rigidities and therefore reduce the value of ϕ, thereby increasing x_N.

crucial step in the completion of the theoretical apparatus of NKEmi; a step, moreover, made easier by the numerous 'micro-based' theoretical analyses that labour economists have been producing in recent years.

Because of the institutional features of our labour markets, in Europe the fullest development has been given to the approach based on trade unions bargaining power.[29] This is an approach of Marxian or Kaleckian origins, but it has received new impetus (and found wider academic acceptance) since it was equipped with micro-foundations based on the maximization of the trade-union membership's utility and on (either axiomatic or strategic) theories of bargaining.

One can briefly describe the approach by assuming that the objective function of the single union operating in each industry (sectoral trade union)[30] is utilitarian; that is to say, the union's objective function can be specified as the sum of the utility functions of its members (which amounts to saying that the union gives the same weight to all its members). As it bargains with each firm in the sector, the union seeks to maximize:

$$V = N [V(w)^v - (V(\hat{w})^v] \quad N \leq N^0$$

where N are the employees belonging to the union, N^0 is the total number of the union's members, w is the real wage of the employees and ($\hat{w}$) is the reservation wage. The aim of the firm is to maximize profit (Π).

The outcomes of the bargaining process between the union and each firm can be determined using a generalized Nash solution, representable as follows:

$$Max\Omega = N [\overset{v}{V} (w) - (\overset{v}{V} (\hat{w})]^s \Pi^{1-s}$$
$$sub N \leq N^0$$

where s denotes the union's bargaining power and (1-s) that of the firm. Note that this is a very general situation in which the trade union and the firm bargain over both wages and employment ('efficient bargaining' according to Leontief, 1946, and McDonald and Solow, 1981). The result of efficient bargaining will be a point in the space (w, N) to the right of the firm's labour demand relation, a tangent point between a curve of the firm's iso-profit and a trade-union indifference curve (for example E in Figure 1.6); that is, a point along the contracts curve (CDC) determined by relative bargaining power.[31] If s = 0, the

---

[29] Useful surveys are by Oswald (1985), Pencavel (1985) and Farber (1987). An integrated micro-macro approach can be found in Layard, Nickell and Jackman (1991).

[30] One may also assume, although less realistically, that there is a craft union or syndicate in each sector (Blanchard and Kiyotaki, 1987), or a single national union. However, whereas with syndicates it is possible to achieve a positively sloping WW curve, the single national union generates horizontal WWs.

[31] Note that the position of CDC in the plane depends on the value of the reservation wage, which may in turn depend — as will become clearer below — on the unemployment rate.

workers obtain the reservation wage and the firm maximizes profits (point B); as s increases, the contract point moves rightwards along CDC.

If bargaining is restricted to wages, and if the task of setting employment is assigned to the firm alone, one has the 'right to manage' case (Nickell and Andrews, 1983): the maximization of Ω only occurs with respect to w, and it is subject to the further constraint that the firm is on its labour demand curve. The outcome of the bargaining is represented by a point like RM in Figure 1.6.

Finally, if the firm's bargaining power is nil (s = 1), then one has a case of a 'monopoly union'. The objective function of firms disappears from the maximization of Ω and so too does bargaining, although the labour demand constraint is obviously still binding. The result would be a higher wage and a lower level of employment than in the 'right to manage' case, which in its turn entails (in general) a higher wage and a lower level of employment than in the case of efficient bargaining.

So far the partial equilibrium analysis, with an exogenous reservation wage. It is precisely because of the exogeneity of ($\hat{w}$) that WW is parallel to the axis N (in the 'right to manage' case of Figure 1.6). However, one needs only assume that ($\hat{w}$) depends on the present unemployment rate to obtain, in all three cases mentioned above, an increasing WW in the space (w, N); a WW which can be shown to be invariably located to the left of the perfect competition labour supply curve;[32] a WW, finally, whose position in the 'efficient bargaining' and 'right to manage' cases depends on the relative bargaining powers of trade unions and firms[33].

Trade-union models as the micro-foundations of involuntary unemployment have been criticised because they fail to explain why non-unionized unemployed workers do not offer to work for a wage lower than that negotiated by the union. This objection can be met by pointing out that the unions seek to discourage firms from bargaining individually with non-unionized workers, and that the possibility of this kind of behaviour generates 'institutions' which protect both the union and firms against the possible consequences of 'non-cooperation'.

However, models with labour market imperfections have been developed which omit the trade unions and seek to explain the rigidity of real wages on the basis of the individual incentives of firms and workers. We are referring here to the 'efficiency wages' and 'insider-outsider' models.[34]

---

[32] A proof which requires specification of the form of the union's utility function, the production function, and the firm's demand function (see Boitani and Damiani, 1994).

[33] Notice that the over-full-employment result of efficient bargaining in a partial equilibrium context does not carry over to the general equilibrium context. Under general equilibrium, right to manage and efficient bargaining give rise to the same WW schedule (see Boitani and Damiani, 1995).

[34] There is a massive literature on the subject. Excellent points of reference are Akerlof and Yellen (1986) and Weiss (1991) for 'efficiency wages' models, and Lindbeck and Snower (1988) for 'insider-outsider' models.

'Efficiency wages' models attribute the departure from the perfect competition paradigm to the presence of asymmetric information between firm and worker, which gives rise to the well-known problems of 'adverse selection' (when the information asymmetry concerns the characteristics of the employees) and 'moral hazard' (when it concerns the effort squandered in work). The simplest 'efficiency wages' model (Solow, 1979) contains a worker's effort variable or productive efficiency variable which enters the firm's production function in a multiplicative way. Effort is an increasing and concave function of the real wage.[35]

Profits are maximized when the elasticity of effort to the real wage is equal to one (the Solow condition). It is easily shown that this corresponds to the minimization of the cost per unit of effort. The Solow condition univocally determines the real wage, which will be an 'efficiency wage' in the sense that firms derive no economic advantage from accepting workers who offer to work for a lower wage.[36]

In efficiency wage models, power in the labour market lies entirely in the hands of firms. However, it is possible to incorporate a model *à la* Solow into a more general bargaining model, showing that efficiency wage considerations and union bargaining power do reinforce one another in determining higher wages and lower employment levels (Boitani and Damiani, 1995).

Some of the variants and extensions of the efficiency wages theory yield a positively sloping WW curve. A first possibility consists in introducing the turnover hypothesis (Salop, 1979). Alternatively one may resort, using a 'moral hazard' approach, to the 'shirking' hypothesis (Shapiro and Stiglitz, 1984), in which case a 'no shirking constraint' is obtained which slopes positively in the plane (w, N) because, as employment increases, the 'stick' of unemployment becomes less effective, and firms find it increasingly necessary to use the 'carrot' of high wages in order to induce workers not to shirk: workers who are caught shirking and are therefore dismissed would fall from a higher income level than that represented by the Walrasian wage.[37] There are other models which stress the problem of adverse selection stemming from firms' inability to distinguish *ex ante* between high-productivity and low-productivity workers, so that they find it convenient to pay high wages in order to increase the probability that they will attract high-productivity workers (Weiss, 1980; Malcomson, 1981).

---

[35] The original reason for the positive slope of the effort function is Leibenstein's (1957) nutritional hypothesis. But see also Marshall (1890) and Webb (1897).

[36] The Solow condition is valid whatever form of market prevails in the goods market. Obviously, under monopoly (and also under monopolistic competition), the price rule lies entirely beneath the perfect competition labour demand curve. Therefore, given the efficiency wage, imperfect competition is distinguished from perfect competition only by a lower level of employment.

[37] A largely similar result is obtained by those working within the Marxian tradition of the 'work process' (Bowles, 1985).

Unlike 'efficiency wages' models, 'insider-outsider' models assume that a large part of labour market power is in the hands of the workers and, more precisely, of the employed. And this is because every firm must sustain more than negligible costs in transforming an outsider into a worker equipped with the training suited to its particular needs, not to mention the costs of dismissal. Taken together, these costs (called 'turnover' costs) generate rents which may be appropriated by the employed workers if they claim wages higher than that of outsiders (equal to the reservation wage) by an amount equal to the marginal costs of turnover.[38] It is possible to obtain a positively sloping WW curve in some of these models, too, if the reservation wage stands in relation to the unemployment rate.

The insider-outsider approach is, by itself, able to sustain an under-employment equilibrium. It can also be employed to tackle the question of why 'firms do not bargain with individual workers ignoring unions' (Lindbeck and Snower, 1988, p. 46). The answer is that the unions (as insiders) can help to increase turnover costs and to regulate cooperation and boycott relationships with newly-hired workers (thus also influencing firms' costs) to an extent such that they cannot be ignored. Furthermore the insider-outsider approach can be combined with the efficiency wages approach in a integrated Nash model of bargaining in which the predominance of one or the other wage-setting mechanism depends on the (employed) workers bargaining power (Lindbeck and Snower, 1991).

It should also be stressed that the market power of the insiders may render the effects of demand shocks asymmetrically persistent. Thus, a negative shock — one which is not immediately absorbed by proportional changes in prices and wages because of the joint presence of nominal and real rigidities — will engender a permanent increase in unemployment. By becoming outsiders, the newly unemployed will lack the power to push wages down, so that when a new negative shock appears the economy will display an (equilibrium) unemployment rate higher than that obtained prior to the shock. This is the phenomenon known as hysteresis, which seems to have been a typical feature of unemployment in Europe during the 1980s (see Lindbeck and Snower, 1988, chapters 9, 10; Blanchard and Summers, 1986).

In all the above three approaches — efficiency wages, insider-outsider, and trade union — real wages are relatively insensitive to the business cycle. For this reason it is customary to speak of wage 'rigidity'. It should be borne in mind, however, that in all three cases the real wage is the result of optimizing behaviour. The wages thus determined 'are no more rigid than an optimally chosen price of a monopolist is "rigid". The terminology of rigidity takes an unexplained auctioneer as a reference point and not the rational agent' (Hahn,

---

[38] Various hypotheses relative to turnover costs can be found in the various papers by Lindbeck and Snower collected in their book of 1988.

27

1987, pp. 8-9). The market failures implied by labour market imperfections are more profound and significant than those that derive from simple rigidities and frictions in an otherwise Walrasian world.

2.6. Multiple equilibria and coordination problems

A number of authors (Garretsen, 1992; Dore, 1993; Silvestre, 1993) distinguish between the NKEmi models discussed so far, in which nominal rigidities have a predominant role, and those characterized by multiple equilibria. Only the latter qualify as the legitimate heirs of Leijonhufvud (1968, 1981), who places 'coordination failures' at the centre of a truly Keynesian economics. The core of Keynesian policy is therefore the problem of equilibrium selection; that is, the problem of creating institutions and conventions which encourage coordination in order to reach the best equilibrium, rather than the problem of utilizing the traditional levers of monetary and fiscal policy.[39]

The argument runs as follows. When one single (Nash) equilibrium exists, inefficiency arises because of the presence of reciprocal externalities and the difficulties of cooperation. The macroeconomic externality discussed earlier exists because there is a problem of cooperation, not because there is a problem of coordination. Pareto-efficient outcomes are not equilibria. When, by contrast, there exist multiple equilibria, an equilibrium selection problem arises. If the equilibria are Pareto-ranked, coordination failures may mean that the economy is trapped in an inefficient equilibrium even though the Pareto-efficient outcomes are equilibria as well.

The Pareto-ranking of the equilibria is in its turn due to the existence of strategic complementarity which arises when the changes in one agent's strategy influence *in the same direction* the marginal pay-off of each of the others. Strategic complementarity entails that the reaction function of all agents is positively sloping. Although strategic complementarity is necessary for multiple symmetrical equilibria to come about, it is not sufficient for it.[40] Indeed, strategic complementarity is also present in the 'standard' NKEmi models with monopolistic competition or oligopoly, although it does not give rise to the multiple equilibria and coordination failures as just described.[41]

---

[39] On this see Boitani and Delli Gatti (1991); Silvestre (1993).

[40] When changes in one agent's strategy influence the marginal pay-offs of each of the other agents in the reverse direction, then one has strategic substitutability. Strategic substitutability implies that the reaction function of each and all the agents is negatively sloping. Recall that in our context agents (firms) are all equal; therefore the Nash equilibria must be symmetrical. It is not difficult to envisage multiple equilibria in the presence of strategic substitutability, but in this case they would not be symmetrical. The notions of strategic complementarity and substitutability were introduced by Bulow, Geanakoplos and Klemperer (1985). On games characterized by strategic complementarity see Milgrom and Roberts (1990), Vives (1990) and Fudenberg and Tirole (1991). On coordination problems in games see the contributions in Friedman (1993).

[41] See Boitani, Delli Gatti and Mezzomo (1992).

Figure 1.7a shows two agents' Bertrand-type linear reaction functions which exhibit strategic complementarity with a unique equilibrium, while Figure 1.7b depicts two symmetric equilibria due to the non linearity of both reaction functions.

The notion of 'coordination failure' introduced by Leijonhufvud to replace the Walrasian auctioneer, and the consequent inability of economic subjects (operating in different markets) to communicate with each other, is thus given rigorous specification. But at the same time, the fact that the notion pivots on the existence of multiple equilibria restricts its range, since this property is by no means generally shared by NKEmi models and it is, moreover, often based on very specific assumptions needed in order to get multiple intersections of the reaction functions.

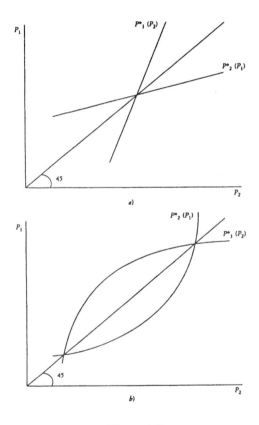

Figure 1.7

Without going into details, it should be pointed out that a number of models obtain multiplicity by eschewing a monetary economy (Heller, 1986; Cooper and John, 1988; Roberts, 1989; Pagano, 1990; Boitani and Delli Gatti, 1991). However, the absence of a nominal *anchor* is not enough to generate multiple equilibria; more simply, it renders the equilibrium indeterminate. Thus, Heller (1986) uses a model with constant marginal costs, Cournot, oligopoly and Stone Geary preferences while Boitani and Delli Gatti have mark-up pricing and rigid wages. If any one of these hypotheses is dropped, the multiplicity disappears. Roberts (1989) bases his model on a specific timing of price-quantity and wage-employment choices and is thus able to relinquish imperfect competition as well. It is sufficient to have a different timing for different results to be obtained (for example, all efficient equilibria, or a single equilibrium). Pagano (1990) introduces the hypothesis that, although the labour market is perfectly competitive, the elasticity of the aggregate labour supply curve is high and the share of GDP accounted for by wage-earners is more than 1/2.

Manning (1990) although preserving the nominal anchor, obtains multiple equilibria by means of a special form of increasing returns technology: namely, a production function of the type $Y=AN^{\alpha}$ with $\alpha>1$, as opposed to the production function introduced by Weitzman (1982) of the type $Y=(AN-f)^{\alpha}$ with $\alpha<1$[42]. Frank (1990) also preserves the nominal anchor, and achieves multiplicity by combining imperfect competition with the hypothesis of risk aversion by firms — in the specific form of decreasing relative risk aversion, without which there would be one single equilibrium.[43]

Perhaps the most Keynesian of the models with multiple equilibria has been developed by Bhaskar (1990), who formalizes Keynes' idea of wage relativities within a model of monopoly union.[44] Apart from its Keynesian pedigree, the wage relativities hypothesis seems to possess much greater economic significance than those adopted by the models mentioned above. It is, moreover, based on non-derivability at one point of the utility function; an assumption which is obviously more general than the derivability at all points and which has been confirmed by studies in experimental psychology, for instance by Kahneman and Tversky (1979) and supported by the analyses of Akerlof (1984).

One of the most attractive features of the approach based on wage relativities is that it is able to generate, simultaneously, a range of equilibria

---

[42] As a consequence of the hypothesis that $\alpha<1$, Manning is also obliged to assume very low elasticity of demand for the goods produced by the firm in order to obtain a well-defined problem of profit maximization (see Manning, 1990, p. 152).

[43] Frank's approach is also interesting because it creates a bridge between NKEmi and NKEai. The latter, as we shall see, adheres closely to the hypothesis that the firm behaves as if it were risk averse.

[44] The same result can be obtained by introducing the hypothesis of wage relativities into an efficiency wages model.

with involuntary unemployment and the non-neutrality of money, if the workers (trade unions) are Keynesian and expect (rationally) monetary shocks to have major effects on quantities and minor ones on prices. If there exists a small number of workers (trade unions) who do not have perfectly rational expectations, it is possible to show that the expectations of these workers facilitate coordination and make it possible to achieve one single equilibrium within the range (see Haltiwanger and Waldman, 1985). This is an equilibrium in which the expectations of everyone will be fulfilled but which, once again, may well be an under-employment equilibrium on which monetary shocks will have typically Keynesian effects.[45]

As regards the contraposition between models with nominal rigidities and those with coordination failures, it is worth pointing out that nominal rigidity may arise in a model with strategic complementarity and multiple equilibria in price adjustment (Ball and Romer, 1991).

The model examined by Ball and Romer is, in fact, entirely similar to the one illustrated in section 2.3. It is possible to show in this context that 'nominal rigidity arises from a failure to coordinate price changes. (...) Flexibility in one firm's price increases the incentives for other firms to make their prices flexible. This strategic complementarity leads to multiple equilibria in the degree of nominal rigidity' (Ball and Romer, 1991: 539).[46]

Thus an equilibrium with full price adjustment may occur if the shock surpasses a certain critical threshold size; while another equilibrium with perfect rigidity may occur if the shock is very small and no firm finds it

---

[45] The literature on coordination failures and multiple equilibria contains at least three different classes of dynamic models.

First, there are studies of self-fulfilling expectations and sunspots (the expectation of the event that engenders the event is a Keynesian theme). If more than one equilibrium exists, then even variables of marginal importance can produce real effects (Woodford, 1991). The cycles thus obtained are in equilibrium and endogenous, in the sense that they depend on the existence of some form of market failure. Unlike the Slutsky-Frisch models based on the existence of a "mythical steady state", models of endogenous equilibrium fluctuations do not need either an initial impulse to generate recurring oscillations or, like deterministic disequilibrium models, feedback mechanisms (often non-rational) which enable the cycle to reproduce itself.

There is then a body of literature which revives the theme of increasing returns: given that when aggregate demand is high increasing returns lower production costs, agents are stimulated to produce more. As they do so, individual actions produce externalities and therefore multiple equilibria (a model in Shleifer, 1986). If analysis concentrates on demand expectations in particular, it is possible to show that externalities stimulate cycles in different sectors and that, ulitmately, externalities govern the duration of the cycle.

The third class comprises models which demonstrate that economies with incomplete markets and close complementarities may generate path dependent fluctuations. This occurs when the effect of a shock on aggregate production is permanent (Durlauf, 1991). These models show that there may be multiple equilibria which differ in average and variance of output; that fluctuations in output are persistent because shocks provoke changes in the equilibria; and that these changes take the form of cyclical oscillations.

[46] Resuming the analysis in note 31, if the i-th firm adjusts its price and the others adjust as well, then $Di=1$, $P=M$, $M/P=1$, $P_i/P=1$, therefore $\Pi i = \Pi (1,1)-z$. On the other hand, if the i-th firm

---

31

convenient to sustain the adjustment cost. In the case of intermediate shocks,[47] a firm will adjust its prices if and only if the others adjust theirs. Thus, for a given quantity of money, there will be only one equilibrium. However, as the quantity of money changes, the economy may assume a variety of equilibria, depending on whether individual firms 'coordinate themselves' in deciding whether to adjust quantities or prices. In a dynamic context, moreover, strategic complementarity may give rise to multiple equilibria in the frequency of price adjustments and therefore in the dynamics of quantities (Ball and Romer, 1991: 548-9). In contrast to static models, effects on quantities in the dynamic model are closely dependent on the size of the monetary shock: a certainly more realistic outcome.

One notes, finally, that when coordination failures give rise to an equilibrium with nominal rigidities the response may consist not just in the defining of institutions and conventions which facilitate coordination, but also in the standard Keynesian policies designed to augment (or restrict) aggregate demand. These policies become necessary (and are effective) when the institutions and conventions fail: just as nominal rigidities and coordination failures are complementary explanations of fluctuations, so traditional policies are complementary, not alternative, to those designed to encourage coordination by means of announcement and signalling effects.

3. NEW KEYNESIAN ECONOMICS: ASYMMETRIC INFORMATION AND THE INEFFICIENCY OF CAPITAL MARKETS

3.1. Introduction

The microeconomic implications of market imperfections deriving from asymmetric information were originally described by Stigler (1961)[48]. Akerlof

---

does *not* adjust but the others do adjust, $D_i=0$, P=M, M/P=1, $P_i/P=1/M$, therefore $\Pi_i = \Pi (1,1/M)$. One may thus define an earning function $L_A = \Pi (1,1) - \Pi (1,1/M)$, which should be greater than z (the cost of adjustment) because the firm i adjusts its price. Using a second-order Taylor approximation around M=1 yields:

$$x_A = \sqrt{\frac{2z}{\Pi_{12}}}$$

Combining the expression for x_N in note 31 with x_A yields $x_N=x_A(1/\phi)$. Given the meaning of ϕ, it follows that $x_N>x_A$. If, therefore, the monetary shock |x| lies between x_A and x_N both rigidity and flexibility are equilibria.

[47] That is, if the monetary shock |x| lies between x_A and x_N.

[48] The assumption of asymmetric information is based on a stylized fact and not derived from first principles. In this it resembles the assumption of market power in NKEmi. The stylized fact is the background 'noise' which disturbs (and obscures) the market context and makes it difficult to ascertain the positions of individuals — that is, it impedes discrimination between

(1970) developed the topic with reference to the used car market and the purchaser's risk of buying a 'lemon'. If the principle of asymmetric information had been used only to analyse specific markets such as that studied by Akerlof, the literature that sprang from it would have soon become of only marginal economic relevance. In the 1980s, however, the importance of information asymmetries in capital markets was discovered, starting from the commonsense observation that certain shares and investment projects may sometimes prove to be 'lemons' for, respectively, the underwriter or the financier.

The micro and macroeconomic implications of informational imperfections in capital markets are numerous. We shall restrict ourselves here to listing and describing only three of them: in terms of firms' behaviour, the functioning of markets, and the effectiveness of monetary policy.

The most important consequence of informational imperfections in capital markets for the theory of firms' behaviour is the *falsification of the Modigliani-Miller theorem*, which holds that the financial structure does not influence production and investment decisions.[49] In the 1960s and 1970s the Modigliani-Miller theorem conquered the profession 'like the Inquisition conquered Spain', to use Keynes' metaphor,[50] opening a yawning chasm of incomprehension between economists and businessmen, whose behaviour constitutes *per se* an irrefutable counter-example.[51]

The rejection of the hypothesis of perfect markets led to renewed exploration of the role performed by the financial structure of firms in the determination of investments and production in the course of fluctuations (Bernanke, 1983; Bernanke and Blinder, 1988; Gertler, 1988; Bernanke and Gertler, 1990). On the basis of the empirical evidence available, sources of financing can be classified, in decreasing order of cost, into a *financing hierarchy* or *pecking order*, with the accumulation of internal resources (self-financing or cash flow) at the top, followed by bank credit and the issue of new shares (Myers and Majluf, 1984; Fazzari, Hubbard and Petersen, 1988).

The most important consequence of information asymmetry for the working of the capital markets is the possibility of *equilibrium rationing of funds*. The persistent surplus of demand for capital stems principally from the

---

the 'good' and the 'bad' — thereby inducing risk averse behaviour. Individuals can deal with information asymmetry by procuring extra information, although this is a costly process which may also be inhibited by free riding behaviour.

[49] For a retrospective assessment of the theorem and of its implications see Modigliani (1988), Miller (1988), Stiglitz (1988) and Bhattacharya (1988).

[50] Keynes' metaphor (1936: 32) referred to the acceptance by English economists of Say's law after its authoritative endorsement by Ricardo.

[51] Before the Modigliani-Miller theorem took over, the relevance of cash flow to firms' investment decisions was generally recognized, as shown by the writings of the Charles River School (see the contributions by Kuh and Meyer). The role of financial variables in the generation and propagation of fluctuations has been the central theme of the Debt Deflation School of Fisher (1933), Kindleberger (1978) and Minsky (1975, 1982, 1986).

fact that the 'price' (the interest rate in the credit market, the stock exchange index for securities) does not transmit information about scarcity; that is, it is no longer able to perform its allocative function. In both this context and that of efficiency wages theory, the direct linkage with the method and conclusions of Akerlof's approach to the market for 'lemons' is fairly evident (Stiglitz, 1987).

In the presence of rationing, output and investment decisions are constrained by the level and the nature of available capital. Monetary policy is therefore transmitted through the equity base of firms and/or the availability of credit. Thus, the major consequence of information asymmetry for monetary policy is the importance of transmission channels other than the one based on portfolio choices.[52]

In section 3.2 we shall briefly describe the consequences of asymmetric information between the managers of a firm and potential shareholders for the working of the stock market, setting out the conditions under which *equity rationing* can occur. We shall then, in section 3.3, consider the implications of the information asymmetry between firms and financial intermediaries for the functioning of the credit market, setting out the conditions under which *credit rationing* may occur.

The consequences of equity rationing and credit rationing on macroeconomic equilibrium and on the mechanism for transmission of monetary policy are briefly described and commented on in section 3.4. Finally, in section 3.5 we discuss the NKEai theory of fluctuations.

3.2. Equity rationing and the financial structure of firms

The simplest and most effective description of the consequences of asymmetric information on the working of the stock market reproduces Akerlof's analysis of the market for 'lemons' and applies it to the stock market. If firms' managers 'know more' than potential shareholders about the net present value of investment projects — if, that is, there is an *information asymmetry* between borrowers and lenders of funds in the stock market — given the impossibility of ascertaining the value of each individual project, investors will be willing to purchase the new shares of all firms at the same price, and they will therefore implicitly require the 'good' firms to pay a *lemon premium* which compensates them for those losses they incur by financing 'bad' firms as well. The lemon premium therefore takes the form of a 'discount' on the purchasing price of shares issued by good firms which may dissuade the latter from raising capital

---

[52] Already in the 1950s, the 'doctrine of availability' had stressed the limits on funds procurement and suggested that other aspects apart from the interest rate should be examined when assessing credit market conditions.

on the stock market. In other words, a lemon premium in the form of too low a price (that is the under-valuation of the issuing firm) triggers a typical adverse selection effect. If only bad projects (firms) are left in the market, a firm issuing new shares reveals itself as saddled with a low net present value investment project; that is, it sends a negative signal to potential investors who therefore interpret the announcement of an equity issue as a collapse in the value of shares.[53]

Similar conclusions can be reached from different theoretical starting points. For example, Jensen and Meckling (1976) have stressed the role of the firm's financial structure in generating managerial incentives. Shareholders may discourage the financing of investments by means of share issues and favour indebtedness because it spurs the managers to greater effort under the sword of Damocles of bankruptcy, thus attenuating the problem of moral hazard implicit in the relationship between owners and managers. It is widely known, in fact, that whereas an equity issue entails co-participation in profits and therefore a distribution of risks among the shareholders, a debt contract entails a fixed-sum obligation: the creditor assumes none of the risks associated with the firm's activity, since these accrue entirely to the debtor firm.

The issue of new shares may also send out a negative signal to potential investors. They may, for example, interpret the raising of risk capital as an attempt to avert bankruptcy (Ross, 1977; Greenwald, Stiglitz and Weiss, 1984). The situation here is one of a snake biting its own tail: if managers use the stock market unwillingly and only in the last resort to avoid the under-valuation of their firm, and if this is known to stock exchange operators, the decision to issue shares signals an irremediable financial difficulty which potential investors recognize and ratify by refusing to purchase these shares.

In order to illustrate the conditions under which recourse to the stock market to finance an investment project is inhibited, we take as an example — following Myers and Majluf (1984) — a firm possessing installed capital with a market value K and an investment project whose net present value is R. By hypothesis both K and R are random variables which can only take positive values, with a certain joint distribution of probability which we denote as F(.). The firm must decide whether to finance the investment project by placing new shares on the market or whether to abandon both the share issue and the project on the assumption that internal financial resources (self-financing) are not available and that it will not resort to credit.

If the management and the potential investors had the same information, the firm would always have to proceed with the investment because the investors would always be ready to finance a project with positive net present value. In this case, in fact, share prices would not fall, and the value of the

---

[53]   The empirical evidence for the depressive effect of the announcement of a new equity issue is analysed by Asquith and Mullins (1986).

capital raised on the stock market would correspond exactly to the net present value of the investment.

If, instead, the managers of the issuing firm possess an information *advantage* over the investors concerning the net present value of the investment project — if, that is, there is an information asymmetry between borrowers and lenders of funds in the stock market — a conflict of interest arises between old and new shareholders. Old shareholders must compare the benefit of issuing new shares — which consists in participation in the firm's increased capital value — against the cost of the participation of new shareholders in the firm's already-installed capital. Let us suppose that managers maximize the value of the shares already placed on the market — that is, they act in the interest of the old shareholders — and that the latter do not purchase the newly-issued shares and are therefore passive with respect to management's attempt to raise risk capital. In this case, managers may decide not to make an investment — even if its net present value is positive — should the cost of the share issue to the old shareholders prove to be higher than the benefit.

Let E be the value of the newly-issued shares and by hypothesis let E be equal to the investment project to finance (I=E). If the firm decides not to issue shares, the value of the shares held by the old shareholders will be $V_n=K$. If, instead, the firm does issue shares, the value of the old shares will be

$$V_e = \frac{V'}{V'+E}(E+K+R),$$ where V' is the market value of the old shares if the firm issues new ones,[54] and V'+E is the market value of all the shares, old and new. The management resorts to the stock market if $V_e > V_n$; that is, once the appropriate substitutions have been made, if: $E\,K/(V'+E) < V'\,(E+R)/(V'+E)$ where the left-hand side of the inequality is the share of installed capital appropriated by the new shareholders, while the right-hand side is the share of the increase in the firm's value distributed among the old shareholders. The management therefore places new shares on the market only if the increase in the firm's value accruing to the old shareholders is greater than the share of the firm's capital acquired by the new shareholders.

The above inequality may be written as:

$R > R'$ where $R' = (E/V')K-E$.

In other words, the management will go ahead with the share issue and undertake the investment project only if the net present value of the latter is greater than the critical threshold R', which depends linearly on K, given E and V'. Hence, as Figure 1.8 shows, only combinations (K, R) represented by the points in the region M' will induce the firm to invest and to issue shares. If,

---

[54] Using V to denote the market value of the old shares, if the firm does not issue new ones it is always the case that V'<V.

instead, the pairs (K, R) are located in region M, the firm will forgo a good investment opportunity rather than issue shares to finance it.

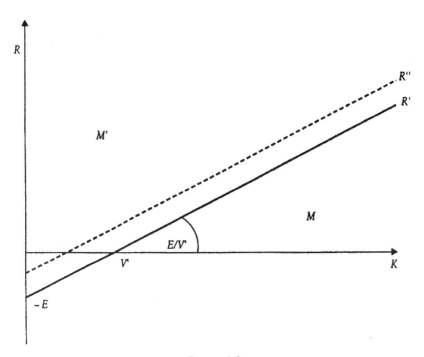

Figure 1.8

Put otherwise, the line representing R' divides the joint probability distribution of K and R into two regions: M and M'. The probability that the management will refrain from an investment so as not to issue new shares is F(M). In this case 'equity rationing' occurs, in the precise sense of an (optimal) decision not to resort to the stock exchange in order to finance investments.

A share issue has an indubitably negative impact on share prices. In fact, the price of old shares when the firm does not issue new ones (V) coincides with the expected value of the random variable K when (K,R) is located in M, which we denote with $\overline{K}$, that is V= $\overline{K}$. A rapid glance at Figure 1.8 is sufficient to show that V>V'.[55]

---

[55] According to Leland and Pyle (1977), the undervaluation of the issuing firm's shares can be attenuated if the entrepreneur or the management invest a part of their personal wealth in the firm and therefore in the financing of the investment project. Potential investors will interpret this commitment by the entrepreneur or managers as a positive signal. They will therefore react accordingly by increasing the price that they are willing to pay for new shares.

37

The non-issue of shares generates an *ex ante* loss of value equal to $L=F(M)\,\overline{R}$, where $\overline{R}$ represents the expected value of R when (K,R) is located in M. If the firm has internal financial resources — that is self-financing — to an amount A, then E=I-A. In this case, $V_n=K+A$.

Moreover, $V_c = V'(E+K+R+A)/(V'+E)$. Following a procedure identical to the one described above, the management will place new shares on the market only if R>R', where R'=(E/V')(K+A)-E (see again Figure 1.8). The accumulation of internal financial resources, therefore, reduces the probability that the firm will issue new shares. This occurs because the self-financing increases the market value of the existing capital and therefore the cost of the share issue to the old shareholders. In the limiting case in which I=A and E=0 (that is the investment is entirely self-financed), no *ex ante* losses occur because recourse to the stock market is averted.

It is possible to show quite straightforwardly (although we shall not dwell on this topic further) that, in the presence of a credit market, it is always in the interest of firms to resort to bank loans instead of issuing new shares. From this a *differentiation of financing sources* follows that gives rise to an ordering in which self-financing is the least 'costly' method of raising capital, followed by bank credit and, lastly, risk capital.[56]

3.3. Credit rationing

As was said at the beginning of section 3.1, asymmetric information is an endemic problem of capital markets (and not only these). In their procurement of credit, firms meet information obstacles just as severe as those already discussed in the equity market. Therefore, the credit market may be characterized by credit rationing. In order to give adequate treatment to the topic we shall distinguish between *ex ante* and *ex post* information asymmetry. In the former case the information advantage of the potential debtor manifests itself before the investment project is undertaken. Not only, therefore, does the potential debtor 'know more' about the yield on the investment for which he is applying for credit, but he knows it before the project is undertaken. With ex-post asymmetric information, the lender and the borrower of funds possess the same information before the project is started, but once it has been realized the borrower is better informed than the lender. The information is symmetrical before the project gets under way, but becomes asymmetrical once it has been financed, so that the debtor can use the funds received to finance an investment

---

[56] Although this differentiation has been confirmed empirically (see Fazzari, Hubbard and Petersen, 1988, and Mayer, 1988), theoretical treatment of it is still in its early stages (Abel, 1990).

of a degree of riskiness different from that for which he has obtained the financing.

The implications of ex *ante* asymmetric information have been studied by, amongst many others, Jaffee and Russell (1976) and Stiglitz and Weiss (1981). The consequences of *ex post* asymmetric information have been explored by Williamson (1986, 1987a) and Gertler (1988). There is a logical (and chronological) concatenation between the two strands of literature that we shall also follow here.

Let us consider a set of firms operating in a regime of perfect competition and which apply to a bank — this too market power — for credit in order to finance investment projects of a fixed and equal size for all applicants (firms are identical in every respect except the riskiness of their investment projects). The relationships between the lenders and borrowers of funds — all by hypothesis risk neutral — are regulated by a standard debt contract which, for simplicity's sake, we may assume as specifying no collateral securities.[57] Associated with each investment project is a distribution function $G(Y,\theta)$ of output (Y) identified by a riskiness parameter θ and characterized by mean preserving spread in θ.[58] In other words, all the investment projects are equal 'on average' but they differ in terms of their associated output, which is increasing in the risk parameter.

According to Stiglitz and Weiss (1981), the output generated by each investment project is not known with certainty even by the firm which undertakes it. But whereas the firm knows its probability of success, and therefore the expected yield, the bank only knows the probabilitis distribution of its potential debtors, and therefore the proportion of debtors that will pay back. The bank, however is unable to discriminate among the investment projects, that is, identify their individual riskiness.[59] The bank must therefore set a limit to its losses by selecting among the requests for financing.[60]

The bank knows that the higher the interest rate that firms are willing to

---

[57] A standard debt contract prescribes a fixed payment (capital and interest) by the debtor or the forfeiting of all its activities in the case of insolvency. The standard debt contract is optimal only under suitable conditions, as we shall see.

[58] This means that for each pair of values of θ there is a corresponding pair of distributions with the same mean but such that the distribution identified by the higher riskiness parameter admits higher probabilities for the extreme values of Y.

[59] Various explanations for the possible differences among potential debtors have been given. Jaffee and Russell (1976) identify two different types of applicants for credit: the 'honest' and the 'dishonest'. The former only accept low interest rates because they want to have a high probability of repaying the loan received. The latter accept high interest rates because they have a low probability of repaying the loan. For Stiglitz and Weiss (1981), by contrast, loan applicants can be classified according to the riskiness of their projects, which is not known to the bank and which can only be 'perceived'; that is, the applicants may be more or less 'optimistic' about the probability of success of their investment projects. Clemenz (1986) argues that applicants can be distinguished according to their 'ability', which is reflected in the project's probability of success.

[60] For a discussion of banks as 'social accountants' and 'screening devices', see Stiglitz (1988).

pay, the riskier will be the investment project for which the financing is requested. The firm, in fact, will accept high-rate loans because they know that their probability of repaying them is low. Therefore, when the bank raises the interest rate, the average riskiness of the set of debtors increases (*adverse selection* effect). Moreover, since the profit expected by the firm is an increasing function of the degree of risk, the higher the rate of interest the riskier (because more profitable) become the investment projects chosen by firms. In other words, when the bank raises the interest rate, the expected riskiness of each project increases (*adverse incentive* effect).[61]

Therefore, as well as the usual direct positive effect on the profit expected by the bank, an increase in the interest rate will produce an indirect negative effect due to adverse selection and adverse incentive. The bank's expected profit will therefore be non-monotonic but typically bell-shaped with respect to the interest rate (r) and it will admit at least one point at which it is maximum. Since the supply of loans (L^s) is a direct function of the profit expected by the bank, it too will be non-monotonic. The demand for loans by firms (L^d) will instead be decreasing (Figure 1.9).

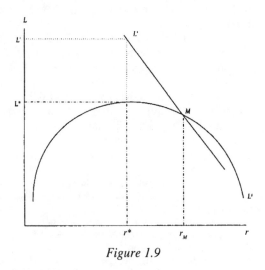

Figure 1.9

---

[61] The adverse incentive effect is based on moral hazard. For an analysis of the possibility of moral hazard with *ex ante* asymmetric information, and of the adverse incentive effect, see Keeton (1979) and Clemenz (1986). A large body of literature (which we shall not consider here) suggests that debt contracts should be viewed as principal-agent relations in which the principal (the creditor) is unable to control the actions of the agent (the debtor). In the terminology of contract theory, these models belong to the 'hidden action' category (Hart and Holmstrom, 1987). An example is provided by 'effort' models, in which it is assumed that the greater the effort of the agent, the greater the final output. An increase in the interest rate charged by the creditor thus induces the debtor to reduce his effort (in that the marginal yield on his effort diminishes).

However, the bank will never choose a point on the downward sloping section of its supply curve. If, in fact, the intersection between the demand and supply of credit were to occur at a point like M, with abscissa r_M, the effective supply of loans would be greater, and equal to L^*. The rate charged by the bank would be $r^*<r_M$ and credit rationing (that is a persistent excess-demand) equal to $L'-L^*$ would come into effect.

The model analysed so far provides a rigorous, and not *ad hoc*, explanation of credit rationing. It thus reveals why the interest rate should not be taken to be the sole or at least the principal transmission mechanism of monetary policy.[62]

Subsequent research, however, has highlighted the restrictive assumptions on which the model is based. Firstly, the standard debt contract is not endogenously determined as the optimal contract.[63] Secondly, under suitable conditions the model may generate *over-investment*, with the banks supplying more than firms desire at a certain rate.[64] Thirdly, if one admits the possibility that banks classify potential debtors, the rationing effect may become negligible.[65]

Finally, Stiglitz and Weiss overlook the possibility that lenders may handle the problem of adverse selection by requiring potential debtors to provide solvency signals (for example, their readiness to accept collateral securities) thereby inducing them to self-selection. Indeed, a credit contract typically specifies not only the rate of interest but also the collateral securities

---

[62] Already in the 1950s and the 1960s, and then in Hodgman (1960), the 'doctrine of availability' stressed that there were limits on the availability of credit, and that the interest rate could not be used as the sole indicator of conditions in the money market. Subsequently, Jaffee and Modigliani (1969) showed that credit rationing entails that the allocation of loans does not take place solely through price mechanisms.

[63] In fact, the standard debt contract is not necessarily optimal. As well shall see below, the models based on risk and on *ex post* asymmetric information endogenously solve the problem of the optimality of the standard debt contract.

[64] The possibility of over-investment has been highlighted by De Meza and Webb (1987), who, on the assumption that investment projects have different expected returns, show that 'good' projects end up by keeping 'bad' ones in play (that is they are not rationed). This is a result which contradicts Stiglitz and Weiss's finding that 'bad' projects force 'good' ones out of the market.

[65] We may suppose that banks are able to partition debtors into risk classes (that is pools of firms with investment projects characterized by identical expected gross yields but different degrees of risk; the degree of risk is a random variable the probability distribution of which is known to the bank). For each rate of interest charged by the bank, there will be non-rationed risk classes, partially rationed classes, and completely rationed ('red-lined') classes. If the partition is extremely fine (with, for example, one firm for each risk class) — as Riley (1987) has shown — there will be rationing for only one class (with one single firm). The lower ranked firms will be entirely excluded (red-lined), while the higher ranked ones will obtain what they require at the equilibrium rate. Rationing *per se* may therefore be negligible. However, as Stiglitz and Weiss (1985, 1987) have shown, many examples can be constructed in which rationing does not disappear even if the number of firms (of different classes) increases.

Financial Constraints and Market Failures

and the size of the loan. Bester (1985) shows that the result of equilibrium credit rationing is *local*, in that a surplus of demand may be in principle covered by an increase in collateral guarantees. However, Bester's assertion that under *separating equilibria* there is *no rationing* does not seem to be generally applicable, as has been repeatedly shown in the literature (Wette, 1983; Stiglitz and Weiss, 1985; Hellwig, 1987).[66]

Unlike the case of *ex ante* asymmteric information, in that of *ex post* asymmetric information the probability of the investment project's success, and therefore of its expected yield, is known both to the firm and to the bank before the project is undertaken. Once the project has been realized, the effective yield is known to the firm but not to the bank, which can only ascertain the yield by sustaining a monitoring cost. This is because the firm may adopt a project different from that declared to the bank (there arises, that is, a typical problem of moral hazard). The presence of monitoring costs characterizes models with costly state verification, in which the financial intermediary is the agent who has the task of monitoring credit contracts because he has a comparative advantage over any other agent in gathering information about the potential debtor.[67]

The implications of moral hazard and costly state verification have been studied by Townsend (1979) and subsequently by Gale and Hellwig (1985) and Williamson (1986, 1987a). In Williamson, an increase in the interest rate

---

[66] According to Stiglitz and Weiss (1985) the degree of risk aversion is inversely correlated to the wealth possessed and committed in guarantee of the loan. The request by the bank for further collateral securities may generate an adverse selection effect for borrowers analogous to that provoked by an increase in the interest rate. The banks thus decide not to make uniform use of the collateral securities lever and thereby give rise to credit rationing.

Hellwig (1987) shows that alternative formalizations which apply game theory to the market with adverse selection lead to different conclusions as regards rationing. The results depend on the type of equilibrium chosen. In the presence of a Nash equilibrium — as Rothschild and Stiglitz (1976) and Wilson (1977) have shown — self-selection takes place through the separation of contracts, and rationing does *not* occur. Alternatively, Wilson (1977) and Riley (1979) have proposed a concept of equilibrium in which the creditors anticipate the debtors' reaction to the introduction of a new contract. With a Riley equilibrium, Milde and Riley (1988) have proved the existence of separating equilibria *with* credit rationing.

[67] In other words, the bank's monitoring costs are lower than those which any other agent must sustain if he wishes to enter the credit market as a lender of funds. The contract which minimizes monitoring costs with the debtor's expected profit remaining equal — that is the optimal contract — is the standard debt contract. If, in fact, the contract establishes in which state one has monitoring (where by 'state' is meant the yield on the project), and if the state in which monitoring is accepted is interpreted as a state of insolvency, then the bank's monitoring cost is equal to the cost it incurs when the firm which obtains the financing goes bankrupt.

The optimal contract is defined as that pair of values of capital and interest which maximizes the profit expected by the debtor under the constraint that the profit expected by the creditor is at least equal to his opportunity cost (the yield on a risk-free security). It can be shown that this pair of values is in fact constant, in that the capital does not depend on the profit from the project financed and the contract is consequently a standard debt contract (Williamson, 1987a).

42

not only boosts profits of the lender in states not subject to monitoring (that is when insolvency does not occur) but also the likelihood of insolvency. There is, therefore, a trade-off between an increase in expected profit and an increase in bankruptcy costs. This entails the non-monotonicity of the expected profit function. If the rate of interest which maximizes the creditor's pay-off is lower than the market clearing level, then the bank has no incentive to increase it in order to absorb the market excess-demand, and rationing therefore occurs.

Williamson's approach is based on a unifying principle for use in studying the credit market: financial contracts, intermediation and allocative inefficiencies are all explained by the existence of monitoring costs. However, it has been argued that, in practice, these costs are not typically large. Moreover, it can be shown that standard debt contracts are optimal only if monitoring is deterministic and only if firms' revenues are not correlated to any other observable variable, in which case the debt contract would take some other contractual form which specifies extra information.

3.4. Financial structure, aggregate supply and monetary policy

We now examine the behaviour of firms in a context in which they are subject to equity rationing because of asymmetric information: the context, that is, of the stock exchange. Let us assume, however, that firms have unlimited access to credit: the banking system accommodates the demand for loans with a supply that is infinitely elastic given the contractual rate of interest. Firms' production decisions are therefore influenced by the form (credit, precisely) in which funds are made available, not by their overall amount.[68]

The theory of firms' behaviour presented in this section is a simplified version of the model set out by Greenwald and Stiglitz in a number of works (Greenwald and Stiglitz 1988a, 1989a, 1990, 1993b). The representative firm, which operates under perfect competition, produces a good (the GDP) wholly destined for consumption, using labour as its sole production factor and a technology with decreasing returns. Not considered, therefore — at least for the moment — is fixed capital, either as stock or as flow (investment). Greenwald and Stiglitz assume that firms must pay for labour before they have received revenues from sales. They are therefore forced to incur debts in order to pay wages.[69] In order to render the fundamental differences between the NKEmi and NKEai approaches clear and distinct, for the moment we shall ignore the time structure of Greenwald and Stiglitz's model, although we shall

---

[68] If, besides equity rationing, there is credit rationing as well, production decisions will be constrained by the overall amount of the financial resources available, as we shall see below.

[69] This, of course, is a revival in modern guise of the classical theory of capital as wages fund. The same kind of sequence (employment-production-sales) provides the basis for the 'monetary circuit' approach (Graziani, 1988).

continue to assume that labour is paid through indebtedness.[70]

Asking for bank credit exposes the firm to the risk of bankruptcy, which arises when the equity base or net worth is lower than the stock of debts.[71] Associated with bankruptcy are costs proportional to the quantity produced.[72] The likelihood of bankruptcy is negatively correlated with the equity base in real terms.[73]

In this context the firm's problem is to maximize real profit with respect to the quantity produced; that is:

$$\underset{q}{Max} \ \pi = q - (1+r) \ [w\phi(q) - a] - gq\psi(\alpha)$$

where q is the quantity produced, r is the real interest rate, w is the real wage, ϕ (q) = n is employment (an inverse of the production function), g is the real unitary cost of bankruptcy, a is the equity base in real terms, and $\psi(\alpha)$ is the

---

[70] In other words, we assume that employment, production, selling and borrowing decisions take place simultaneously. The simplification proposed may be justified by supposing that payments (wages) and earnings (revenues) are not synchronous — they therefore give rise to a financial shortfall — but that the interval between them is so short that it is negligible from the modelling point of view. Of course, if we distinguish between current expenditure (wages, intermediate goods) and fixed capital expenditure (investment) in the firm's costs structure, the need for borrowing only arises in relation to investment; that is, in relation to costs incurred today which generate revenues only in the future. Greenwald and Stiglitz consider the analytical apparatus that we are about to describe as immediately applicable to the case of capital goods purchasing, although they do not explicitly address the problem.

[71] The possibility of bankruptcy is closely connected to equity rationing: in this case, in fact, firms are unable to share the risks they assume in production with other agents (investors).

[72] Greenwald and Stiglitz propose two explanations for bankruptcy costs. First, given that in the presence of imperfect information outside observers are unable to distinguish between bad luck and incompetent management, rightly or wrongly the bankruptcy damages the reputation of the managers. The bankruptcy costs are therefore represented by the impact of this loss of reputation on the managers' future earnings. Alternatively, the costs of the bankruptcy can be expressly stipulated in the managers' contracts as a form of disincentive.

[73] Greenwald and Stiglitz assume that the firm operates in a 'disturbed' (uncertain) context which prevents them from knowing with certainty how much they will be able to sell at every price level; that is at what price the firm will manage to sell its product (in other words, the firm's infinitely elastic demand curve is affected by a stochastic disturbance). The firm has therefore limited information, and the competition, although perfect, is not pure. For the firm, the relative price of its product compared with its competitors' price is a random variable with unitary expected value and finite variance. In a context such as this, the price that the firm obtains on the market may prove so low as to prevent it from honouring its debts with the banks. Therefore, the likelihood of bankruptcy coincides with the likelihood that the relative price will be lower than the limit-price required to avert it (that is the minimum relative price that ensures solvency), which in turn depends negatively on the equity base in real terms: the greater the equity base, the lower the limit-price and therefore the likelihood of bankruptcy. Of course, the real equity base is not the sole determinant of the limit price: in the main text we have used a simplification of Greenwald and Stiglitz's model.

probability of bankruptcy with $\psi'(\alpha)<0$. Each period debt, which is equal to the wage-fund minus internal financing $(wn-\alpha)$ is entirely paid back within the same period.[74]

The interest rate r is the *real rate expected by the banks*; that is, the contractual (nominal) rate applied to the loans net of the inflation rate expected by the banks. Greenwald and Stiglitz assume that the latter are perfectly informed and risk-neutral, and that they will fix the contractual rate (i) so as to generate, given their expectations of inflation, a constant real rate r. However, the nominal interest rate is not indexed to the inflation rate. Hence, a rate of inflation different from the one expected by firms will entail changes in the real rate borne by firms, and will have relevant effects on the economy as a whole.[75]

From the first-order condition (that is: $1-(1+r)w\phi'(q) - g\,\psi(\alpha) = 0$) the real wage w is obtained as a decreasing function of n, given the equity base and the interest rate. This is the firm's labour demand curve. Summing horizontally the individual labour demand curves yields the market labour demand curve in the presence of bankruptcy risk (N_b^d), which — in the plane (w,N) — lies beneath the labour demand curve in the absence of bankruptcy risks (Figure 1.10). *Ceteris paribus*, under risk of bankruptcy firms demand less labour for every level of the real wage. The risk of bankruptcy induces in firms — which are formally risk neutral — a behaviour which is *de facto* risk averse.[76]

The financial structure of firms, therefore, is anything but irrelevant to employment and production decisions, contrary to the contentions of the Modigliani-Miller theorem. The generation of internal financial resources is the prime source of funds that can be invested in extra wages and therefore in

---

[74] Thanks to this simplifying assumption, Greenwald and Stiglitz rule out by hypothesis the accumulation of debt by firms. They thus neglect a crucial vehicle for the transmission of shocks, and an important factor in their persistence. The dynamic implications of the accumulation of debt are presented and discussed in Delli Gatti, Gallegati and Gardini (1993).

[75] That is, $i = (1+r)(1+p^e) - 1$, where p^e is the rate of inflation expected by the banks. The procedure whereby the contractual rate is determined on the basis of the expected real rate is much more complex than this, but for our purposes the simplification proposed here will suffice. It is not clear in Greenwald and Stiglitz's work whether the hypothesis of perfect information also entails perfect foresight on the part of the banks, in which case the expected inflation rate should be equal to the effective rate in every period.

The hypothesis of constancy of the real rate correponds to a stylized fact frequently cited by the authors in their works (for example Stiglitz, 1992). In this context such a hypothesis is justified by the constancy of the time preference rate obtained by maximization of the representative consumers' intertemporal utility.

[76] By issuing shares, firms share the risk (as well as profits) with investors. By raising loans, instead, they incur a fixed-sum obligation which, if it proves impossible to honour, will force them into bankruptcy. Financing by means of share issues is inhibited by the signalling effect discussed in section 3.2. The impossibility of procuring risk capital entails recourse to bank debt which induces behaviour which is the more risk averse the greater the exposure and the risk of bankruptcy. It is apparent why Greenwald and Stiglitz (1993b) claim that they have elaborated a theory of supply based on risk aversion.

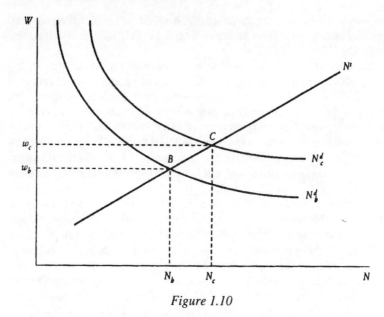

Figure 1.10

new employment. From this implicitly derives a hierarchy of financing sources.

Let us suppose that the labour supply function (N^s) is well behaved, that is, positively sloped. The intersection between demand and supply determines the real wage and equilibrium employment in the presence of bankruptcy costs (point B), which will be lower than those obtained in the absence of bankruptcy costs (point C). The level of employment N_b therefore implicitly defines an *asymmetric information natural rate of unemployment*, which is obviously higher than the natural rate as formulated by Friedman. Bankruptcy costs therefore entail inefficiency at the macroeconomic level. The parallelism with the case of imperfect competition is evident.[77]

The market labour demand curve is parametrized — and so is the real interest rate — to the equity base (A).[78] An increase in the latter will shift the demand curve upwards because it reduces the likelihood of bankruptcy.

On variations in the equity base, equilibrium in the labour market and the

---

[77] Of course, if we were to consider imperfect competition and asymmetric information jointly, the labour demand curve would lie below the curve associated with the costs of bankruptcy, and the real wage and equilibrium employment would therefore be even lower.

[78] The letter 'a' denotes the firm's real equity base; 'A' instead denotes the aggregate real equity base. The market labour demand curve (N), obtained by horizontally summing the individual demand curves (n) — each of which parametrized to the individual equity base (a) — will be in its turn parameterized to the aggregate real equity base (A). We assume, of course, that the regularity conditions necessary for the aggregation are satisfied.

production function will produce an increasing relation between Y,[79] and A (Figure 1.11),[80] which is parametrized to the real rate r. In other words, $Y=Y(A,r)$ with $Y_A>0$ and $Y_r<0$.

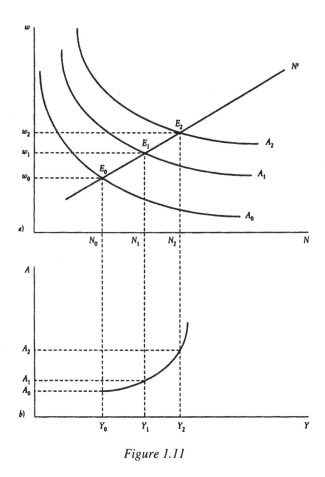

Figure 1.11

    The real equity base is the difference between the quantity produced and the real costs that the firm expects to incur in redeeming its debts and paying dividends, which can be considered, in its turn, an increasing function of the

---

[79]   The letter q denotes the output of the individual firm, while Y denotes total income.
[80]   According to Greenwald and Stiglitz, the function is concave: at relatively low (high) levels of the equity base — that is, in economies with high (low) amounts of indebtedness — the output multiplier is very high (low).

Financial Constraints and Market Failures

equity base: D=mA.[81] Ultimately, therefore:

$$A = Y - \frac{1+r}{\eta}[w\phi(Y)-A]-mA$$

where η denotes the ratio between the effective future level of prices and that expected by firms (η= P/P^e). Expression (1+r/η) represents the real interest factor *for firms*. The real interest rate may be interpreted as the difference between the real rate charged on loans by the banks and the error in forecasting the inflation rate made by firms.

Both Y and w are increasing functions of A and decreasing functions of r. The above equation should therefore be interpreted as an implicit function of A in η and r, that is: A=A(h,r) with A_h>0, A_r<0. Substituting this expression in the relation between Y and A obtained above and represented in Figure 1.11 yields income as an increasing function of the expectation parameter η and a decreasing function of the real interest rate r: Y=Y(h,r) with A_h>0, A_r<0. Linearizing the function by means of logarithmic transformation, we may write:[82]

$$Y = Y(r) + \beta(P-P^e).$$

This equation can be interpreted as an *aggregate supply curve à la Greenwald-Stiglitz* which shares with the Lucas curve the presence of a price shock among the determinants of production decisions, but differs from it in that full employment income — which depends on firms' equity base as well as on technology — is affected by changes in the real interest rate charged by the banks.

An unexpected monetary expansion — that is a positive price shock — increases the equity base by reducing the real debt service for firms.[83] The increase in the firm's net worth reduces, in its turn, the probability of

---

[81] The presence of asymmetric information on the equity market and the connected problems of adverse selection and moral hazard explain not only equity rationing but also the dividends policy of firms, which is generally intended to provide a constant flow of dividends to the shareholders in order not to emit negative signals to investors. For our present purposes, we shall restrict ourselves — following Greenwald and Stiglitz — to the assumption that this flow depends positively on the equity base. This expression may be seen as the steady state condition of the dynamic equation that defines the equity base in Greenwald-Stiglitz' model (see section 3.5).

[82] In order to economize on notation, the symbols which have so far denoted levels will be used in the following equation to denote logarithms.

[83] By hypothesis, the banks keep the real interest rate constant. Assuming that they always anticipate the effects of monetary measures, this implies that the nominal rate is index-linked to the effective inflation rate. However, the *ex post* debt service in real terms for firms — that is after the monetary shock — is influenced by the price shock. Hence, if the expected inflation rate is lower than the effective rate, the real debt service for firms diminishes.

insolvency and boosts labour demand. The labour demand curve moves along the labour supply curve and generates a higher equilibrium level of employment and real wage. This engenders an increase in aggregate supply which — under the hypothesis that the demand for consumption goods adjusts to supply in order to maintain equilibrium in the goods market[84] — produces an increase in income.[85]

This result has obvious affinities with the conclusions of NCM, as Greenwald and Stiglitz themselves acknowledge. However, they hasten to attribute a crucial role to aggregate demand, and especially to mixed demand and supply shocks. There are at least two channels through which demand and supply shocks merge. First, a supply shock, for example a positive 'price surprise' to a firm, causes an increase in output which increases income and therefore demand for the goods produced by other firms.[86] Second, shocks which hit the equity base influence not only the firm's production decisions but also its investment plans and therefore aggregate demand.[87]

We have so far assumed that asymmetric information occurs only in the equity market. We can, however, extend the model to take account of asymmetric information on the labour market as well, by introducing a wage setting rule obtained from one of the efficiency wage theories. As we have already seen,[88] under the turnover or shirking hypotheses, the wage rule turns out to be an increasing relation between real wage and employment[89] (WW in Figure 1.10) which lies entirely above the labour supply curve. Equilibrium in the labour market — that is, the intersection between labour demand and the wage rule — generates a level of employment N* and therefore involuntary unemployment equal to N'-N*. Asymmetric information in the labour market

---

[84] In Greenwald and Stiglitz (1993b), the equilibrium between aggregate demand (in this case, only for consumption goods) and aggregate supply is assumed, but the adjustment mechanism is not discussed.

[85] It is worth dwelling briefly on the mechanism which transmits impulses from the real interest rate. An increase in the real interest rate influences production decisions through two channels: firstly, it directly increases the marginal cost of labour; secondly, it reduces the equity base and thereby increases the probability of bankruptcy. Both effects tend to reduce labour demand for every level of the real wage. The labour demand curve shifts along the supply curve and generates a lower rate of employment and of real wage. Aggregate supply diminishes as a consequence.

[86] This mechanism is based on a typical demand spillover (a firm's employment decisions influence the demand addressed to other firms through the income and the consumption of its workers) which, in a dynamic context, generates a positive externality. The consequences of this 'Keynesian game' in terms of multiple equilibria parametrized to the 'state of confidence' are analysed in Boitani and Delli Gatti (1991).

[87] The impact of changes in the equity base on investment requires an extension of the model of the firm's behaviour which takes into account uncertainty over the future return on the investment itself.

[88] See section 2.5.

[89] In the case of shirking, this is the 'no shirking constraint'.

therefore plays a decisive role in generating involuntary employment in Greenwald and Stiglitz's model.

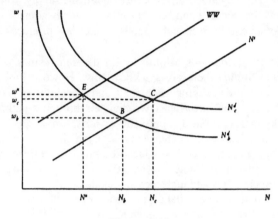

Figure 1.12

Asymmetric information in the stock market is implicit, as we know, in the presence of the equity base among the determinants of labour demand. As the equity base changes, equilibrium in the labour market — jointly with the production function — will produce a relation between Y and A lying above the equilibrium relation obtained from the intersection between labour demand and supply. In other words, *for every level of the equity base*, equilibrium employment will be lower than that which would occur in the absence of asymmetric information in the labour market, the difference being involuntary unemployment.

Following the same procedure as used above to construct the aggregate supply curve *à la* Greenwald-Stiglitz, we reach the conclusion that the equilibrium income — which continues to be parametrized to the price shock and to the real interest rate — is characterized by involuntary unemployment. *Mutatis mutandis*, the basic result obtained above is robust with respect to the change to the model proposed here: a monetary shock is not neutral only if it is unexpected. In this case, however, changes in income and in employment are accompanied by changes in the reverse direction in involuntary unemployment.

The model analysed so far lends itself to a straightforward extension which takes account of the implications of asymmetric information, not only on the equity and the labour markets, but also on the credit market. If the firm is subject to twofold rationing — if, that is, it is unable to procure risk capital and unable to obtain sufficient credit — the *financing constraint* becomes binding: the overall amount of funds available inflexibly restricts production

50

and investment decisions. Greenwald and Stiglitz (1990) examine the consequences of this financing constraint in a suitably modified IS-LM model,[90] of which we here briefly outline a simplified version in order to show the effects of monetary policy on the transmission mechanisms. We begin with the version of the model with fixed prices (for simplicity's sake, we may posit P=1) and idle productive capacity. The variables that appear in the functions presented below are therefore valued in real terms.

The effective level of the credit supplied is the product of the banks' assets multiplied by the share loaned to firms. In the case of a balance-sheet simplified to the extreme, in which assets consist of government securities and loans to firms,[91] while liabilities consist of deposits,[92] by accounting coherence the banks' assets are equal to the level of their deposits. If we assume, for simplicity, that the quantity of money coincides with the level of deposits,[93] the banks' assets are equal to the quantity of money. In other words, the quantity of money functions as a scale variable of the credit supplied.

The proportion of assets invested in loans depends positively on the equity base of firms and negatively on the rate of interest on Government securities. An increase in the equity base — that is, a strengthening of the financial structure — reduces the probability of insolvency and therefore improves the quality of the pool of borrowers, and this induces the banks to grant more credit.[94-95] A reduction in the rate of interest on Government securities has the same expansionary effect on the credit supplied, given the substitutability between Government securities and credit to firms in the banks' assets. The quantity of money, the equity base of firms, and the rate of interest on Government securities can be interpreted as factors which shift the bell-shaped curve representing the bank's supply of loans with asymmetric information in the credit market. Therefore, the level of credit associated with the maximum point of this curve — that is the volume of effective loans (B) in the presence of credit rationing — will depend on the above-mentioned variables:

$$B = B(M, r_G, A) \text{ with } B_M > 0, \ B_r < 0; \ B_A > 0$$

[90] For a similarly modified ISLM model — that is one intended for analysis of the specificity of credit in macroeconomic equilibrium — see Bernanke and Blinder (1988).
[91] For the sake of simplicity, we ignore bank reserves.
[92] For the sake of simplicity, we consider the net capital of banks to be negligible.
[93] This hypothesis entails the absence of currency: all transactions are regulated by means of cheques drawn on bank accounts.
[94] In the presence of equity rationing and an accommodating credit policy, however, the granting of loans by the banks by definition does not depend on the firms' assets structures: the banks grant all the credit that firms apply for at a given real rate, without considering the effects of the risk of bankruptcy.
[95] In this context, the equity base performs a similar function to that of collateral guarantees.

The rate of interest on loans is an increasing function of the rate on government securities, which are considered to be risk-free assets, that is $r=a(r_G)$.[96]

On the goods market, aggregate demand is the sum of consumption — which depends, according to a standard hypothesis, on income — public spending (G) and investment (I). Assuming that there is rationing in the credit market, the level of investment will be limited by the volume of funds made available by the banks (I=B).[97] Equilibrium in the goods market, taking account of the credit supplied by the banks, generates an equilibrium relation between the interest rate and income parametrized to the equity base of firms and to the quantity of money. This is the IS curve:[98]

$$r^G = g\ (Y;M,G,A)\ with\ g_y<0,\ g_M>0,\ g_G>0,\ g_A>0 \qquad (IS)$$

Equilibrium on the market for money generates a relation between the interest rate, income and the quantity of money; that is, a standard LM curve:

$$r^G = l(Y;M)\ with\ l_Y>0,\ l_M<0 \qquad (LM)$$

We now examine the effects of a monetary expansion. In the new context, this shock manifests itself as a rightward shift in both the LM and the IS curves. This inevitably gives rise to an increase in income while the effect on the interest rate remains indeterminate (see Figure 1.11).

The increase in liquidity is transmitted through numerous channels. First, the means of payment available to the public increase: the rearrangement of household portfolios produces an immediate reduction in the interest rate on Government securities which positively influences the supply of credit, given the substitutability between loans and Government securities in the banks' portfolios, and therefore investment. Furthermore, the quantity of money is a scale variable of the supply of loans. An increase in it will therefore increase the amount of funds available to firms for investment. The principal transmission mechanism therefore becomes the *availability of credit*. The increase in income deriving from the extra spending on investment goods, however, and the associated increase in the transactions demand for money, may more than

---

[96] Greenwald and Stiglitz derive this proposition within a simple mean-variance model applied to banks' investment choices in loans and Government securities.

[97] All the determinants of the effective level of credit supplied by the banks thus become determinants of investment as well. Hence it follows that investment depends, amongst other things, also on the equity base. In this new context, the correlation passes through credit rationing and does not derive from the reformulation of the firm problem to take account of capital spending.

[98] In Bernanke and Blinder's (1988) model, an equilibrium relation is generated between the interest rate and income, with joint consideration of equilibrium on the goods and credit markets, and is indicated with CC.

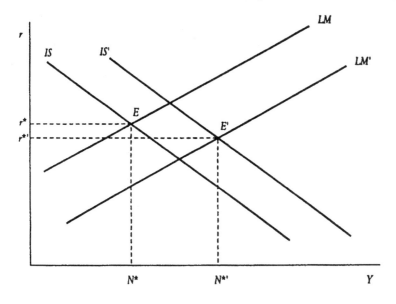

Figure 1.13

offset the initial impact on the interest rate, leaving it unchanged or even pushing it up.

In a context of price flexibility, Greenwald and Stiglitz's reduced form of the IS-LM model yields an aggregate demand curve in the plane (P,Y) which is *parameterized to the equity base of firms*, to public spending and to the quantity of money. A shock which hits the equity base, therefore, has demand effects which manifest themselves through firms' investment plans.

Once the aggregate demand curve has been constructed, the temptation immediately arises of using the supply curve *à la* Greenwald-Stiglitz as developed above in order to 'close' the model. However, there is still a great deal of analytical work to be done before a thoroughly satisfactory AD-AS model can be achieved. For example, the supply curve in the new context would have to be modified in order to take account not only of equity rationing, but of credit rationing as well.

Moreover, in defining the real equity base one cannot assume that the real rate charged by banks is constant (perhaps because it coincides with the time preference rate) without addressing the problem of the relation between the rate of interest on Government securities and the rate *on investments*.

Nevertheless, at least at the conjectural level, we can identify the principal effects of an unexpected monetary shock: the price surprise and the change in the equity base will influence aggregate demand through the supply of credit by the banks and spending on investment goods; but it will also influence demand through its impact on the likelihood of bankruptcy and on firms' investment plans. This provides substantial confirmation of the conclusions reached earlier.

3.5. Income fluctuations and deterministic cycles

In the analysis of economic fluctuations, 'most macro-economist now share the same framework', that is, the Slutsky-Frisch approach (Blanchard and Fischer, 1989: 277).[99] The impulse-propagation methodology holds that serially non-correlated shocks, the *impulses*, influence output through a *propagation* mechanism (that is a relation with distributed lags). Because of 'Ockham's rule', as well as its econometric successes, the Slutsky-Frisch approach has progressively supplanted the non-linear methodology of the Kaldor-Hicks-Goodwin tradition.

According to the thesis underlying the impulse-propagation approach, the capitalist system is intrinsically stable, albeit subject to the exogenous shocks of 'nature' or of economic policy. Conversely, the non-linear theories have the repetitive nature of cyclical fluctuations depend on the endogenous properties of an unstable system. Whereas NKEmi, with the possible exception of sunspot theories, adheres to the former research methodology, the NKEai school adopts a more eclectic and general approach which, by combining endogenous dynamics and stochastic elements, supports Keynes' assertion that capitalism is a system subject to periodic fluctuations which, although violent, do not degenerate into structural collapse.

This approach can be analysed better if we reformulate the model of section 3.3 in order to consider (following Greenwald and Stiglitz, 1993b) a change in the equity base:

$$A_{t+1} = Y - [(1+r)/\eta] \, [w\phi(Y) - A] - mA$$

As will be remembered from the previous section, the real wage and employment are determined by the intersection between the 'no shirking constraint' and labour demand. Since the latter is parametrized to the equity base, the real wage and equilibrium employment (and therefore income) are

---

[99] In the Slutsky-Frisch approach, small deviations from the steady state are analysed (for a critique of the assumptions underlying this methodology see Woodford, 1992). In order to obtain the steady-state equilibrium position, numerous restrictions must be introduced: specifically, one must assume that equilibrium exists, that it is unique, and that it is stable. Moreover, if the presence of imperfect information is hypothesised, the concept itself of equilibrium with rational expectations remains undefined (Phelps, 1992). The effects of the introduction of stochastic disturbances in NKEai models are analysed in Delli Gatti, Gallegati and Gardini, (1993); Gallegati and Stiglitz, (1992, 1993).

increasing functions of the equity base. Bearing this in mind, the previous expression translates into a non-linear first-order difference equation in A,

$$A_{t+1} = \Gamma_1 A - \Gamma_2(A^2)$$

which can display the shapes shown in Figure 1.14

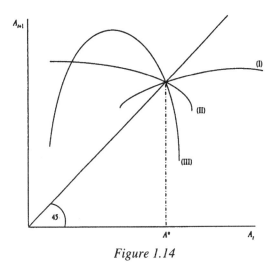

Figure 1.14

In Figure 1.14, assuming that the equation of the At+1 curve intersects the 45 degrees line from above (that is that its slope is less than 1 in absolute value), there is a convergence, either monotonic or with damped oscillations, towards the steady state equilibrium. Conversely, in order to obtain endogenous dynamic behaviour — behaviour, that is, which does not depend on an initial shock — the value of Γ_1 must lie within a specific interval. If the parameter assumes values between 3.45 and 4, the model generates endogenous disequilibrium dynamics which are *chaotic* in nature (Grandmont, 1985; Goodwin and Pacini, 1992).

During the upward phase of the cycle, the increment in production is reflected in an increase in labour demand and therefore in wages. In the long run, increased indebtedness reduces profits and the equity base. In the presence of financing constraints, this reduction generates an increase in bankruptcy risk and a fall in present output which reduces the demand for labour: wages decline while the increase in self-financing that ensues restores the initial conditions of profitability. When profits begin to grow, in fact, also the quantity produced and employment will progressively increase, with expansionary effects on wages. If in an initial phase the increase in wages stimulates aggregate demand, it thereafter causes profits and output to shrink, thereby restoring the conditions of cycle reversal.

This dynamics to a large extent reproduces the results obtained by Goodwin's Lotka-Volterra models, with 'new' hypotheses based on first principles and the not uninfluential variant of the a-periodicity of the fluctuations, although they are still not derived from the optimizing behaviour of agents. For this purpose, NKEai must take a further step forward by abandoning the hypothesis, analytically very useful but incoherent in a context of asymmetric information, of the representative agent.[100]

In the case in which convergence to equilibrium is not such as to generate endogenous behaviours, the dynamics of the system may still be analysed using the impulses-propagation instrument by linearizing around the steady state. Those who adopt the Slutsky-Frisch methodology must address three questions: the *origin*, the *transmission* mechanism and the factors of impulse *amplification-attenuation*.

In the absence of perfect capital markets — that is, of those markets which transfer risk over time and among agents — it may happen that if firms are risk-averse, small shocks will have major macroeconomic consequences (Stiglitz, 1992b, 1993). A shock which reduces firms' equity base, in the absence of conditions which validate the Modigliani-Miller theorem, leads to a reduced availability of capital and an increase in financial fragility and therefore in bankruptcy risk. If the elasticity of production to the risk of bankruptcy is high (which is usually the case if firms are risk-averse: for empirical verification see Fazzari et al., 1988), every disturbance will have broad effects on production because the marginal cost of an additional unit of output diminishes when the equity base increases and grows when it decreases. If this is true, then the origin of fluctuations becomes in some way secondary (from time to time, it may be real, monetary or expectations-based) to the fact that the structure of the economy either amplifies the effects of these disturbances or distributes them among sectors and firms.[101-102]

---

[100] Greenwald and Stiglitz (1993b) do not consider the effects stemming from the accumulation of capital and from technical progress, and consider only growthless fluctuations. NKEai cyclical growth models with an explicitly modelled investment function are presented in Gallegati (1993b) and Ardeni and Gallegati (1994).

[101] See, for instance Greenwald and Stiglitz (1988b: 255). Oddly enough, NKEai theory lacks an analysis of the financial multiplier (Roe, 1973). Aggregate fluctuations which derive solely from the composition effect are studied in Gallegati (1993a).

[102] Apart from methodological eclecticism, what induces NKEai not to identify the origin of shocks is the difficulty of distinguishing between demand shocks and supply shocks. From a microeconomic point of view, in fact, demand and supply are often indistinguishable because the variables which influence the former are the same as those which determine changes in the latter. Consider investments, for example: the decision to augment capital is a decision which simultaneously affects demand and aggregate supply. More generally, because the equity base enters the aggregate functions of demand and supply, every shock that affects it will induce both curves to shift. Contrary to the Blanchard-Quah methodology, NKEai (Stiglitz, 1992b: 70; Greenwald and Stiglitz, 1988b: 259) sets out to verify the validity of macroeconomic models not only in aggregate but also in their individual microeconomic propositions.

Consider a negative shock on prices as a result of which the current price is lower than the expected level. If, as Greenwald and Stiglitz assume, contracts are not index-linked, a redistribution of wealth between borrowers and creditors will come about which, given the context of information asymmetry and risk-averse firms, has significant effects on production. With a present price lower than the expected one, the level of net worth, and therefore of output, will immediately fall below the steady-state value and will return to the equilibrium value only slowly. In fact, in order to accelerate adjustment, firms must produce more, and they therefore incur excessive risks in the presence of bankruptcy costs.[103] Firms expand their production only if they are able to rely on an adequate level of self-financing: in the presence of imperfect capital markets, in fact, no firm is willing to increase its financial fragility and, since self-financing accumulates slowly, strongly persistent shocks are generated.

Rather oddly for models of Keynesian inspiration, the source of impulses is almost entirely real (see also Hall, 1988: 262). This is due to two aspects which have not yet been entirely accounted for in NKEai models (index-linking and transmission mechanisms) and also to the consideration that the distinction between demand and supply is, at best, misleading.

4. ACHIEVEMENTS AND SHORTCOMINGS OF NEW KEYNESIAN ECONOMICS

In anticipation of certain of our conclusions, we may say that, since NKE has still not produced a general macroeconomic model with solid microfoundations, it is far from having completed its research programme. The piecemeal approach about which Stiglitz (1992b) complains characterizes analyses which often go no further than formulating partial equilibrium models. We believe, however, that the foundations have now been laid for a general NKE model based on contributions which have yielded extremely important findings, such as coordination failures, multiple equilibria in non-competitive contexts, the rationing of funds and the differentiation of sources of financing on the basis of asymmetric information. All insights which undermine the foundations of the Walrasian model, but that ought to be carefully put together in order to have a unified New Keynesian theory capable of effectively competing with its Neoclassical rival, which is still dominant in textbooks and journals.

---

[103] In NKEai models, the production function becomes almost concave as full employment is approached because of bankruptcy costs. This phenomenon may generate asymmetry in the system's response to impulses depending on whether a firm's financial position is close to concavity or whether it is not: the same shock hitting the equity base may have much more evident effects in curtailing the expansion of production.

4.1. An overview

Despite their differing pre-analytical convictions, NKE and the neoclassical schools share two methodological premises: that macroeconomics must be grounded on solid microeconomic bases, and that understanding macroeconomic behaviour requires the construction of a simple general equilibrium model. To this NKE adds a 'validation' criterion which goes beyond the pure and simple goodness of fit of a macroeconomic model and requires microeconometric estimates and the verification of every individual forecast. Our assessment of the successes and failures of NKE — an assessment which is necessarily provisional given that research is still in progress — is predicated on the methodological premises and empirical discriminants just mentioned.

We shall not be concerned with establishing the extent to which NKE is Keynesian, since this is an issue which, on the one hand, can be considered purely semantic and, on the other, requires much more space than available here for its thorough treatment.

Mankiw and Romer (1991) view NKE's contribution as an attempt to explain the nominal rigidities of prices, wages and the interest rate in a context of widespread market imperfections. They distinguish between the NKEmi and NKEai strands of inquiry on the basis of types of markets and of imperfections.[104] Under this interpretation, whereas NKEmi emphasises imperfections in the goods market, NKEai concentrates on the informational imperfections in the capital market, with the labour market acting as the link between the two lines of thought. The difference between the two schools, therefore, is principally a matter of emphasis; and it is a difference so subtle that such distinguished economists as Phelps and Gordon (1990) apparently failed to notice it , concentrating on NKEmi alone. Needless to say, this interpretation strikes us as highly reductive.

In this paper we have sought to show that NKE analysis goes well beyond a microeconomic explanation of only nominal rigidities. However, the proliferation and fragmentation of approaches has so far prevented identification of a *causa causans* acting as the guiding principle for research (McCallum, 1993).[105] To borrow an expression from Blanchard and Fischer (1989: 383),

---

[104] Commenting on Greenwald and Stiglitz (1988a), Hall proposes the distinction, not between NCM-RBC and NKE, but between the real macroeconomic school of Prescott and Greenwald-Stiglitz and the *nominal* school of Ball, Mankiw and Romer, where the differentiation is based on the origin of impulses.

[105] Stiglitz (1992b: 276) criticises the piecemeal approach of NKEmi by saying: 'The piecemeal approach is not only unattractive, in requiring a myriad of explanations, but the explanations seem sometimes at odds with one another'. One may suspect that Stiglitz is convinced to be able to avoid this criticism by assuming asymmetric information as the basic principle for his own models.

NKE paradoxically suffers from an *embarras de richesses*. The search for a unifying principle certainly continues to be one of its priorities, but the NKE paradigm is still highly fragmented, and this is only in part due to its youthfulness. This fragmentation obviously invites Ockham's razor and, even when the various 'theories' do not conflict with each other, they may generate wholly contradictory outcomes. Thus, for example, whereas for NKEmi price flexibility has stabilizing effects, NKEai endorses Keynes' contention that more flexible prices entail greater instability.[106] NKE theory must also explain (as a corollary to price flexibility) the issue of the absence of index-linking, and this because contracts are not tied to a real index. The existence, and the definition itself, of a general price level is highly dubious if multiple equilibria exist, or if different information sets are able to generate different convergence paths to equilibrium (of rational expectations) (Phelps, 1992).

The attempt by NKE to derive aggregate relations from 'first principles' via analysis of non-competitive markets enables interpretation of Keynesian propositions in terms of strategic interaction and, ultimately, of macroeconomic externalities. The possibility of multiple equilibria also implies that the concept of a natural rate of unemployment loses the central position it has in neoclassical models. Lastly, the existence of asymmetric information is yet another reason for abandoning the Walrasian paradigm, and it demands some methodological thoughts on the foundations of the traditional approach based on the representative agent, since this is a concept at odds with the very premises of the NKE approach. And yet both NKEmi (with its assumptions of *symmetric* agents) and NKEai (which, though it acknowledges the problem, takes refuge in the old instrument of perfect competition 'for analytical convenience') continue to use it.

Formal recognition is granted to composition effects, problems of income distribution and those relative to change in the productive structure but, following the Marshallian tradition, they are relegated to the footnotes and hedged with caveats. It should instead be accepted that any microfoundation which uses the representative agent is an *ad hoc* procedure open to the same criticisms as levelled against old-style Keynesian methodology. It follows, therefore, that the NKE revolution has yet to be accomplished.[107]

It is likely that the proponents of NKE have underestimated the implications of the simultaneous abandonment of perfect markets and symmetrical information. It is precisely in this direction, we believe, that a unifying principle should be pursued. A principle which allows the theory not to rely on needlessly tortuous explanations for the most important stylized facts.

---

[106] Price flexibility is pro-cyclical, and therefore destabilizing, for the NKEai authors who — like the Fisher-Minsky-Kindleberger school — stress the importance of the Fisher effect. NKEmi instead almost exclusively emphasises the Pigou effect, which is anti-cyclical and stabilizing.

[107] On the need of rejecting macro-models based on the representative agent see Kirman (1992). A first step in this direction is due to Haltiwanger and Waldman (1985, 1991).

Nonetheless, the richness of the NKE microfoundations and their analytical detail is impressive and represents one of the outstanding successes of the theory, which today takes the form of a New Keynesian Microeconomics more than anything else (Rotemberg, 1987). Although it has failed to produce a general equilibrium model, this literature has laid its basis and built its main components.

The main goal of NKE is to construct an aggregate supply function with adequate microfoundations in order to replace the obsolete Phillips-Lipsey function. On the demand side, it preserves most of the IS-LM apparatus. Aggregate demand is thus derived from the consumption function in Modigliani's version of the life-cycle (Campbell and Mankiw, 1989a,b; Mankiw, 1982) and from Tobin's q-theory of investment, or from some version of the accelerator theory (Fazzari et al.,1988). The microfoundation of NKE requires a dynamic model in order to encompass intertemporal optimization, and therefore a mechanism of *expectations* formation. It is on the first point that NKEmi models fail, because they are static; while, although NKEai goes beyond the static environment, it still has not resolved the problems created by the mechanism of expectations formation (Leijonhufvud, 1992; King, 1993). Strategic interaction and spillover effects may give rise to multiple equilibria even in the presence of rational expectations. It is perhaps necessary to abandon this hypothesis, which was in any case adopted 'for lack of anything better'.

NKE has so far been unable to model investment demand and capital accumulation within a general equilibrium model.[108] As was pointed out in section 3, without investment demand it is difficult to grasp all the implications of financing constraints in a context of asymmetric information, and the importance itself of equity and credit rationing diminishes. Furthermore, since aggregate demand in such a context is not micro-founded, the supply side of the model is also incomplete and the analytical horizon is restricted to the short run.[109] Also from this point of view, therefore, the 'revolution' is still far from accomplished, and it is not difficult to imagine that the modelling of expectations and of investment will be a key focus of future NKE research.

The aggregate supply curve of NKEai is in any case different from Lucas's curve because it depends, apart from technology, on the financial structure of firms: supply and demand shocks therefore both have permanent effects. As for the aggregate supply curve of NKEmi, this differs from the

---

[108] The relations between investment demand and asymmetric information have bred numerous models of partial equilibrium as well as empirical studies, beginning with Fazzari, Hubbard and Petersen (1988).

[109] In the long run, whereas NKEmi continues to use Solow's growth model with various modifications (Mankiw, Romer and Weil, 1992), NKEai has recently begun to propose models alternative to the neoclassical prototype (Stiglitz, 1993; Greenwald, Kohn and Stiglitz, 1991; Greenwald, Salinger and Stiglitz, 1991)

neoclassical curve in that it is shifted 'to the left' in correspondence to production levels lower than the Walrasian ones. Demand shocks only have effects in the short period in the presence of frictions which restrict or delay the adjustment of prices and nominal wages. The persistence of these effects is tied to the existence of hysteresis (Blanchard and Summers, 1986).

The neoclassical synthesis has provided the basis for the macroeconometric 'structural' models developed since those of the Cowles Commission in the 1940s — models consisting of two conceptual blocks, that of aggregate demand derived from the IS-LM model and that of aggregate supply derived from the Phillips curve. As is well known the neoclassical synthesis was harshly criticised by Lucas. NCM has emphasised the definition of models coherent with the rational expectations assumption and therefore has favoured the interpretation of disturbances as unexpected changes in exogenous magnitudes by agents incapable of distinguishing between aggregate and individual shocks. At the econometric level, this approach was combined with that of completely 'destructured' models like VAR, by means of which it is possible to show the interaction among unexplained components (residual) interpreted as shocks.

The decline of NCM has undoubtedly been prompted by unfavorable econometric results showing, for example, the weak predictive ability of unexpected changes in the money stock on changes in income. Thus, the correlation between money and income which led to the rise of NCM (Lucas, 1972; Sims, 1972) paradoxically turned out to be the empirical ground on which it displayed its shortcomings (Mishkin, 1982; Gordon, 1982).

More recently, two mutually incompatible hypotheses have been advanced which view the money-income correlation as non-spurious: namely the NKE and RBC hypotheses. The latter reverses the causality relation between money and income, and fluctuations (which are handled in a dynamic model of general economic equilibrium) are attributed wholly to technological shocks. Nominal shocks are therefore irrelevant to changes in real magnitudes. In the RBC models, money plays a passive role, and the apparently high money-income correlation is greatly reduced if the nominal interest rate is taken into account.

NKE, for its part, is unable to offer convincing explanations of the weak pro-cyclicity of real wages, although it has modelled other stylized facts properly (Greenwald and Stiglitz, 1988b). However, it is worth pointing out that complete empirical validation of NKE theories has not yet been carried out, basically because there is no *full* macroeconomic model whose reduced testable form has been explicitly set out. The available empirical studies address individual propositions or blocks of the theory: menu costs (Cecchetti, 1986; Blinder, 1991), the cyclicity of mark-ups (Rotemberg and Woodford, 1991), multiple equilibria (Durlauf, 1989; Manning, 1990), the theory of investment (Fazzari et al., 1988), financial crises (Bernanke 1983; Mishkin,

1992), credit rationing (Calomiris and Hubbard, 1990; Bordo, Rappoport and Schwartz, 1991) with generally promising results.[110]

In most of the recent macroeconometric literature, the breakdown of the observed series into a cycle and a trend component has been interpreted in the light of the antithesis between NKE models and RBC ones. Since the work of Nelson and Plosser (1982), the traditional view that fluctuations occur around a deterministic trend which identifies a steady-state growth rate has been opposed by the view that GDP can be more satisfactorily explained by a stochastic process which tends not to return to an average long-period value; that is, a stationary process which, in its simplest representation, contains a unitary root and therefore follows a stochastic trend. This decomposition of the time series has received growing empirical and theoretical support from the proponents of RBC, for whom the economy is always in equilibrium (on the trend path) and a cycle (that is a divergence from this trend) does not exist.

Although the empirical evidence in favour of the non-stationary nature of the series and of stochastic trends is not conclusive, the presence of a unitary root in real GDP no longer seems in doubt. Attention has therefore shifted from identification of unitary roots to the persistence of shocks. Certain authors have argued that it is possible to infer from the degree of persistence of shocks the nature of the impulses that drive the economic cycle: a low (high) degree of persistence indicates mainly aggregate demand (supply) shocks. In the approach used by Blanchard and Quah (1989: 655) disturbances with a temporary effect on output can be interpreted as demand shocks, while those with a permanent effect derive from supply impulses. This view concurs with certain NCM propositions as well as NKEmi ones. The NKEai approach tends to predict a potentially different outcome, although one not yet subjected to empirical testing: solely demand or solely supply shocks do not exist because in the real world the two types of shocks interweave.

4.2. On NKEmi

The merit of NKEmi is that it has shown how market imperfections may produce macroeconomic results substantially different from those obtained in a Walrasian environment: the inefficiency of aggregate equilibria and their possible multiplicity, albeit in the presence of optimizing individuals, undermine certain key components of NCM, including — in the case of multiple equilibria — the role and the meaning itself of rational expectations and of the natural rate of unemployment. However, even with a unique equilibrium, the consequences of market imperfections are much more profound than those of 'frictions' or 'rigidities' in a Walrasian context (where, moreover, they are left

---

[110] See also the essays in Hubbard, (1990a,b).

unaccounted for), because in imperfect markets the individual optimum does not necessarily correspond to the collective optimum, and there are no automatic mechanisms able to eliminate the inefficiencies of (Nash) equilibria. Dynamics outside equilibrium, if convergent, do not in any case lead to an efficient position; not to mention the possibility of hysteresis and path dependence.

In the light of the preceding discussion, the benevolence — if not the outright sympathy — shown by Mankiw (1992) for Friedman's 'natural rate' hypothesis does not do justice to NKE research, which is implicitly relegated to the short period, with its array of frictions, adjustment costs and limited information, and ready to retreat to the long period in order to make room for classical propositions. This is a thesis not entirely new in the literature, since it was propounded at the end of the last century by Alfred Marshall, but it is one which becomes highly disputable when the models utilized incorporate structural, and not transitory, market imperfections.

Market imperfections also render macroeconomic results sensitive to the presence of extremely small nominal frictions which in a Walrasian context would be entirely negligible. On the other hand, attributing the non-neutrality of monetary shocks entirely to small menu costs is unwise. Small menu costs explanations of neutrality are in fact not robust, because it is not clear why firms should not assess the costs that they must sustain to adjust quantities. Moreover — though combined with real rigidities — small menu costs generate non-neutrality only in the presence of shocks of minor size. Lastly — in a dynamic context — they are inhibiting only if prices and wages follow time-dependent adjustment rules while they are not inhibiting in the case of state-dependent adjustments. However, there do exist explanations of nominal rigidities, or at least of inertia, which are more persuasive, for example those based on relative wages or on lags in input-output models (Lindbeck and Snower, 1992).

One may plausibly expect small menu costs or near rationality to become part of a more complex and satisfactory explanation of why prices and wages are not perfectly indexed. This explanation, however, requires examination of less rudimentary economies than those typical of NKEmi.[111] Research, both theoretical and empirical, is far from complete.

The role played by money in this class of models is also open to criticism. Money, in fact, is conceived as a non-produced good which enters the utility functions of individuals directly; from this assumption follows a sort of Fisher equation which ties the quantity of money and prices together in the presence of a nominal shock. The long-period neutrality of monetary policy is thus demonstrated by construction. Conversely, according to NKEmi, fiscal policy

---

[111] Amongst other things, as Tobin (1993) has argued, a simple inertial factor in prices is sufficient to ensure effects analogous to those deriving from small menu costs of price adjustment.

is effective even in the absence of nominal rigidities, but only insofar as it affects the 'supply side' by shifting the price rule upwards or the wages rule downwards,[112] or insofar as it alters the distribution of resources among subjects with differing propensities to spend.

The static models used by NKEmi has frequently been criticised (McCallum, 1990, 1993) for being unworkable. A static model is obviously unsuitable for analysis of the business cycle, and NKEmi restricts itself to studying the mechanism of adjustment 'around' the steady state.[113] On closer scrutiny, the aggregate demand side also suffers from the restrictions imposed by the static nature of the model. It is, in fact, difficult to conciliate an intertemporal theory of consumption or investment with this scheme. Extending analysis to aggregate demand entails abandonment of the static environment and, ultimately, the reformulation of NKEmi models in an explicitly dynamic context.[114]

4.3. On NKEai

NKEai has stressed the role of credit, capital markets and financial institutions in the economic system. Overall, and rather oddly, NKEai has concentrated on areas where the contribution of NKEmi has been least positive; that is, the interrelations between productive activities and forms of firms' financing and the role of money. As a matter of fact, Stiglitz (1987, 1988) has repeatedly stressed that credit, not money, is the most important financial activity in a capitalist economy.[115] This contention stems directly from the asymmetric information hypothesis,[116] which, according to NKEai, can legitimately aspire to becoming the unifying principle.

---

[112] This implication of economic policy is not a novelty: consider the 'active labour policies' associated with the Phillips curve, or the efficiency of fiscal policy to the extent that it influences the incentive to work in the supply *side economics.*

[113] NKEai has produced models which exhibit stochastic fluctuations and deterministic cycles (Greenwald and Stiglitz, 1993b), or jointly deterministic and stochastic dynamics (Gallegati and Stiglitz, 1992).

[114] There is a recent body of literature on the dynamic relations between aggregate demand and output in NKEmi models: Caplin and Leahy (1991); Bertola and Caballero (1990). For a dynamic model of menu costs see Caballero and Engel (1992).

[115] There is a rich tradition of thought on the importance of credit which began with the Radcliffe Report: see, for example, Minsky (1975, 1982, 1986), B. Friedman (1986). In NKEai, monetary policy is effective if it influences the equity base of firms and by this means pushes up labour demand. This happens as long as financing contracts are not indexed. The transmission mechanisms, which are much richer than in NKEmi, are based mainly on the *availability of credit* (in the presence of rationing).

[116] The problem of information differentials is an enduring one in economic theory, especially financial theory. Bagehot (1873) and Marshall (1992) analyse the problem of the existence of operators in the financial markets with different amounts of knowledge. Keynes (1913) identifies the existence of an information problem taking the form of control by the lenders of

The notion of asymmetric information presupposes that agents are different. According to Leijonhufvud, this distinction is a sufficient condition to generate coordination failures, and this allows to abandon the Arrow-Debreu model. More specifically, with complete information, banks and firms would constitute a single aggregate in which every debt-credit relationship is cancelled and money has no role to perform. Similarly, if firms and households coincided, investment decisions and saving decisions would not be qualitatively distinct acts.

The hypothesis of asymmetric information has other implications as well. First, the Modigliani-Miller theorem is no longer valid. Investment is thus constrained by the availability of funds, and this is a factor which enters production decisions. Put otherwise, the nominal quantity of money has real effects on income, independently of nominal rigidities, even if the lack of a theory of investment demand renders this assertion only potentially valid. If money is not neutral, the final outcomes of the economic process, and therefore the equilibrium position, are influenced by the nominal quantity of means of payment. The granting of credit has effects on the realization of investment projects, and therefore on income.

If and only if money is neutral (and in the Walrasian world it is neutral by construction), the dichotomy between the real and monetary sectors holds. It is therefore no coincidence that NKEmi, when it does not use information asymmetries, manages at most to establish non Pareto-optimal outcomes in the presence of different degrees of imperfection. If agents are different from one another, 'composition effects' may exist and, above all, the role of the *representative agent* may enter into crisis. This analytical tool makes it possible to extend, by means of simple summation, microeconomic behaviour to macrorelations, thereby enabling optimization to be used in analysis of aggregate data.

What no longer holds in a non-representative agent context, and also in that of strategic interaction in imperfect markets, is the invisible hand which makes the individual optimum coincide with the collective optimum (Kirman, 1992).

Game theory has shown that rational behaviour may generate multiple equilibria. One may argue along the same lines that if asymmetric information exists, problems of adverse selection impede a decentralized system from achieving Pareto-optimal positions (Akerlof, 1970; Stiglitz and Weiss, 1981) and thus give rise to coordination failures. The 'Greenwald-Stiglitz theorem' in fact asserts that if limited information exists, the economy is not even in a constrained Paretian optimum (Greenwald and Stiglitz, 1986).

---

funds on the use of them by their borrowers: the banks' monitoring of credit can only be partial, however, because they rely on information which is *limited*, in that no-one knows the future, and *asymmetric*, in that one party has an informational advantage over the other.

Although extremely promising in terms of the recovery of Keynesian themes as well as for the explanation of numerous stylized facts, NKEai is still characterized by models which are largely partial and — as we saw in section 3 — not without problems of internal coherence. Nor should it be forgotten that their almost exclusive focus on financial markets ends up by reducing goods markets to mere appendages of them. It does not appear that NKEai authors have explored all the consequences of their assumptions. The way to a fairly general New Keynesian macro-model based on first principles is still very long.

BIBLIOGRAPHY

Abel, A. B. (1990), "Consumption and Investment", in Friedman, B.M. and Hahn. F.H. (eds) (1990), 725-778.

Akerlof, G. A. (1970), "The Market for 'Lemons': Quality Uncertainty and the Market Mechanism", *Quarterly Journal of Economics,* 85, 488-500.

Akerlof, G. A. (1984), "Gift Exchange and Efficiency Wage Theory: Four Views", *American Economic Review P&P*, 74, 79-83.

Akerlof, G. A. and Yellen, J. L. (1985), "A Near-Rational Model of the Business Cycle with Wage and Price Inertia", *Quarterly Journal of Economics*, 100 823-838.

Akerlof, G. A. and Yellen, J. L. , P. (eds) (1986), *Efficiency Wage Models of the Labour Market*, Cambridge, Cambridge University Press.

Andersen, T.M. (1990), "Comment on McCallum, B.T., New Classical Macroeconomics: A Sympathetic Account", *Scandinavian Journal of Economics*.

Ando A. (1983), "Equilibrium Business-Cycle Models: An Appraisal", in F.G.Adams, B.Hickman, *Global Econometrics*, MIT Press, Cambridge.

Ardeni, P.G. (1992), "Investment and Debt Contracting under Asymmetric Information. I.The Static Case", *Quaderni di Economia, Matematica and Statistica*, Facoltà di Economia and Commercio, Università di Urbino, n.15, febbraio.

Ardeni P.G., M.Gallegati (1994), *Investimenti, Fluttuazioni e Crescita*, Il Mulino, Bologna.

Ashenfelter, O. and R. Layard, (eds) (1987), *Handbook of Labour Economics*, Amsterdam, North Holland.

Asquith, P. and W. Mullins, (1986), "Equity Issues and Offering Dilution", *Journal of Financial Economics*, 15, 61-89.

Bagehot, W. (1873), *Lombard Street*, trad. it. 1905, UTET, Torino.

Ball, L. and D. Romer, (1990), "Real Rigidities and the Non-Neutrality of Money", *Review of Economic Studies*, 57, 183-203.

Ball, L. and D. Romer, (1991), "Sticky Prices as Coordination Failures", *American Economic Review*, 81, 539-552.

Ball, L., N. G. Mankiw, and D. Romer, (1988), "The New Keynesian Economics and the Output-Inflation Trade-Off", *Brookings Papers on Economic Activity*, 1, 1-79.

Barro R.J. (1972), "A Theory of Monopolistic Price Adjustment", *Review of Economic Studies*, 34, 17-26.

Barro R.J., H.Grossman, (1971), "A General Disequilibrium Model of Income and Employment", *American Economic Review*, 61, 82-93.

Beckerman, W.(eds) (1986), *Wage Rigidity and Unemployment*, Oxford, Duckworth.

Benassy, J.P., (1975), "Neo-Keynesian Disequilibrium Theory in a Monetary Economy", *Review of Economic Studies*, 42, 503-523.

Benassy, J.P. (1987), "Imperfect Competition, Unemployment and Policy", *European Economic Review*, 31, 417-426.

Benassy J.P., (1990), "Non-Walrasian Equilibria, Money and Macroeconomics", in F.Hahn, B.Friedman (eds).

Bernanke B. (1983), "Nonmonetary Effects of the Financial Crisis in the Propagation of the Great Depression", *American Economic Review*, 73, 257-76.

Bernanke, B.S. and A.S. Blinder, (1988), "Credit, Money and Aggregate Demand", *American Economic Review* , 78, 435-439.

Bernanke, B.S. and M. Gertler, (1989), "Agency Costs, Net Worth and Business Fluctuations", *American Economic Review* , 79, 14-31.

Bernanke, B.S. and Gertler, M. (1990), "Financial Fragility and Economic Performance", *Quarterly Journal of Economics*, 105, 87-114.

Bertola, G. and R.J. Caballero, (1990), "Kinked Adjustment Cost and Aggregate Dynamics", *NBER Macroeconomics Annual*

Bester, H. (1985), "Screening versus Rationing in Credit Markets with Imperfect Information", *American Economic Review* , 75, 850-855.

Bewley, T.F.(eds) (1987), *Advances in Economic Theory: Fifth World Congress*, Cambridge, Cambridge University Press.

Bhaskar, V. (1990), "Wage Relativities and the Natural range of Unemployment", *Economic Journal*, 100, Su, 60-66.

Bhattacharya, S. (1988), "Coroporate Finance and the Legacy of Miller and Modigliani", *Journal of Economic Perspectives*, 2, 135-147.

67

Bils, M. (1987), "The Cyclical Behaviour of Marginal Cost and Price" , *American Economic Review*, 77, 838-55.

Bils, M. (1989), "Pricing in a Customer Market", *Quarterly Journal of Economics*, 104, 699-718.

Blanchard, O.J. (1983), "Price Asynchronization and Price Level Inertia", in R. Dornbusch and M. Simonsen (eds).

Blanchard, O.J (1986), "The Wage-Price Spiral", *Quarterly Journal of Economics*, 101, 543-65.

Blanchard, O.J. (1990), "Why Does Money Affect Output?", in Friedman, B. and F. Hahn, (eds), 779-835.

Blanchard, O.J. and D. Quah, (1989), "The Dynamic Effects of Aggregate Demand and Supply Disturbances", *American Economic Review*, 79, 655-673.

Blanchard, O.J. and S.Fischer, (1989), *Lectures on Macroeconomics*, MIT Press, Cambridge.

Blanchard, O.J. and N. Kiyotaki, (1987), "Monopolistic Competition and the Effects of Aggregate Demand", *American Economic Review*, 77, 647-66.

Blanchard, O.J. and L.H. Summers, (1986) ,"Hysteresis and the European Unemployment Problem", *NBER Macroeconomics Annual*, 15-77.

Blanchard, O.J and L.H. Summers, (1987a) , "Beyond the Natural rate Hypothesis", *American Economic Review , P.&P.* , 77, 182-7.

Blanchard, O.J and L.H. Summers, (1987b) , "Hysteresis in Unemployment ", *European Economic Review ,* 31, 288-95.

Blinder, A.S., (1988), "The Fall and Rise of Keynesian Economics", *The Economic Record*, 64, 278-94.

Blinder, A. (1991), "Why are Prices Sticky? Preliminary Evidence from an Interview Survey", *American Economic Review*, 81, 89-96.

Boitani, A. (1991), "Post Keynesians versus New Keynesians on Imperfect Competition and Unemployment Equilibrium", in Sebastiani M. (ed), *The Notion of Equilibrium in the Keynesian Theory*, London, Macmillan.

Boitani, A. and M. Damiani, (1994), "Mercato del lavoro e Nuova Economia Keynesiana", in Amendola A. (ed), ESI, Napoli.

Boitani, A. and M. Damiani, (1995), "Market Imperfections, Unemployment Equilibria and Nominal Rigidities". This volume, ch. 5.

Boitani, A. and D. Delli Gatti, (1991), "Equilibrio di sottoccupazione e stato di fiducia in un gioco keynesiano", *Economia Politica*, 8, 45-71

Boitani, A., D. Delli Gatti, and Mezzomo, L. (1992), "Concorrenza imperfetta, esternalità e spiegazioni delle rigidità nella Nuova Economia Keynesiana", *Economia Politica*, 9, 299-361.

Boitani, A. and A. Salanti, (1994), "The Multifarious Role of Theories in Economics: The Case of Different Keynesianism", in P.A. Klein (ed.), *The Role of Theories in Economies*, Boston, Kluwer, 121-158.

Bordo, M., P. Rappoport, and A. Schwartz, (1991), "Money versus Credit Rationing: Evidence for the National Banking Era 1880-1914", *NBER Working Paper n.3689.*

Bowles, S. (1985), "The Production Process in a Competitive Economy: Walrasian, Neo-Hobbesian and Marxian Models", *American Economic Review,* 75, 16-36.

Bowles, S. and R. Boyer, (1988), "Labor Discipline and Aggregate Demand: A Macroeconomic Model", *American Economic Review, P.&P.,* 78, 395-400.

Brander, J. and T.R. Lewis, (1986), "Oligopoly and Financial Structure: the Limited Liability Effect", *American Economic Review,* 76, 956-970.

Bulow, J.I, J.D. Geanakoplos, and P.D. Klemperer, (1985), "Multimarket Oligopoly: Strategic Substitutes and Complements", *Journal of Political Economy*, 93, 488-511.

Caballero, R.J., and E.M.R.A. Engel (1992), "Heterogeneity and Output Fluctuations in a Dynamic Menu Cost Model", *Review of Economic Studies*

Calomiris, C.W. and R.G. Hubbard, (1990), "Firm Heterogeneity, Internal Finance and Credit Rationing", *Economic Journal*, 100, 90-104

Campbell, J.Y. and G.N.Mankiw (1989a), "Consumption, Income and Interest Rates: Reinterpreting the Time Series Evidence", *NBER Macroeconomic Annual*, 185-215.

Campbell, J.Y. and G.N.Mankiw (1989b), *Permanent Income, Current Income and Consumption*, NBER working paper 2436.

Caplin, A. and J. Leahy, (1991), "State Dependent Pricing and the Dynamics of Money and Output", *Quarterly Journal of Economics*.

Caplin, A. and D. Spulber, (1987), "Menu Costs and the Neutraliy of Money", *Quarterly Journal of Economics,* 102, 703-726.

Cecchetti S. (1986), "The Frequency of Price Adjustment: A Study of the News stand Prices of Magazines, 1953 to 1979", *Journal of Econometrics*, 31, 255-74.

Chamberlin E. (1933), *The Theory of Monopolistic Competition*, Harvard University Press, Cambridge Mass.

Clemenz, G. (1986), *Credit Markets with Asymmetric Information*, Londra, Springer Verlag.

Clower, R.W. (1965), "The Keynesian Counterrevolution: A Theoretical Appraisal", in F. Hahn, F. Brechling (eds), 103-125.

Cooper, R. and John, A. (1988), "Coordinating Coordination Failures in Keynesian Models", *Quarterly Journal of Economics*, 103, 441-63.

Delli Gatti, D., M.Gallegati and L.Gardini, (1993), "Investment Confidence, Corporate Debt and Income Fluctuations", *Journal of Economic Behaviour and Organization.*

De Meza, D. and D.C. Webb, (1987), "Too Much Investment in Problems of Asymmetric Information",*Quarterly Journal of Economics*, 102, 281-292.

Dixon, H.D. and N. Ranklin (1994) "Imperfect Competition and Macroeconomics: A Survey", *Oxford Economic Papers*, 46, 171-195.

Dore, M.H.I. (1993), *The Macrodynamics of Business Cycles*, Blackwell, Oxford.

Dornbusch, R. and R. Layard, (eds) (1987), *The Performance of the British Economy*, Oxford, Clarendon Press.

Dornbusch, R.and M. Simonsen, (eds) (1983), *Inflation, Debt and Indexation*, Cambridge (Mass.), MIT Press.

Durlauf, S. (1989), "Output Persistence, Economic Structure and the Choice of Stabilization Policy", *Brookings Papers on Economic Activity*, 69-111.

Durlauf, S, (1991), "Path Dependence in Aggregate Output", *NBER Working Paper*, n.3718.

Farber, H. (1987), "The Analysis of Union Behaviour", in O. Ashenfelter, and R. Layard, (eds) (1987).

Fazzari, S., G. Hubbard, and Petersen, B. (1988), "Financing Constraints and Corporate Investment", *Brookings Papers on Economic Activity*, 1, 141-206.

Feiwel, G. (eds) (1989), *The Economics of Imperfect Competition and Employment: Joan Robinson and Beyond*, London, Macmillan.

Fischer, S. (1977), "Long Term Contracts, Rational Expectations and the Optimal Money Supply Rule", *Journal of Political Economy*, 85, 191-205.

Fisher, I. (1933), "The Debt Deflation Theory of the Great Depression", *Econometrica.*

Frank, J. (1990), "Monopolistic Competition, Risk Aversion and Equilibrium Recessions", *Quarterly Journal of Economics*, 105, 163-90.

Friedman, B., (1986), "Money, Credit, and Interest Rate in the Business Cycle", in R.Gordon (a c. di), *The American Business Cycle*, University of Chicago Press, Chicago.

Friedman, B and F. Hahn, (eds) (1990), *Handbook of Monetary Economics*, Vol.II, Amsterdam, North-Holland.

Friedman, J.W. (ed) (1993), Problems of Coordination in Economic Activity, Boston, Kluwer.

Friedman, M. (1953), *Essays in Positive Economics*, University of Chicago Press, Chicago.

Friedman, M., (1968), "The Role of Monetary Policy", *American Economic Review*, 58, 1-17.

Frydman, R., E.Phelps, (1983), "Individual Expectations and Aggregate Outcome: An Introduction to the Problem", in R. Frydman and E. Phelps (eds), *Individual Forecasting and Aggregate Outcome*, Cambridge University Press, Cambridge.

Fudenberg, D. and J. Tirole, (1983), "Capital as a Commitment: Strategic Investment to Deter Mobility", *Journal of Economic Theory*, 31, 227-250

Fudenberg, D. and J. Tirole, (1991), *Game Theory*, MIT Press, Cambridge.

Gale, D. and M. Hellwig, (1985), "Incentive Compatible Debt Contracts: The One Period Problem", *Review of Economic Studies*, 52, 647-663.

Gallegati, M. (1993a), "Composition Effect and Economic Fluctuations", *Economic Letters*.

Gallegati, M. (1993b), "Endogenous Growth, Economic Fluctuations, and Capital Accumulation", *Moneta and Credito Quarterly Review*.

Gallegati, M. and J.E. Stiglitz (1992), "Stochastic and Deterministic Fluctuations in a Non-Linear Model with Equity Rationing", *Giornale degli Economisti ed Annali di Economia*, 51, 97-108.

Gallegati, M. and J.E. Stiglitz (1993), *Irregular Business Cycles*, working paper, Stanford.

Garretsen, H. (1992), *Keynes, Coordination and Beyond*, E. Elgar, Aldershot.

Gertler, M. (1988). "Financial Structure and Real Economic Activity", *Journal of Money, Credit and Banking*, 20, 559-588.

Gertner, R., R. Gibbons and D. Scharfstein, (1988), "Simultaneous Signalling to the Capital and Product markets", *Rand Journal of Economics*, 19, 173-190.

Goodwin, R.M. and P.M.Pacini (1992), "Nonlinear Economic Dynamics and Chaos", in A. Vercelli and N. Dimitri (eds).

Gordon R.J., (1976), "Recent Development in the Theory of Inflation and Unemployment", *Journal of Monetary Economics*, 2, 185-219.

Gordon, R.J. (1982), "Price Inertia and Policy Ineffectiveness in the United States", *Journal of Political Economy*, 90, 1087-1117.

Gordon, R. J. (1990), "What is the New Keynesian Economics?", *Journal of Economic Literature,* 28, 1115-71.

Grandmont J.M., (1985), "On Endogenous Competitive Business Cycles," *Econometrica,* 53, 995-1045.

Graziani, A. (1988), "Il circuito monetario" in Messori, M. (ed.), *Moneta e Produzione,* Einaudi, Torino

Greenwald, B., M. Kohn and J.E. Stiglitz (1991), "Financial Market Imperfections and Productivity Growth", *Journal of Economic Behavior and Organization,* 13, 321-45.

Greenwald, B., M. Salinger and J.E. Stiglitz (1991), *Imperfect Capital Markets and Productivity Growth,* mimeo, Stanford.

Greenwald, B. and J.E. Stiglitz, (1986), "Externalities in Economies with Imperfect Information and Incomplete Markets", *Quarterly Journal of Economics,* 105, 87-114.

Greenwald, B. and J.E. Stiglitz (1987), "Keynesian, New Keynesian and New Classical Economics", *Oxford Economic Papers,* 39, 119-32.

Greenwald, B. C. and J.E. Stiglitz, (1988a), "Imperfect Information, Finance Constraints and Business Fluctuations", in Kohn, M. and Tsiang, S.C. (eds) (1988), 103-140.

Greenwald, B. and J.E. Stiglitz (1988b), "Examining Alternative Economic Theories", *Brookings Papers on Economic Activity,* 1, 207-60.

Greenwald, B.C. and J.E. Stiglitz,(1989a), "Toward a Theory of Rigidities", *American Economic Review,* 79, 364-369.

Greenwald, B.C. and J.E. Stiglitz, (1990), "Macroeconomic Models with Equity and Credit Rationing", in Hubbard, R. G. (eds) (1990), 15-42.

Greenwald, B.C. and J.E. Stiglitz, (1993a), "New and Old Keynesians", *Journal of Economic Perspectives,* 7, 23-44.

Greenwald, B.C. and J.E. Stiglitz, (1993b), "Financial Market Imperfections and Business Cycles", *Quarterly Journal of Economics,* 108, 77-114.

Greenwald, B.C. and J.E. Stiglitz, and Weiss, A. (1984), "Informational Imperfections in the Capital Markets and Macroeconomic Fluctuations", *American Economic Review,* 74, 194-200.

Grossman, S. (1975), *The Existence of Future Markets, Noisi Rational Expectations, and Informational Externalities,* IMSSS 182, Stanford University.

Grossman S.J. and J.E. Stiglitz, (1976), "Information and Competitive Price System", *American Economic Review P&P,* 66, 246-53.

Grossman S.J. and J.E. Stiglitz, (1980), "On the Impossibility of Informationally Efficient Markets", *American Economic Review,* 70, 393-408.

Hahn, F.H. (1987), "On Involuntary Unemployment", *Economic Journal*, 97, Su 1-16

Hahn F., Brechling F. (eds) (1965), *The Theory of Interest Rates*, Macmillan, London.

Hall R.E., (1988), "Comment" on Greenwald, Stiglitz (1988), 261-4.

Haltiwanger J. and M. Waldman (1985), "Rational Expectations and the Limits of Rationality: An Analysis of Heterogeneity", *American Economic Review*, 75, 326-340.

Haltiwanger J. and M. Waldman (1991), "Responders versus Non-Responders: A New Perspective on Heterogeneity", *Economic Journal*, 101, 1085-1102.

Hargreaves Heap, S. (1992), *The New Keynesian Macroeconomics*, Aldershot, Elgar.

Hart, O. (1982), "A Model of Imperfect Competition with Keynesian Features", *Quarterly Journal of Economics*, 97, 109-138.

Hart, O. and B. Holmstrom, (1987), "The Theory of Contracts" in Bewley, T.F. (eds) (1987), 71-155.

Heinkel, R. (1982), "A Theory of Capital Structure Relevance Under Imperfect Information", *Journal of Finance*, 37, 1141-1150.

Heller, W.P. (1986), "Coordination Failure under Complete Markets with Applications to Effective Demand", in Heller, Starr and Starret (eds), 155-75.

Heller, W.P., R.M. Starr, and D.R. Starrett, (eds) (1986), *Equilibrium Analysis: Essays in Honor of Kenneth J. Arrow, II*, Cambridge, Cambridge University Press.

Hellwig, M. (1987), "Some Recent Developments in the Theory of Competition in Markets with Adverse Selection", *European Economic Review*, 31, 319-325.

Hicks J., (1965), *Capital and Growth*, Oxford University Press, Oxford.

Hodgman, D.R. (1960), "Credit Risk and Credit Rationing", *Quarterly Journal of Economics*, 74, 258-278.

Hubbard, R.G. (eds) (1990a), *Asymmetric Information, Corporate Finance and Investment*, Chicago, University of Chicago Press.

Hubbard, R.G. (eds) (1990b), *Financial Markets and Financial Crises*, NBER, Chicago.

Jaffee, D. and F. Modigliani, (1969), "A Theory and Test of Credit Rationing", *American Economic Review*, 59, 850-872.

Jaffee, D. and T. Russell, (1976), "Imperfect Information, Uncertainty and Credit Rationing", *Quarterly Journal of Economics*, 91, 651-666.

Jaffee, D. and J.E. Stiglitz, (1990), "Credit Rationing", in B. Friedman, and F. Hahn, (eds) (1990), 837-888.

Jensen, M.C. and W. Meckling, (1976), "Theory of the Firm, Managerial Behavior, Agency Costs and Ownership Structure", *Journal of Financial Economics*, 3, 305-360.

Kahneman, D. and A. Tversky (1979), "Prospect Theory: An Analysis of Decisions under Risk", *Econometrica*, 47, 263-91.

Kaldor, N. (1978), *Further Essays in Economic Theory,* Londra, Duckworth.

Kaldor, N. (1983), "Keynesian Economics After Fifty Years", in Worswick and Trevithick (eds) (1983), 1-28.

Katz, L. (1987), "Efficiency Wage Theories: A Partial Evaluation", *NBER Macroeconomics Annual,* 235-76.

Keeton, W.R. (1979), *Equilibrium Credit Rationing*, New York, Garland Publ. Inc.

Keynes, J.M. (1913), "How Far Are the Bankers Responsible for the Alternations of Crisis and Depression?", in J.M. Keynes (1973).

Keynes, J.M., (1933), *A Monetary Theory of Production*, in J.M. Keynes (1975).

Keynes, J.M. (1936), *The General Theory of Employment, Interest and Money*, Londra, Macmillan.

Keynes, J.M., (1973), *Collected Writings*, Macmillan, London.

Kindleberger, C.P. (1978), *Manias, Panics and Crashes. A History of Financial Crises*, New York, Basic Books.

King, R.G. (1993), "Will the New Keynesian Economics Resurrect the IS-LM Model?", *Journal of Economic Perspectives*, 7, 67-82.

Kirman, A. (1992), "Whom or What does the Representative Consumer Represents?", *Journal of Economic Perspectives*, 6, 117-36.

Kohn, M. and S.C. Tsiang, (1988), *Finance Constraints, Expectations and Macroeconomics*, Oxford, Oxford University Press.

Layard, R. and S. Nickell, (1986), "Unemployment in the UK", *Economica,* 53, 121-66.

Layard, R. and S. Nickell, (1987), "The Labour Market", in R. Dornbusch and R. Layard (eds)(1987).

Layard, R., S. Nickell, and R. Jackman (1991), *Unemployment Macroeconomic Performance and the Labour Market*, Oxford, OUP. (1987),

Leibenstein, H. (1957), "The Theory of Unederdevelopment in Densely Populated Backward Areas", in H. Leibenstein (ed.), *Economic Backwardness and Growth*, New York, Wiley.

Leijonhufvud, A. (1967), "Keynes and the Keynesians: A Suggested Interpretation", *American Economic Review*.

Leijonhufvud, A. (1968), *On Keynesian Economics and the Economics of Keynes*, London, Oxford University Press.

Leijonhufvud, A. (1973), "Effective Demand Failures", *Swedish Economic Journal*.

Leijonhufvud, A. (1981), *Information and Coordination*, Oxford University Press, Oxford.

Leijonhufvud A., (1992), "Keynesian Economics: Past Confusion, Future Prospects", in A. Vercelli and N. Dimitri (eds).

Leland, H. and D. Pyle, (1977), "Informational Asymmetries, Financial Structure and Financial Intermediation", *Journal of Finance*, 32, 371-387.

Leontief, W. (1946), "The Pure Theory of the Guaranteed Annual Wage Contract", *Journal of Political Economy*, 54, 76-79.

Lindbeck, A. (1992), "Macroeconomic Theory and the Labour Market", *European Economic Review*, 36, 209-235.

Lindbeck, A. and Snower, D.J. (1986a), "Wage Setting, Unemployment and Insider-Outsider Relations", *American Economic Review*, 76, 235-239.

Lindbeck, A. and D.J. Snower, (1986b), "Involuntary Unemployment as an Insider-Outsider Dilemma" in W. Beckerman (eds) (1986).

Lindbeck, A. and D. J. Snower, (1987), "Efficiency Wages Versus Insider-Outsider Relations", *European Economic Review*, 31, 157-67.

Lindbeck, A. and D. J. Snower, (1988), *The Insider-Outsider Theory of Employment and Unemployment*, Cambridge (Mass.), MIT Press.

Lindbeck, A. and D. J. Snower, (1992), "Price Inertia and Production Lags", *Institute for International Economic Studies Seminar Paper* n.494

Lucas R.E. (1972), "Expectations and the Neutrality of Money", *Journal of Economic Theory*, 4, 103-24.

Lucas R.E. (1973), "Some International Evidence on Output-Inflation Tradeoffs", *American Economic Review*, 63, 326-34.

McCallum, B.T. (1990), "New Classical Macroeconomics: A Sympathetic Account", *Scandinavian Journal of Economics*.

McCallum, B.T. (1993), *Macroeconomics After Two Decades of Rational Expectation*, NBER working paper 4367.

McDonald, I. and R. Solow, (1981), "Wage Bargaining and Employment", *American Economic Review*, 71, 896-908.

Madden, P. (1983), "Keynesian Unemployment as a Nash Equilibrium with

Endogenous Wage/Price Setting, *Economics Letters*, 12, 109-114.

Malcomson, J. (1981), "Unemployment and the Efficiency Wage Hypothesis", *Economic Journal*, 91, 848-866.

Mankiw, N.G. (1982), "The Permanent Income Hypothesis and the Real Interest Rate", *Economic Letters*, 7, 307-311.

Mankiw, N. G. (1985), "Small Menu Costs and Large Business Cycles: A Macroeconomic Model of Monopoly", *Quarterly Journal of Economics*, 100, 529-39.

Mankiw, N.G. (1992), "The Reincarnation of Keynesian Economics", *European Economic Review*.

Mankiw, N.G. and D.Romer (eds) (1991), *New Keynesian Economics*, MIT Press, Cambridge.

Mankiw, N.G., D. Romer and D.N. Wiel (1992), "On the Empirics of Economic Growth", *Quarterly Journal of Economics*, 107, 403-37.

Manning, A. (1990), "Imperfect Competition, Multiple Equilibria and Unemployment Policy", *Economic Journal*, 100, Su, 151-62.

Marshall (1890) Principles of Economics, MacMillan, London.

Marshall, A. (1975), *The Early Economic Writings*, (eds) J.K.Whitaker, MacMillan, London.

Marshall, A. (1992), in M. Dardi and M.Gallegati, "Alfred Marshall on Speculation", *History of Political Economy*, 3, 31-50

Mayer, C. (1988), "New Issues in Corporate Finance", *European Economic Review*, 32, 1167-1189.

Milde, H. and J.C. Riley, (1988), "Signalling in the Credit Markets", *Quarterly Journal of Economics*, 103, 101-129.

Milgrom, P. and J. Roberts, (1990), "Rationalizability, Learning and Equilibrium in Games with Strategic Complementarities", *Econometrica*, 58, 1255-78.

Miller, M.H. (1988), "The Modigliani-Miller Propositions After Thirty Years", *Journal of Economic Perspectives*, 2, 99-120.

Minsky, H.P. (1975), *John Maynard Keynes*, New York, Columbia University Press

Minsky, H.P. (1982), *Can "It" Happen Again? Essays on Instability and Finance,* Armonk N.Y., M.E. Sharpe.

Minsky, H.P. (1986), *Stabilizing an Unstable Economy,* New Haven, Yale University Press.

Mishkin, F.S. (1982), "Does Monetary Policy Matter? An Econometric Investigation", *Journal of Political Economy*, 90, 22-51.

Mishkin, F.S., (1990), *Asymmetric information and financial crises: Historical evidence*, NBER working paper.

Modigliani, F., (1963), "The Monetary Mechanism and its Interation with Real Phenomena", *Review of Economics and Statistics*.

Modigliani, F. (1988), "MM — Past, Present, Future", *Journal of Economic Perspectives*, 2, 149-158.

Muth, J.F. (1961), "Rational Expectations and the Theory of Price Movements", *Econometrica*, 29, 315-35.

Myers, S.C. and Majluf, N.S. (1984), "Corporate Financing and Investment Decisions when Firms Have Information that Investors Do Not Have", *Journal of Financial Economics*, 13, 187-221.

Nelson, C.R.and C.I. Plosser, (1982), "Trend and Random Walk in Macroeconomic Time Series. Some Evidence and Implications", *Journal of Monetary Economics*, 10, 139-162.

Nickell, S.J. and M. Andrews, (1983), "Unions, Real Wages and Employment in Britain 1951-79", *Oxford Economic Papers*, 35, Su, 183-206.

Oswald, A. (1985), "The Economic Theory of trade Unions: An Introductory Survey", *Scandinavian Journal of Economics*, 87, 160-93

Pagano, M. (1990), "Imperfect Competition, Underemployment Equilibria and Fiscal Policy", *Economic Journal*, 100, 440-63.

Parkin, M. (1984), *Macroeconomics*, Englewood Cliffs, Prentice-Hall.

Pencavel, J. (1985), "Wages and Employment Under Trade Unionism: Microeconomic Models and Macroeconomic Applications", *Scandinavian Journal of Economics*, 87, 197-225.

Phelps, E.S. (1967), "Phillips Curve, Expectations of Inflation and Optimal Unemployment Over Time", *Economica*, 34, 254-81.

Phelps, E.S. (1970), *Microeconomic Foundations of Employment and Inflation Theory*, Norton, New York.

Phelps, E.S. (1990), *Seven School of Macroeconomic Thought*, Oxford, Oxford University Press.

Phelps, E.S. (1992), "Expectations in Macroeconomics and the Rational Expectation Debate", in Vercelli A., N.Dimitri (eds).

Riley, J.C. (1979). "Informational Equilibrium", *Econometrica*, 47, 331-386.

Riley, J.C. (1987), "Credit Rationing: A Further Remark", *American Economic Review*, 77, 224-227.

Roberts, J. (1989), "Involuntary Unemployment and Imperfect Competition: A Game Theoretic Macromodel", in Feiwel (eds), 146-165.

Roe, A.R. (1973), "The Case for Flow of Funds and National Balance Sheet Accounts", *Economic Journal*.

Romer, C. and D.Romer, (1989), "Does Monetary Policy Matter? A New Test in the Spirit of Friedman and Schwartz", *NBER Macroeconomics Annual*, 121-70.

Romer, D. (1993), "The New Keynesian Synthesis", *Journal of Economic Perspectives*, 1, 5-22.

Ross, S.A. (1977), "The Determination of Financial Structure: the Incentive Signalling Approach", *Bell Journal of Economics*, 8, 23-40.

Rotemberg, J. (1987), "The New Keynesian Microfoundations", *NBER Macroeconomics Annual*, 2, 69-104.

Rotemberg, J. and Saloner, G. (1986), "A Supergame-Theoretic Model of Price Wars during Booms", *American Economic Review*, 76, 390-407.

Rotemberg, J. and Woodford, M. (1991), "Markups and the Business Cycle", *NBER Macroeconomics Annual*, 63-140.

Rothschild, M. and Stiglitz, J.E. (1976), "Equilibrium in Competitive Insurance Markets with Imperfect Information", *Quarterly Journal of Economics*, 91, 628-649.

Salop, S. (1979), "A Model of the Natural rate of Unemployment", *American Economic Review*, 69, 117-25

Schumpeter, J. A. (1954), *History of Economic Analysis*, Oxford University Press, Oxford.

Schleifer, A. (1986), "Implementation Cycles", in Mankiw, N.G. and Romer, D. (1991)

Shapiro, C. and J. Stiglitz, (1984), "Equilibrium Unemployment as a Worker Discipline Device", *American Economic Review*, 74, 433-44.

Sheshinski, E. and Y. Weiss (1977), "Inflation and Cost of Price Adjustment", *Review of Economic Studies*, 44, 287-303.

Sheshinski E. and Y. Weiss (1979), "Demand for Fixed Factors, Inflation, and Adjustment Costs", *Review of Economic Studies*, 46, 31-45.

Sims, C. (1972), "Money, Income and Causality", *American Economic Review*, 62, 540-552.

Silvestre, J. (1993), "The Market Power Foundations of Macroeconomic Policy", *Journal of Economic Literature*, 31, 105-141.

Solow, R. (1979) "Another Possible Source of Wage Stickiness", *Journal of Macroeconomics*, 1, 79-82.

Solow, R. (1980), "On Theories of Unemployment", *American Economic Review*, 70, 1-11.

Startz, R. (1989), "Monopolistic Competition as a Foundation for Keynesian Macroeconomic Models, *Quarterly Journal of Economics*, 104, 737-752.

Stigler, G. (1961), "The Economics of Information", *Journal of Political Economy*, 69.

Stiglitz, J.E. (1971), *Perfect and Imperfect Capital Markets*, mimeo.

Stiglitz, J.E. (1974), *Information and Capital Markets*, mimeo, Oxford University.

Stiglitz, J.E. (1984), "Price Rigidities and Market Structure", *American Economic Review*, 74, 350-356.

Stiglitz, J.E. (1985), "Information and Economic Analysis: A Perspective", *Economic Journal*.

Stiglitz, J.E. (1987), "The Causes and Consequences of the Dependence of Quality on Price", *Journal of Economic Literature*, 25, 1-48.

Stiglitz, J.E. (1988), "Money, Credit and Business Fluctuations", *Economic Record*, 307-22.

Stiglitz, J.E. (1989), "Money, Credit and Business Fluctuations", *NBER Working Papers*, n. 2823

Stiglitz, J.E. (1992a), "Capital Markets and Economic Fluctuations in Capitalist Economies", *European Economic Review*, 236-86.

Stiglitz, J.E. (1992b), "Methodological Issues and New Keynesian Economics", in Vercelli A., N.Dimitri (eds).

Stiglitz, J.E. (1992c), "Una spiegazione della crescita: concorrenza and struttura finanziaria", *Rivista di politica economica*, 82, 207-44.

Stiglitz, J.E. (1993), *Endogenous Growth and Cycles*, NBER working paper 4286.

Stiglitz, J.E. and Weiss, A. (1981), "Credit Rationing in Markets with Imperfect Information", *American Economic Review*, 71, 393-410.

Stiglitz, J.E. and A. Weiss, (1985), "Credit Rationing and Collateral", *Bell Communications Research Discussion Paper*.

Stiglitz, J.E. and A. Weiss, (1987), "Credit Rationing: Reply", *American Economic Review*, 77, 228-231.

Taylor, J. (1979), "Staggered Wage Setting in a Macro Model", *American Economic Review*, 69, 108-113.

Taylor, J. (1980), "Aggregate Dynamics and Staggered Contracts", *Journal of Political Economy,* 88, 1-23.

Tobin J. (1993), "Price Flexibility and Output Stability: An Old Keynesian View", *Journal of Economic Perspectives*, 7, 45-65.

Townsend, R. (1979), "Optimal Contracts and competitive Markets with Costly State Verification", *Journal of Economic Theory*, 21, 265-293.

Vercelli, A. and N. Dimitri (ed.) (1992), *Macroeconomics*, Oxford University Press, Oxford.

Vives, X. (1990), "Nash Equilibrium with Strategic Complementarities", *Journal of Mathematical Economics*, 19, 305-321.

Webb, S. and B. Webb (1897), *Industrial Democracy*, London.

Weiss, A. (1980), "Job Queues and Layoffs in Labor Markets with Flexible Wages", *Journal of Political Economy*, 88, 526-38.

Weiss, A. (1991), *Efficiency Wages,* Oxford, Clarendon Press.

Weitzman, M.L. (1982), "Increasing Returns and the Foundations of Unemployment Theory", *Economic Journal*, 92, 787-804.

Wette, H. (1983), "Collateral and Credit Rationing in Markets with Imperfect Information: A Note", *American Economic Review*, 73, 442-445.

Williamson, S.D. (1986), "Costly Monitoring, Financial Intermediation and Equilibrium Credit Rationing", *Journal of Monetary Economics*, 18, 159-179.

Williamson, S.D. (1987a), "Recent Developments in Modelling Financial Intermediation", *Federal Reserve Bank of Minneapolis Quarterly Review*, 19-29.

Williamson, S.D. (1987b), "Financial Intermediation, Business Failures and Real Business Cycles", *Journal of Political Economy*, 95, 1196-1216.

Wilson, C.A. (1977), "A Model of Insurance Markets with Imperfect Information", *Journal of Economic Theory*, 16, 167-207.

Woglom, G. (1982), "Underemployment with Rational Expectations", *Quarterly Journal of Economics*, 97, 89-108.

Woodford, M. (1991), "Self Fulfilling Expectations and Fluctuations in Aggregate Demand", in Mankiw N.G. and Romer, D. (1991)

Woodford, M. (1992), "Equilibrium Models of Endogenous Fluctuations: An Introduction", in Vercelli A., N.Dimitri (eds).

Worswick, G. and Trevithick, J. (eds) (1983), *Keynes and the Modern World*, Cambridge, Cambridge University Press.

Yellen, J. L. (1984), "Efficiency Wage Models of Unemployment", *American Economic Review,* 74, 200-205.

2. An Investigation into the New Keynesian Macroeconomics of Imperfect Capital Markets[*]

Roberto Tamborini

1. INTRODUCTION

The strand of macroeconomic theory with which this paper is concerned is part of the so-called New Keynesian (NK) economics, that is to say, a large body of literature which aims at showing that major macroeconomic phenomena of the Keynesian type are rooted either in imperfectly competitive markets for goods and labour or in imperfectly informed markets for capital (Mankiw and Romer, 1991). The NK macroeconomics of imperfect capital markets rests on a few basic features of the market economy that usually do not appear in the standard list of ingredients of macro-modelling (for example Greenwald and Stiglitz, 1987, 1990; Stiglitz, 1991):

1. The economy is sequential in nature, that is to say, there exists a finite, sizeable time lag between agents' decisions and their realizations. When future markets are absent, most notably in the case of consumption goods, agents' decisions are fallible.[1]
2. In a sequential economy, means of payment are necessary to bridge the gap that may arise between payments and receipts. The focus is on firms which

* An earlier version of this paper appeared with same title in the series Quaderni del Dipartimento di Scienze Economiche, Università di Padova, n.34, 1994. I wish to thank the participants in the C.N.R. (National Research Council) Group on New Keynesian Economics for their helpful comments, and in particular Piergiorgio Ardeni, Domenico Delli Gatti, Marcello Messori. I am also indebted to Ottorino Chillemi, Axel Leijonhufvud, Michele Moretto, Maurizio Pugno and Guglielmo Weber for their comments in private conversations or during seminars. I bear full responsibility for this paper.
1 Though fallibility is often used interchangeably with risk by NK authors, the former concept stresses the fact that, because of the absence of future markets, agents cannot insure optimally against risk. Those decisions which turn out to be wrong after any uncertainty is resolved, generally entail that the agent bear positive adjustment costs.

have to pay for production inputs (circulating as well as fixed capital) before being able to sell output.
3. The various financial instruments whereby firms may raise means of payment are not perfect substitutes because of informational imperfections in capital markets. The firms' decisions about employment and production are conditional on the financial instrument that firms choose (or have to choose).

These features are regarded as sufficient for market economies to exhibit Keynesian macroeconomic behaviour. In particular, it is strongly argued that capital market imperfections are a fundamental cause of the non-neutrality of money on output and employment even when labour and goods markets are perfectly competitive. The reason can be sketched as follows. Because of their inability to obtain all the desirable risk capital on the equity market, firms resort to debt as their main financial instrument, and debt forces firms to take bankruptcy into account in their plans. All the factors raising the probability of bankruptcy for firms, namely higher real interest rates, greater price uncertainty, lower equity base, and so on, lead them to reduce output and employment. Money is effective on output and employment, not through the usual channel of the money balances held by the public, but to the extent that changes in monetary policy alter the supply of credit and eventually the probability of bankruptcy of firms (see in particular Blinder and Stiglitz, 1983; Greenwald and Stiglitz, 1988b, 1991).

This alternative view of the role of money in the macroeconomic process rests on a large body of microeconomic models of the behaviour of borrowers and lenders under imperfect information. However, the production of full-blown macroeconomic models is much less developed. One can find a few reformulations of the IS-LM model where the credit channel of monetary policy is made explicit (for example Blinder, 1987; Bernanke and Blinder, 1988; Greenwald and Stiglitz, 1990) or Greenwald and Stiglitz's 'risk-based aggregate supply' models (for example 1988a, 1990, 1993) more akin to the modern macro-modelling introduced by New-Classical and Real-business-cycle theorists. The Greenwald and Stiglitz (1993) paper (GS hereafter) appears to be the most advanced contribution in this direction. Yet, whereas the authors are mostly concerned with showing how financial factors help 'account for many widely observed aspects of actual business cycles' (p.77), on reading that paper one may feel that some basic issues in macroeconomic theory (say those in the Macro I course) need careful reconsideration too.

Therefore my contribution aims at two targets: first, to present a model for studying the conditions of general macroeconomic equilibrium in an economy with characteristics such as those embodied in the GS class of models; second, to put under examination the claim that imperfect capital markets are sufficient for 'financial factors' to be non-neutral on output and employment in this class of models.

The task of bringing together the essentials of such a number of different and highly specialized models as those produced in the NK approach is not an easy one, and has required some unavoidable (over)simplifications. Section 1 describes the structure of a sequential production economy where firms hire labour and produce in each period, and sell a single homogenous output in the subsequent one. To give substance to the sequential structure of transactions, overlapping generations of workers-consumers with a life-cycle of 2 periods are also assumed. As is typical of NK models, emphasis is placed on the contractual arrangements in the economy and the way they constrain agents' decisions. The key feature of the model is that the firms are owned by entrepreneurs-managers and are not publicly quoted, so that they have to borrow their working capital and cannot divest themselves of the bankruptcy risk. For simplicity there is only one lender in the economy: the central bank. Hence there are two key 'financial factors' in this economy: the bank-managed interest rate, as the capital cost to firms, and the related bankruptcy risk.

Sequential models generally admit a temporary equilibrium solution, where price expectations are taken as given and a sequential equilibrium solution, where it is imposed that one period's price expectations are fulfilled in the next (Hicks, 1939; Grandmont, 1983). Thus section 3 first introduces the individual plans of firms and workers, and then section 4 presents the temporary general equilibrium solutions for the markets of labour, credit and output. These solutions reproduce the main features of the NK macro-models with imperfect capital markets in such a way that the issue of the non-neutrality of the financial factors can be discussed in detail. Section 5 examines the issue of sequential equilibrium, this raises some interesting problems as to expectations formation -which are neglected in the NK literature. The main content of section 5, is to show that the non-neutrality of the 'financial factors' under rational expectations depends on the specification of the labour supply function, and that there are cases in which non-neutrality may no longer hold. Section 6 summarizes the main results of the paper and attempts an assessment of the NK macroeconomics of imperfect capital markets at its present stage of development.

2. STRUCTURE OF THE ECONOMY

Let us consider a sequential economy where discrete periods of time are indexed with t. In each period t, a constant population of W workers are born with no endowment except their work force. Such workers have a life cycle of 2 periods: the period of work (t) and the period of retirement ($t+1$). Hence in each t there exists a constant (arbitrarily large) population of agents:

$$A = W + W' = 2W \qquad (2.1)$$

where W' denotes the retired workers.

In each t there also exists an arbitrarily large population of firms. Firms are not quoted, and each is directed by a worker-manager (manager for short) $j \in \underline{W}$ who belongs to the active population $\underline{W}$ and claims on the firm's profit and losses. A firm's life coincides with the manager's. Firms produce competitively one single non-storable consumption good, called 'the output' of the economy, by means of homogeneous labour. The production cycle of each firm takes one period, regardless of the scale of output. Therefore, in each t the markets for labour and output are opened: on the former, the firms buy labour from active workers in function of the output planned for sale at $t+1$; on the latter market, the firms sell the output planned at t-1 to the consumers (active and retired workers), and so on as in the chart below:

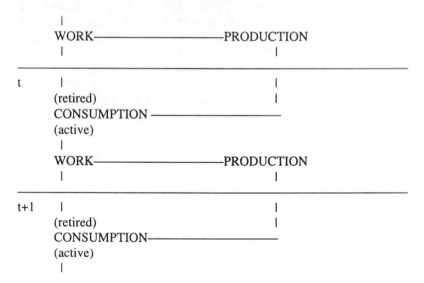

Figure 2.1 Work, production and consumption in the sequence economy

The time structure of transactions is such that the firms must be able to pay for their desired workforce before being able to sell output. This requirement by firms, which disappears in standard macroeconomic models based on simultaneous transactions on all markets, is viewed as a key factor in the NK macroeconomics (for example Blinder and Stiglitz, 1983; Blinder, 1987; Greenwald and Stiglitz, 1987). In order to accommodate this factor in the model, I posit the following characterizing assumptions:

(A1) There exists a general means of payment in the form of fiat money issued by a government agency called 'the central bank'.

(A2) Workers and firms stipulate 'standard labour contracts', that is to say, contracts in terms of money which are resolved through payment within the working period.

(A3) The central bank operates a credit window at the beginning of each t. Any borrower j receives the contractual amount of credit B_{jt} against its commitment to pay $B_{jt}(1 + R_t)$ in $t+1$,[2] where R_t is the bank nominal interest rate, $B_{jt} = (1 - \theta)S_t L_{jt}$, θ is the fraction of the working capital self-financed by j, S_t the contractual money wage rate, L_{jt} the labour input.

First of all, (A1) and (A2) are implied by one another, and they can be taken to represent the NK imperfect capital markets hypothesis. In fact, look at the chart of the economy in Figure 2.1: if an agent wishes to consume throughout his life, he may choose to sell labour in t at the market wage rate and use labour income to buy consumption in $t+1$. Any desirable intertemporal distribution of consumption is allowed for by trades between workers and firms at every date, *provided that workers' claims on output act as store of value* in view of the fact that the economy's output is non-storable.[3] Hence one might design labour contracts like Arrow and Debreu pure securities and the wage rate as their price,[4] in which case (A1) and (A2) would be dropped together. The latter would be viewed as a case of perfect capital markets, with workers in a position of suppliers of firms' (working) capital. Hence (A1) and (A2) amount to assuming that Arrow and Debreu labour contracts are not feasible,[5] or more loosely speaking, that firms are 'fully rationed on the equity market' (see for example Greenwald and Stiglitz, 1990, 1993).

---

[2] Workers do not borrow because they live only two periods and they do not have incomes in the second period.

[3] This point follows the well-known general principle that in a sequential economy any means of payment should also act as store of value, though the reverse may not be true: Hicks (1967), Radner (1968), Hahn (1982, ch.1).

[4] For instance, each worker in t receives from the hiring firm S_t labour bonds per unit of labour services; each labour bond will be convertible into the consumption good in $t+1$ at the market price.

[5] As far as I know, the New-Keynesian literature does not provide explicit and formal explanation of the reason why Arrow and Debreu labour contracts are non existent in real life, though one might claim that the informational imperfections behind equity rationing also operate against Arrow-Debreu labour contracts. See also Tamborini (1995).

Under 'full equity rationing', firms may finance their wage bill either from their internal funds or by borrowing on the credit market. (A3) states the credit conditions for those firms which resort to borrowing. The credit market is the pivot of the NK macroeconomics of imperfect capital markets, which is in fact rooted in a vast and detailed literature on the microeconomics of credit (for example Jaffee and Stiglitz, 1990; Greenwald and Stiglitz, 1988b, 1990; Gertler and Gilchrist, 1993). Most of this literature concentrates on informational imperfections leading to credit market failures, such as credit rationing. However, it is now widely held that credit rationing, or other market imperfections, are not necessary for credit variables to exert real effects (for example Gertler and Gilchrist, 1993). Therefore I shall follow GS's modelling strategy, who in the first instance consider a single market-clearing interest rate determined by competitive commercial banks with an infinitely elastic credit supply. Instead of commercial banks, I simply have the sole central bank as the institution wich sets the interest rate in each period.[6] Moreover, since in this economy firms live two periods, in each t each old firms' cash-flow is fully exhausted by profit and debt payments due from t-1, and each new firms' internal funds are always zero, that is $\theta = 0$ so that new production requires B_{jt} = $S_r L_{jt}$. Thus we obtain another typical feature of the NK macroeconomics, namely that 'credit is special' because it is the only source of funds for most firms (see for example Gertler-Gilchrist, 1993). Here we are only assuming that this is true for all firms.[7]

An important point in the NK macroeconomics is that macro-outcomes are sensitive to the the way in which contracts bind individual behaviour at the micro-level. Thus the specification of the debt contracts stipulated by firms, and the ensuing managers' earnings schemes, is a crucial step. Let the j-th manager's earnings scheme be the following

$$S_t \qquad\qquad \text{when active} \qquad\qquad\qquad \text{(A4)}$$

$$\left.\begin{array}{ll} Z_{jt+1} & \text{if } Z_{jt+1} \geq 0 \\[2mm] Z_{jt+1} - \kappa_j S_t L_{jt}(1 + R_t) & \text{if } Z_{jt+1} < 0 \end{array}\right\} \text{ when retired}$$

where $Z_{jt+1} = P_{jt+1}Y(t)_{jt+1} - S_t L_{jt}(1 + R_t)$ is profit, $Y(t)_{jt+1}$ is the output produced in t and sold in t+1, P_{jt+1} is the selling price, $Z_{jt+1} < 0$ is a state of bankruptcy, and $0 \leq \kappa_j \leq 1$ is the incidence of bankruptcy on the manager's personal resources.

(A4) is simply meant to justify the profit-maximizing hypothesis (see below)

---

6 For an extension of this model to a competitive credit market see Tamborini (1995).
7 In the GS model, the firm's internal funds, or 'equity base', do play an important role in connection with business fluctuations, which however fall outside the scope of this paper.

and at the same time to introduce bankruptcy risk into the firm's decision making as a consequence of 'equity rationing'. In fact, the manager is paid at the market price of labour when active, and then seizes the firm's whole profit, if positive, or subtracts the firm's liability from his personal resources, when retired. k_j would be 0 only in a limited liability contract. Microeconomic analyses have shown that the optimal one-period debt contracts are generally limited liability contracts, such that the firm's liability in case of default is limited up to its revenue (see for example Gale and Hellwig, 1985). The GS macro-model, however, does not specify the debt contract but assumes a positive cost of bankruptcy as an increasing function in the firm's output. The authors put forward a number of justifications for this assumption, though perhaps the most important argument is that 'having bankruptcy costs depend on [output] is necessary in order to ensure that the possibility of bankruptcy is never ignored' (p.89). (A4) shows that this may be the case with $k_j > 0$.[8]

We now need an explanation of why bankruptcy may occur, and possibly a probability measure of it. First of all, we are obviously not interested in situations where all firms either go bankrupt or make profits; in other words, we need an economy where firms may differ in their performance. Indeed, the heterogeneity of agents, as opposed to the representative agent methodology, is central to the NK micro- and macroeconomics (for example Greenwald and Stiglitz, 1987; Stiglitz, 1991). Heterogeneity may be introduced *ex post,* as (stochastic) differences in firms' realizations or *ex ante* as differences in firms' plans. The GS model is an example of the former type, since each firm *ex post* faces an individual selling price which is a stochastic deviation from the output average market price.[9] More formally:

(A5) Let the individual selling price P_{jt+1} of any firm j be a random realization of a distribution with mean value P_{t+1}. Each active manager j and worker w in t has a probability distribution over possible output prices in $t+1$, with density function $f_{jt}(P_{jt+1})$, $f_{wt}(P_{jt+1})$ respectively, and with mean values

$$P^e(t)_{jt+1} = P^e(t)_{wt+1} = P^e(t)_{t+1} \qquad \text{for all } j, w$$

$P^e(t)_{t+1}$ will be read as the economy's expected price, conditional on informaton available at t. The equality of the expected price among firms and workers is only a simplifying assumption that prevents phenomena that may arise at the aggregate level from differences in this parameter. Though potentially interesting, these phenomena fall outside the scope of the present paper.

---

[8]   An alternative strategy would be to set k as a fixed cost and let the bankruptcy probability to increase with output (see also GS, p.86, and below, fn. 10).

[9]   Therefore, it seems that the GS needs an imperfect output market too. This additional imperfection is unnecessary if firms heterogeneity is introduced *ex ante* as shown in Tamborini (1995).

A bankruptcy state occurs whenever $P_{jt+1} < C_{jt}$ where $C_{jt} = S_t L_{jt}(1 + R_t)/Y(t)_{jt+1}$ is the firm's average cost of producing $Y(t)_{jt+1}$. Given $f_{jt}(P_{jt+1})$, $\phi_{jt} = \text{Prob}(P_{jt+1} \leq C_{jt})$ is the bankruptcy probability. Therefore, $\kappa_j S_t L_{jt}(1 + R_t)\phi_{jt}$ is the manager's *expected* bankruptcy cost.[10]

3. INDIVIDUAL PLANS

3.1. Firms

It is assumed that the managers are risk-neutral and wish to maximize profit over their life-cyle. Given the above time structure of production and transactions, however, the manager has to plan production in period t whereas sales and profit will materialize in period $t+1$. From (A4) and (A5), the manager's expected profit will be (see GS, equation (13)):

$$Z^e_{jt+1} = [P^e(t)_{jt+1} Y(t)_{jt+1} - S_t L_{jt}(1 + R_t)] - \kappa_j S_t L_{jt}(1 + R_t)\phi_{jt} \qquad (3.1)$$

The firm's programme is:

$$\max_L Z^e_{jt+1} \qquad (3.2)$$

given the production function

$$Y(t)_{jt+1} = L^\eta_{jt} \qquad (3.3)$$

for all firms, with $0 < \eta < 1$.

For the sake of comparison with standard macroeconomic models, it is convenient to compute the log-linear solution of the firm's programme, which yields the following labour demand function (unless otherwise stated, the log of each variable will be denoted by converting the notation from capital to small-case letters):

$$l_{jt} = \delta - \phi_{jt} - \gamma(s_t + r_t - p^e(t)_{jt+1}) \qquad (3.4)$$

---

[10] Under suitable assumptions, ϕ_{jt} may be expressed as a continuous and differentiable function $\phi_{jt}(C_{jt}, \sigma_{jt})$, where σ_{jt} is the standard deviation of the price distribution, with derivatives $\phi'_1 > 0$, $\phi'_2 > 0$. If C_{jt} is increasing in output, then also ϕ_{jt} is, which makes the expected bankruptcy cost increasing in output (even in the presence of a fixed charge on the manager's personal resources). For reasons of analytical parsimony I shall not make this further assumption, and I shall treat ϕ_{jt} as an exogenous parameter.

with $\quad \delta = \dfrac{\ln\eta}{1-\eta}$, $-\varphi_{jt} = \dfrac{\ln(1+\kappa_j\phi_{jt})}{1-\eta}$, $\gamma = \dfrac{1}{1-\eta}$ $\quad r_t = \ln(1 + R_t)$

Equation (3.4) displays some typical features of the NK models of firm with credit (for example Greenwald and Stiglitz, 1990, 1993). First, because of the time lag between production and sale, the firm's employment decision is ruled by its *expected* real cost (the term in brackets), not the current one. Second, the real cost includes the bank interest rate r_t. Third, the optimal employment rule now also includes the expected bankruptcy marginal cost $|\varphi_{jt}$ $|\in [0, \infty]$, bankruptcy risk for short, which increases as ϕ_{jt} or κ_j increase. That is to say, an increase in the bankruptcy probability or in personal bankruptcy costs induces the manager to reduce employment and output. On the other hand, (3.4) becomes the standard labour demand function when $r_t = 0$, $\phi_{jt} = 0$ or $\kappa_j = 0$.

3.2. Workers

Workers are assumed to choose rationally between leisure and consumption in a competitive labour market. I shall adapt to the present context the general life-cycle choice model elaborated by Lucas and Rapping (1969) and Sargent (1979), where active workers w at any t are characterized by an individual system of preferences over the quantity of leisure H_{wt} and of consumption Y_{wt} in t and onwards, represented by the utility function

$$U_t(H_{wt}, Y_{wt}, ...) \qquad (3.5)$$

monotonically increasing and twice differentiable in each argument, with $H_{wt} \in [0, H]$ and H as the social maximum working time.

Given the structure of transactions in the economy, the opportunities for each worker at birth are constrained as follows:

$$L_{wt} = H - H_{wt} \qquad (3.6a)$$

$$P_t Y_{wt} + M_{wt} = S_t L_{wt} \qquad (3.6b)$$

$$P_{wt+1} Y_{w't+1} = M_{wt} \qquad (3.6c)$$

where L_{wt} is labour supply in t, M_{wt} are money balances, and $Y_{w't+1}$ is consumption in $t+1$.

The worker's programme is:

Financial Constraints and Market Failures

$$\max_{H,Y} U_t \text{ s.t. } (3.6a\text{--}3.6c) \tag{3.6}$$

and under the assumptions that leisure and consumption are normal goods and that an internal solution exists, the Lucas-Rapping-Sargent model yields:

$$L_{wt} = L_w(S/P_t,\ P^e_{wt+1}/P_t) \tag{3.7a}$$

$$Y_{wt} = Y_w(S/P_t,\ P^e_{wt+1}/P_t) \tag{3.7b}$$

$$Y_{w't+1} = M_{wt}/P_{t+1} \tag{3.7c}$$

with $L'_{w1} > 0, L'_{w2} < 0, Y'_{w1} > 0, Y'_{w2} < 0$. Note that P^e_{wt+1}/P_t is 1 + the expected inflation rate (expected inflation rate for short).

The worker's choice between leisure and consumption and between present and future consumption is ruled by the current real wage rate and the expected inflation rate as usual. But the cross-elasticity between *present* leisure and *future* consumption is not nil: an increase in P^e_{wt+1} which raises P^e_{wt+1}/P_t amounts to a fall in S/P^e_{wt+1}, the expected real wage rate, hence L^s_{wt} is decreasing in P^e_{wt+1}/P_t or else increasing in S/P^e_{wt+1}.

Always following Lucas-Rapping and Sargent we may also assume that a log-linear specification of (2.7a) exists and is the following:

$$l_{wt} = \alpha + \beta_1(s_t - p_t) - \beta_2 q^e(t)_{wt+1} \tag{3.8}$$

where $q^e(t)_{wt+1} = p^e(t)_{wt+1} - p_t$ is w's expected inflation. It is worth noting that this specification of the labour supply function encompasses different specializations that can be found in macro-models. Here we shall consider the 'New Keyensian case' and the 'New Classical case'.

The *New Keyenesian case* obtains for $\beta_2 = 0$, that is if only the *current* real wage rate appears in (3.8).[11]

The *New Classical case* obtains for $\beta_1 = \beta_2 = \beta$, that is if only the *expected* real wage rate $(s_t - p^e(t)_{wt+1})$ appears in (3.8).[12]

---

[11] This is common to many NK macro-models, though is made explicit through a choice model of workers in the GS model. The reason is that GS (p.96) adopt a particular utility function which is quasi-linear in contemporaneous consumption and leisure, and linear in present and future consumption (i.e. the marginal rate of intertemporal substitution is constant and equal to the individual factor of time discount). By *imposing* that the real interest rate $(P/P^e_{wt+1} - 1$ in our model) be equal to the time discount, GS obtain that the worker is *indifferent* as to the allocation of real labour income between present and future consumption, so that the worker only has to choose the optimal amount of labour supply in function of the *current* real wage. The authors do not explain why they restrain their competitive equilibrium to the case when the real interest rate is just equal to the time discount. Competitive equilibrium would equally hold for any other level of the real interest rate, with the worker choosing a corner solution.

[12] See the expectations-augmented labour supply function originated by Friedman and Phelps and adopted in the New Classical models (for example Sargent and Wallace, 1975). The restrictions on the parameters in (2.7) implies that the income effect and the intertemporal effect on the worker's choice have the same magnitude.

Both special cases of course have pros and cons. Paradoxically, the NK case does not seem to fit well in its own analytical framework. Workers and firms result in having an asymmetric attitude towards future prices. However, as the present analysis makes clear, as a consequence of the sequential structure of transactions, workers should display a forward-looking attitude like firms: they should also be concerned with their future purchasing power. This is perhaps inconvenient analytically because, as Keynes argued (1936, ch.19), in a forward-looking, competitive labour market nobody can set the real wage rate. The New Classical case, combined with equation (3.4), allows for a consistent symmetric forward-looking behaviour of firms and workers, though this is obtained at the cost of a strong restriction on the parameters of the labour supply function. On the other hand, some NK authors hold the view that their macroeconomic models with credit are in fact the counterpart of the New Classical models with money neutrality (for example Greenwald and Stiglitz, 1987, 1990, 1993). Yet their different treatment of the labour market does not afford much ground for comparison. In the following it will be important to bear this issue of the specification of the labour supply function in mind, and we shall point out the implications of the different forms whenever it will be the case.

4. TEMPORARY GENERAL EQUILIBRIUM

The model under consideration admits two concepts of equilibrium: *temporary* and *sequential* equilibrium.[13] The former concept refers to the general equilibrium that is established in any period t, given all available information and the relevant expectations; the latter requires that the expectations held in t are fulfilled in $t+1$ (or that the plans of agents chosen in t are actually realized in $t+1$). In this section we first examine the temporary equilibirum solutions.

4.1. Credit, employment and output

First, let us consider the log-linear solutions to the individual maximization programmes in section 2; summation over individuals, given (A5), yields the *average* demand and supply, and the equilibrium conditions for the labour and credit market in t, and follow for convenience:[14]

---

[13] As is well known, this distinction can be traced back to Hicks (1939) and the Swedish tradition. In particular, the present treatment is akin to Grandmont's (1983).

[14] To obtain proper aggregate values one should then apply the relevant scale factors. This operation is left implicit for the sake of simplicity.

Labour market
$$l^d_t = \delta - \varphi_t - \gamma(s_t + r_t - p^e(t)_{t+1})$$
$$l^s_f = \alpha + \beta_1(s_t - p_t) - \beta_2(p^e(t)_{t+1} - p_t)$$
$$l^d_f = l^s_f = l_t$$

Credit market
$$b_t = s_t + l_t$$

Recalling that the output produced in t is $y(t)_{t+1} = \eta l_t$, the temporary equilibrium solutions for the nominal wage rate s_t, the amount of credit b_t and the level of output $y(t)_{t+1}$ are:

$$
\begin{bmatrix} s_t \\ b_t \\ y(t)_t+1 \end{bmatrix} = \begin{bmatrix} s_o \\ b_o \\ y_o \end{bmatrix} + \frac{1}{\Delta} \begin{bmatrix} -1 & -1 & (1-\eta)(\beta_1-\beta_2) & 1+\beta_2(1-\eta) \\ -(1+\beta_1) & -(1+\beta_1) & -\eta(\beta_1-\beta_2) & 1+\beta_1-\beta_2\eta \\ -\beta_{1\eta} & -\beta_{1\eta} & -\eta(\beta_1-\beta_2) & \eta(\beta_1-\beta_2) \end{bmatrix} \begin{bmatrix} \varphi_t \\ r_t \\ p_t \\ p^e(t)_{t+1} \end{bmatrix}
\begin{matrix} (4.1a) \\ \\ (4.1b) \\ \\ (4.1c) \end{matrix}
$$

$\Delta = 1 + \beta_1(1 - \eta) > 0$ (the intercepts, denoted with 'o', are not explicated for brevity).

We can thus draw the following first set of observations. In our economy there are two key respresentative 'financial factors' to which the NK macroeconomics attach great importance: the (average) bankruptcy risk φ_t and the nominal interest rate r_t. Both factors influence the temporary equilibrium values of the endogenous variables. In particular, (P1) *The level of output is negative elastic to changes in the bankruptcy risk and in the nominal interest rate* .

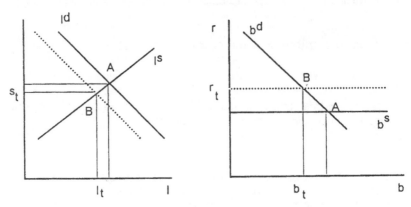

Figure 2.2 An increase in the interest rate

(P1) can be interpreted as a non-neutrality proposition which is central to the NK macroeconomics of imperfect capital markets. However, it should be clear that (P1) does not imply *per se* that there may be involuntary unemployment (the labour market does clear, the nominal wage rate being negative elastic to changes in those same variables). The reason behind (P1) is simply that both variables affect the real marginal cost of firms at a given expected price. The way in which changes in the interest rate affect employment and output can be understood with the help of Figure 2.2. Suppose the central bank raises r_t. *Ceteris paribus*, the expected real marginal cost will rise for all firms, so that labour demand, and hence s_t, l_t, will fall.

The fact that the bankruptcy risk has exactly the same effects as the interest rate is also important both on theoretical and empirical grounds. As is clear from system (4.1), φ_t lends itself to a straightforward interpretation of the source of aggregate supply shocks alternative to the technology/tastes shocks preferred in the New Classical camp (Greenwald and Stiglitz, 1987, 1990, 1993). Shifts in aggregate supply originating in y_o or in φ_t would hardly be distinguishable on empirical grounds, yet the NKs argue that technology/tastes shocks of the magnitude required to reproduce the observed swings in output strain credibility, whereas the bankruptcy risk perceived by firms is typically volatile.[15] Last but not least, this factor is reminiscent of Keynes's original view that business fluctuations are rooted in the instability of the entrepreneurs' state of confidence (Greenwald and Stiglitz, 1987).[16]

Second, the present model shows that the elasticity of output to the 'financial factors' is proportional to its elasticity to labour inputs η and to the elasticity of the labour supply β_1. Indeed, the crucial role of the structural parameters of the labour market in the 'transmission mechanism' from financial impulses to employment and output is largely recognized by the NKs following the GS approach. The claim that this transmission mechanism from the credit cost to output *supply* is likely to be much stronger than the old-Keynesian one of going through asset prices and the asset-prices elasticity of output *demand,* appears largely an empirical matter. However, from a theoretical point of view, it should be noted that the parameters governing the credit-based transmission mechanism are the same as those governing the

---

[15] This paper is not concerned with the business-cycle extensions of the NK macroeconomics, though a growing number of contributions are being addressed to this issue following the GS model. The research strategy opened by the GS model is towards making the business cycle endogenous basically by making the bankruptcy risk itself endogenous. This result may be understood by recalling that the bankruptcy risk is increasing in the amount of borrowing, i.e. decreasing in the amount of internal funds.

[16] Of course, in Keynes's view changes in the entrepreneurs' state of confidence are responsible for aggregate *demand* instability. The shift of focus of the NKs from demand to supply is theoretically and empirically important, and will be discussed in a moment. GS argue that their model can also accommodate the traditional Keynesian investment demand side, but this has been questioned in a paper by.

real business cycle models.[17] Hence the supply side of the economy definitely seems to be the new ground where the controversy over the relevance versus irrelevance of money is played. Yet the controversy is not merely empirical (as many believe it was between Keynesians and Monetarists): it is rooted in the microfoundations of capital markets, depending on whether the financial means are the perfect substitute for the firm or not, and whether the fallibility of firms matters or not.

Third, as is naturally the case in macro-models with credit, the money stock observable in each period is 'endogenous', that is to say it is generated through debt contracts on the credit market, rather than through portfolio shifts on the asset market.[18] The relative importance of 'endogenous' versus 'exogenous' money is a matter of well-known, long-standing, and perhaps never-ending, controversy that we shall not address here. It is instead worth noting how equation (4.1b) looks like it does. This equation gives the amount of credit granted to firms in each t, and in our simple economy it is also the stock of money available to the economy.

Active workers receive the whole available money and then they partly *spend it within t* for current consumption or *hold it till* t+1 for future consumption. Consequently, at any point in time (4.1b) would virtually be undistinguishable to an econometrician from a standard 'M1' demand equation (after some restrictions on the β parameters, see below) whereas it is a credit demand equation. On the other hand, φ_t and $p^e(t)_{t+1}$ could be responsible for the 'breakdown' of the money demand equation if it were in fact mis-estimated in the place of a credit demand equation (or more generally, when the weight of endogenous money were substantial).

Another interesting issue raised by equation (4.1b) is the so-called phenomenon of 'reverse causality'. All exogenous variables that make b_t rise or fall also make $y(t)_{t+1}$ rise or fall. Again, on emprical observation, in our model M1 and output turn out to be positively correlated as in a standard IS-LM model, with 'causation' seemingly going from money supply to output, whereas it is the effect of exogenous variables on employment and ouput that make credit and money adjust themselves endogenously.

4.2. Credit, prices and bankruptcy

System (4.1) gives the output current price p_t and the economy's expected

---

[17] As a matter of fact, King and Plosser (1984) found a significant role of credit and the interest rate, rather than money, in a real business cycle model.

[18] The 'endogenous' view of money creation, though minoritarian, was never fully dismissed. It was revived in the '60s by the Radcliffe Committe (1959), and later by Kaldor's works. The influential paper by King and Plosser (1984) has redirected attention to the issue in the New Classical school too.

price $p^e(t)_{t+1}$ important roles to play. This is a delicate issue both because the NK macro-models are usually expressed in 'real' variables and because we see immediately that the sign of price variables is ambiguous, depending on the relative weight of β_1 and β_2 - that is on the specification of the labour supply function. Following the distinction introduced in section 3.2, we obtain that in the NK case ($\beta_2 = 0$) all endogenous variables depend on both p_t and $p^e(t)_{t+1}$, whereas in the New Classical case ($\beta_1 = \beta_2$) the *nominal* variables, s_t and b_t, only depend on $p^e(t)_{t+1}$ while the *real* variables, l_t and $y(t)_{t+1}$, are fully insulated from price effects.

This difference is only due to the fact that in the NK case the workers are assumed to react to changes in the *current* real wage rate, while in the New Classical case they only react to changes in the *expected* real wage rate (recall that in both cases the firms only react to changes in the *expected* real cost). Among the many issues of potential interest related to price effects, we shall consider only two which seem more relevant to the present context.

A qualifying issue in the NK agenda is that Keynes (1936, ch. 19) idea that the mere downward flexibility of wages and prices could generate no increase in employment and output finds substantial support from consideration of firms' liabilities and bankruptcy risk (for example Greenwald and Stiglitz, 1987).[19] The preferred line of argument in the NK models is that a fall in the current price raises the real value of a firm's outstanding debt,[20] while an expected price fall raises a firm's real marginal cost (see also paragraph 3.1 above).[21] In the present model the first type of effect is absent because firms are assumed to enter each new period with no outstanding debt, while the second is dependent on the labour supply elasticities. Deflationary expectations definitely have a negative impact on employment and output in the NK case - even though a simple manipulation of equation (4.1a) shows that the *real* wage rate ($s_t - p_t$) would *fall* - whereas they are only ininfluential in the New Classical case for the usual reason of the symmetric adjustment of labour demand and supply. In neither case is there a positive effect of deflationary expectations on employment and output, unless the workers' intertemporal substitution effect (less leisure today for more consumption tomorrow) is sufficiently strong ($\beta_1 < \beta_2$).

Another noticeable issue is 'reverse causality' between inflationary expectations and money growth. In the NK case a rise in p_t reduces output and money because workers supply less labour, for a given labour demand; by contrast, a rise in $p^e(t)_{t+1}$ generates greater output and money because it is firms

[19] This issue, too, is not at all new in the macroeconomic debate since it dates back to Fisher's theory of debt deflation: see for example Tobin (1980), and Minsky (1982).

[20] As pointed out by Delli Gatti and Gallegati (1994) the fall in current price should be unanticipated by firms.

[21] Like in Keynes's argument, a fall in the current price and in the expected price may also be correlated.

that demand more labour, for a given labour supply. This phenomenon is even more clear-cut in the New Classical case, where inflationary expectations have no effect on the level of employment, but have full impact on the money wage rate and the money stock, because now *both firms and workers* adjust to the new price expectation. In general, inflationary expectations can be self-fuelled in an 'accommodating' credit market, unless workers display a 'strong' intertemporal substitution effect (less consumption tomorrow for more leisure today) $(\beta_1 < \beta_2 \eta)$.[22]

A question which receives remarkably low attention in the NK literature is whether the credit transmission mechanism has consequences on prices that differ from those of the standard money mechanism. The question is obviously important for its own sake, but also for its bearings upon bankruptcy and, as we shall see later, sequential equilibrium. For instance, in the GS model the average output price is treated as a fully exogenous stochastic variable, with firms' individual sale prices as further stochastic idiosyncratic deviations from the average. This is however not satisfactory if one wishes to build a true general equilibrium solution.

Let us first derive the equilibrium solution for the output price p_{t+1} from system (4.1). This solution will obviously be obtained by equating output demand and supply. The output supply that will materialize in $t+1$ is given by (4.1c). Output demand will consist of two components: one coming from the active population, one coming from the retired population. The second component will amount to the real savings of the retired population plus the real profits earned by the retired managers. As to the component coming from profits, the perfect competition hypothesis in the presence of positive bankruptcy probability should entail that they should *on average* be zero. Hence aggregate demand reduces to

$$WY^d_{wt+1} + (S_t L/P_{t+1} - WY^d_{wt})$$

Now, the average consumption plan of the t-th generation of workers derived from equations (3.6a-c) is (for example Sargent, 1979):

$$y^d_t = \beta'_1(s_t - p_t) - \beta'_2 q^e(t)_{t+1} \tag{4.2}$$

and substituting $(s_t - p_t)$ from equation (4.1a),

---

[22] The dependence of price effects on the specification of the labour supply function has also some bearings upon the controversy over the price-output correlation in the business cycle literature (for example Danthine and Donaldson, 1993). Our previous considerations make it clear that whether price and output should be positively or negatively correlated cannot be established once and for all, independently of whether current or expected prices are considered and of whether price expectations are present or not in labour demand and supply.

$$y^d_t = \varepsilon_0 - \varepsilon_1(\varphi_t + r_t) + \varepsilon_2 q^e(t)_{t+1} \tag{4.3}$$

with $\varepsilon_0 = \beta'_1 s_o$, $\varepsilon_1 = \beta'_1/\Delta$, $\varepsilon_2 = [(1 + \beta_2(1 - \eta)]/\Delta - \beta'_2$

As a consequence, provided that population, technology and tastes do not change, the level of output demand of each generation can only vary if the bankruptcy risk, the interest rate and/or the economy's expected inflation rate vary. These intergenerational changes make the aggregate demand hardly tractable. Yet since we are considering a structurally stationary economy, we may restrict our attention to the set of equilibria that arise when any change that may occur in any exogenous variable in t is once and for all. That is to say, given $\varphi_t, r_t, q^e(t)_{t+1}$, we study the output market equilibrium for $\varphi_{t+\tau} = \varphi_t$, $r_{t+\tau} = r_t$, $q^e(t)_{t+1+\tau} = q^e(t)_{t+1}$, for all $\tau = 1, \ldots$ This restriction implies that the output demand of each generation from t onwards is, *ceteris paribus*, constant over time, so that the demand in $t+1$ reduces to the real money balances of the retired workers $(s_t + l_t - p_{t+1})$. Consequently,

$$\begin{aligned} p_{t+1} &= s_t + l_t - y(t)_{t+1} \tag{4.4} \\ &= p_o - (\varphi_t + r_t) + p^e(t)_{t+1} \\ q_{t+1} &= p_o - (\varphi_t + r_t) + q^e(t)_{t+1} \end{aligned}$$

These results leads us to the following propositions:
(P2) *The price level is negative unit elastic to a once-and-for-all change in the bankruptcy risk or in the interest rate.*
(P3) *The inflation rate is positive unit elastic to a once-and-for-all change in the economy's expected inflation rate.*

The result in (P2) arises from the effects that the 'financial factors' exert on *both* output supply *and* demand. As we have seen previously (see Figure 2.1) an increase in r_t reduces s_t, l_t and consequently $y(t)_{t+1}$. Therefore, in $t+1$ there will be both a lower demand for and a lower supply of output: p_{t+1} will fall too (see Figure 2.3). In general such a fall will be smoother than implied by the sole demand shock. This kind of correlation between demand and supply shifts is an important feature of NK macro-models. The NKs ascribe the well-known fact that price changes are much smoother than output changes more due to co-movements in demand and supply than primarily to price rigidities (Stiglitz, 1992; Greenwald and Stiglitz, 1993).

The result in (P3) follows from the noteworthy feature of (4.4) that the equilibrium price depends on the economy's expected price. This is important for two reasons. The first is that it closes the circle of 'reverse causality' between inflationary expectations and money growth discussed in section 4.1 by translating inflationary expectations into actual inflation. The second is that it paves the way to sequential equilibrium analysis, as we shall see below.

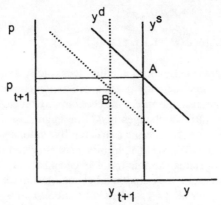

Figure 2.3 The effect of an increased interest rate on output and price

5. SEQUENTIAL GENERAL EQUILIBRIUM

The picture we have drawn from temporary equilibrium analysis is one of an economy where, for a given probability distribution over possible future output prices, 'financial factors' generate important effects on real variables. The NK view is that the non-neutrality of 'financial factors' holds even under rational expectations — that is, even when the old Keynesian non-neutrality of money fails. However, as already remarked previously, the NK macro-models usually do not provide explicit solution for the equilibrium price of output. Given that we obtained such a solution in section 4, our next step will be to examine the sequential equilibrium of the economy. In this analysis, the formation of expectations and their fulfillment take the prominent place.

In the GS model firms in each t are assumed to have rational expectations of the average ouput price, whereas each firm in $t+1$ will face an individual price that may deviate from the mean with positive probability (see section 3). To examine a configuration of our economy which is comparable to that obtained in the GS model, let us restate assumption (A5) by imposing that the agents' probability distribution over output prices coincide with the 'objective' one, so that $p^e(t)_{t+1} = p_{t+1}$. Bankruptcy is still possible for any individual firm if, for instance, the individual selling price is given by $p_{jt+1} = p_{t+1} + v_{jt+1}$ where v_{jt+1} is a random deviation with zero mean.

GS also assume that banks index the nominal interest rate in order to keep the real return to loans unchanged, given the rationally expected inflation. Hence, let the central bank set the nominal interest rate according to a full-indexation 'Fisherian' rule such that, in logs,

$$r_t = \rho + q^e(t)_{bt+1} \qquad (5.1)$$

where $q^e(t)_{bt+1} = p^e(t)_{bt+1} - p_t$ is the central bank's expected inflation. At the moment we need not establish how the 'real anchor' ρ is determined.[23]

The peculiar role of the central bank as a public institution can be characterized by the following assumption:

(A6) The central bank knows (for example by correct sampling and estimaton) the economy's expected price $p^e(t)_{t+1}$.

This ensures that also the central bank has the inflation rational expectation.

After substituting (5.1) and $p^e(t)_{bt+1} = p^e(t)_{t+1} = p_{t+1}$ in system (3.1) we obtain

$$
\begin{bmatrix} s^*_t \\ b^*_t \\ y^*(t)_{+1} \end{bmatrix} = \begin{bmatrix} s'_o \\ b'_o \\ y'_o \end{bmatrix} + \frac{1}{\Delta} \begin{bmatrix} 1+\beta_2(1-\eta) & -1+\beta_2(1-\eta) & \Delta \\ 1+\beta_1-\eta\beta_2 & -1+\beta_1-\beta_2\eta & \Delta \\ -\eta(\beta_1-\beta_2) & -\eta(\beta_1-\beta_2) & 0 \end{bmatrix} \begin{bmatrix} \varphi_t \\ \rho_t \\ p_t \end{bmatrix}
$$

$\qquad\qquad\qquad\qquad\qquad\qquad\qquad\qquad\qquad\qquad\qquad\qquad$ (5.2a)
$\qquad\qquad\qquad\qquad\qquad\qquad\qquad\qquad\qquad\qquad\qquad\qquad$ (5.2b)
$\qquad\qquad\qquad\qquad\qquad\qquad\qquad\qquad\qquad\qquad\qquad\qquad$ (5.2c)

The new equilibrium price associated with system (4.2) is:

$$
p_{t+1} = p'_o - (\varphi_t + \rho_t) + p_t \qquad\qquad\qquad (5.3)
$$

Since technology, population and tastes are constant, the foregoing are also steady-state values provided that φ_t and ρ_t are also constant from t onwards. There follows two conclusions.

First, what is perhaps more of interest to the NK macroeconomics, the steady-state output $y^*(t)_{t+1}$ is indeed a function of ρ_t and φ_t even with rational expectations; however, the sign of the relevant coefficients is ambiguous. It is immediate to observe that the NK contention that ρ_t and φ_t, as components of the real marginal costs for 'equity rationed' firms, have a negative effect on $y^*(t)_{t+1}$ obtains in the NK case of the labour supply function ($\beta_2 = 0$) or only if the labour supply has a sufficiently weak intertemporal substitution effect ($\beta_2 < \beta_1$). If instead one accepts the New Classical specification of the labour supply function ($\beta_2 = \beta_1$), then the standard New Classical proposition holds, namely that the steady-state output only depends on the technology and tastes parameters in y'_o.

Second, the economy will be set on a steady inflationary or deflationary path unless $p'_o - \varphi_t = \rho_t$. In the NK case this implies a choice conflict between inflation and output if the interest rate is to be the sole instrument. For instance, if the central bank chooses the non-inflationary real interest rate $\rho^*_t = p'_o - \varphi_t$,

---

[23]   For instance, GS stick to the neoclassical view of ρ as the 'natural interest rate' derived from the consumer intertemporal preferences (but see fn.11 on this point). Alternatively, one may think of ρ as a conventional rate in the central banker's mind, or a rate established on international markets. Of course, ρ may result not to be equal the actual real interest rate (i.e. $r_t - q_{t+1}$) unless $p^e(t)_{bt+1} = p_{t+1}$.

then the steady-state output will be reduced by $-\eta(\beta_1 - \beta_2)p'_o$. By contrast, the New Classical case takes on a distinct monetarist connotation, with ρ_t in the place of the 'k-rule' of the quantity of money growth. In fact, the central bank's Fisherian rule offsets any real impact of changes in price expectations. The steady-state output being fixed at y'_o, once-and-for-all deviations of ρ_t from ρ^*_t have only Wicksellian effects: the economy is set on a steady inflationary path if $\rho_t < \rho^*_t$, and on a deflationary path if $\rho_t > \rho^*_t$. However, it remains true that, even in the New Classical case, the non-inflationary real interest rate should be computed with reference to the firms' bankruptcy risks, which is ignored in standard models. For instance, this may be relevant to the case when ρ_t is set exogenously by, say, international markets. Or to the case of generational random mutations in φ_t (for example mean preserving spreads in the distribution of prices and hence changes in the bankruptcy probabilities) that should be corrected by adjustments in ρ_t.

6. CONCLUSIONS

This investigation into the macroeconomics of imperfect capital markets delivers a shadowy picture. First of all, one may agree with the proponents of this approach to macroeconomics that the characteristics of the market economy they focus on indeed deserve greater attention by macroeconomists. By bringing together the essential features of a wide array of NK models of imperfect capital markets in a highly stylized model of a sequential credit economy, we have seen that the functioning of the macro-economy is closely related to the specification of factors that usually do not appear in models in the Walrasian, or even the Keynesian, tradition, such as the time profile of transactions, the characteristics of contracts among agents, the way in which money is obtained, the peculiar constraint that debt contracts impose onto firms. In particular, we have examined temporary equilibria in which two key 'financial factors' -the interest rate on bank loans and the related bankruptcy risk- affect employment, output and the price level.

On the other hand, it remains controversial whether the 'financial factors' operate not only outside rational-expectations equilibria. One reason underlying this limitative result may be that the present model as it stands is too simple to encompass all the details of the *modus operandi* of imperfect capital markets. This issue is left for further research and debate.[24] However, to the extent that

---

[24] One point is that commercial banks are key actors in the NK view of the functioning of imperfectly informed markets. An extension of the present analysis to the case of competitive credit market (Tamborini, 1995) gives a more complex picture where, however, a steady state with financial neutrality sill exists. Secondly, the firm's model employed in this paper does not consider internal funds, which are a key variable in the NK macro-models of the GS type. However, internal funds act as a buffer againts the necessity for the firm to resort to credit. One

the present model is taken to reproduce the essential features of the NK macroeconomics, it suggests that the NK use of partial equilibrium models of firm behaviour where there is no explicit endogenous solution for goods prices, wages and interest rates blur the treatment of a few key issues: the relation of wages and interest rates to prices, the causes and consequences of firms' fallibility, and the implications of the rational expectations hypothesis.

The issue of the wage determination has proved to be particularly critical. The NK macro-models generally have firms which demand labour looking at the expected price of output whereas workers sell labour looking at the current price. Our analysis has shown that in a more general representation of workers' behaviour price expectations may affect workers' choice too, and that the impact of 'financial factors' on employment and output is sensitive to the relative weight of the current income effect versus the intertemporal substitution effect in workers' choice. We have seen that the persistence of a negative effect of the cost of credit on the level of output under rational expecations depends on the particular labour supply function adopted in most NK models (no intertemporal substitution effect); by contrast, if one assumes that the two effects are equivalent -which yields the New Classical labour supply function where the only argument is the expected real wage- the cost of credit disappears. This finding suggests that greater attention is needed in disentangling the role of particular specifications of the labour supply function from the genuine role of the 'financial factors'.

Another delicate issue concerns the bankruptcy risk. The problem with plugging the probability of bankruptcy into the firm's optimization programme is how the latter can come to know the probability laws that govern bankruptcy in the economy. At the partial equilibrium level of analysis of most NK models one might think of the probability of bankruptcy as an exogenous parameter on which the firm expresses a subjective belief. Yet in a general-equilibrium macro-context one expects bankruptcy to be related to some endogenous variables to a certain extent, even more so in the GS type of models where the variable governing success or failure is stochastic realizations of the output price. Critical though they are with the New Classical orthodoxy, the NKs seem reluctant to abandon the rational expectations hypothesis for the obvious methodological reason that they wish to show that capital market imperfections, not human misperceptions, are responsible for macroeconomic fluctuations. However, introducing rational expectations seems to undermine, as usual, the non-neutrality propositions even in the extreme case of sole debt finance that has been examined here. I hasten to add that the mere existence of steady-state

---

expects that the greater the internal funds, the weaker the effects of credit finance are. This is not to say that internal finance should not appear as a major ingredient in the NK macroeconomics. On the contrary, the message is that if it is to appear, then the controversial details that we have pointed out become important, and the partial-equilibrium modelling strategy may turn out to be inappropriate.

equilibria where the 'financial factors' have no real effects should not be taken as a sufficient condition for dismissing the whole issue as irrelevant. As is now customary, one may wish to check whether the rational expectations hypothesis in a given context is robust to some reasonable learning processes of agents (see for example Sargent, 1993). For instance, starting from heterogenous expectations, for the economy to converge to steady-state equilibria where the 'financial factors' are neutral the convergence of firms' prior expectations to a common expected value is needed. As the post-rational-expectations literature has made clear, this may become an extremely critical point in a 'self-referential' environment, that is one like equation (4.4), where the realization of a variable depends on the market's expected value. Moreover, the fact that firms may go bankrupt, and that this may well be related to errors during the learning process, it is even less clear that the system will ever have enough 'memory'. Yet at the moment these issues are not in the NK agenda.

REFERENCES

Ardeni, P., et al. (1993), 'La Nuova Economia Keynesiana', paper presented at the XXXIV meeting of the Società Italiana degli Economisti, Naples, October; "The New Keynesian Economics: A Survey", in this volume.

Bernanke B. and A. Blinder, (1988), 'Credit, Money, and Aggregate Demand', *Papers and Proceedings of the American Economic Association, American Economic Review*, 78, 435-439.

Blinder, A. (1987), 'Credit Rationing and Effective Supply Failures', *Economic Journal*, 97, 327-352.

Blinder, A. and J.E. Stiglitz (1983), 'Money, Credit Constraints and Economic Activity', *American Economic Review*, 73, 297-302.

Danthine, J.P. and J.B. Donaldson (1993), 'Methodological and Empirical Issues in Real Business Cycle Theory', *European Economic Review*, 37, 1-35.

Delli Gatti D. and M. Gallegati (1997), 'Financial Constraints, Aggregate Supply, and the Monetary Transmission Mechanism', Manchester School, 65, 101-126.

Gale, D. and M. Hellwig, (1985), 'Incentive-compatible Debt Contracts: The One Period Problem', *Review of Economic Studies*, 52, 647-663.

Gertler, M. and S. Gilchrist (1993), 'The Role of Credit Market Imperfections in the Monetary Transmission Mechanism: Arguments and Evidence', *Scandinavian Journal of Economics*, 93, 43-64.

Gordon, R. (1990), 'What is Keynesian Economics?', *Journal of Economic Literature*, 28, n.3.

Grandmont, J.M. (1983), *Money and Value. A Reconsideration of Classical and Neoclassical Monetary Theory*, Cambridge, Cambridge University Press.

Greenwald, B.C. and J.E. Stiglitz (1987), 'Keynesian, New Keynesian and New Classical Economics', *Oxford Economic Papers*, 39, 119-32.

Greenwald, B.C. and J.E. Stiglitz (1988a), 'Imperfect Information, Finance Constraints and Business Fluctuations', in Kohn, M., Tsiang S.C. (eds.), *Finance Constraints, Expectations, and Macroeconomics*, Oxford, Clarendon Press, 103-140.

Greenwald, B.C. and J.E. Stiglitz (1988b), 'Money, Imperfect Information and Economic Fluctuations', in M. Kohn, and S.C. Tsiang (eds.), *Finance Constraints, Expectations, and Macroeconomics*, Oxford, Clarendon Press, 141-165.

Greenwald, B.C. and J.E. Stiglitz (1990), 'Macroeconomic Models with Equity and Credit Rationing', in R.G. Hubbard, (ed.), *Information, Capital Markets and Investment*, Chicago, Chicago University Press, 15-42.

Greenwald, B.C. and J.E. Stiglitz (1991), *Towards a Reformulation of Monetary Theory*, Caffè Lectures, Milan, Università Bocconi.

Greenwald, B.C., J.E. Stiglitz (1993), 'Financial Market Imperfections and Business Cycles', *Quarterly Journal of Economics*, 108, 77-113.

Hahn, F.H. (1982), *Money and Inflation*, Oxford, Blackwell.

Hicks, J.R. (1939), *Value and Capital. An Inquiry into Some Fundamental Principles of Economic Theory*, Oxford, Clarendon Press, 2nd ed.

Hicks, J.R. (1967), 'The two triads', in *Critical essays in monetary theory*, Oxford, Clarendon Press.

Jaffee, D. and J. Stiglitz (1990), 'Credit Rationing', in B.M. Friedman, and F.H. Hahn, (eds.), *Handbook of Monetary Economics*, Amsterdam, North Holland, 838-888.

Keynes, J.M. (1936), *The General Theory of Employment, Interest and Money*, in *The Collected Writings of John Maynard Keynes*, ed. by E. Moggridge, London, Macmillan, 1973, vol.VII.

King, R.G. and C.I. Plosser (1984), 'Money, Credit and Prices in a Real Business Cycle', *American Economic Review*, 74, pp.363-380.

Lucas, R.E. and L. Rapping (1969), 'Real Wages, Employment and Inflation', *Journal of Political Economy*, 77, 721-754.

Mankiw, N.G. and D. Romer, (eds.) (1991), *New Keynesian Economics*, 2 vols., Cambridge Mass., MIT Press.

Minsky, H.P. (1982), *Can It Happen Again? Essays on Instability and Finance*, New York, Basic Books.

Radcliffe Committee (1959), *Report on the Working of the Monetary System*, London, HMSO.

Radner, R. (1968), 'Competitive Equilibrium under Uncertainty', *Econometrica*, 36, 31-58.

Sargent, T.J. (1979), *Macroeconomic Theory*, New York, Academic Press.

Sargent, T.J. (1993), *Bounded Rationality in Macroeconomics*, Oxford, Clarendon Press.

Sargent, T.J. and N. Wallace (1975), 'Rational Expectations, the Optimal Monetary Instrument, and the Optimal Money Supply Rule', *Journal of Political Economy*, 83, 241-54.

Stiglitz, J.E. (1991), 'Alternative Approaches to Macroeconomics, Methodological Issues and the New Keynesian Economics', *NBER Working Paper*, no.3580.

Stiglitz, J.E. (1992), 'Capital Markets and Economic Fluctuations in Capitalist Economies', *European Economic Review*, 36, 269-306.

Tamborini, R. (1995), 'A General Equilibrium Analysis of the Credit View', *Quaderni del Dipartimento di Scienze Economiche*, Università di Padova, n.46.

Tobin, J. (1980), *Asset Accumulation and Economic Activity*, Oxford, Blackwell.

3. New Keynesian Economics and Sequence Analysis*

Marcello Messori

1. INTRODUCTION

The aim of this chapter is to show why the examination of the variegated approach of new Keynesian economics (NKE) proves interesting from the point of view of both the recent history of economic analysis and the definition of new perspectives for macroeconomics. The theoretical framework, elaborated by so-called New classical macroeconomics (NCM) in the 1970s, reopened problems that orthodox Keynesian macroeconomics treated as definitively solved in the Sixties. The merit of the NKE has been that of accepting the challenge presented by NCM, and of supplying these problems with answers compatible with the Keynesian outcomes. The results obtained by NKE are at times unsatisfactory and almost always incomplete. In any case, they open promising paths of research that are worth taking into serious consideration.

Analogous to the structure of the first chapter, this third chapter starts from the unsolved problems in the Keynesian theory and the relative criticisms raised against it by traditional economics, to arrive at the answers elaborated by the two main strains of NKE: the strain centered on nominal and real rigidities, which has taken root in some well-known universities on the East Coast of the United States, and the strain centered on imperfections in capital markets, which has developed in some of the most famous universities on the West coast of the United States.[1] In the following, I shall not limit myself to

* My paper is an English and revised version of the *Introduzione* (*Introduction*) to an Italian book recently published by il Mulino (*La nuova economia keynesiana*, Bologna) in the series of the '*Società Italiana degli Economisti*' ('Italian economic association'). I wish to thank the *Società Italiana degli Economisti* for the permission to publish the present version of the Italian original paper. I also wish to thank the co-authors of this book as well as Mario Amendola, Giorgio Rodano, and Enrico Saltari for their helpful comments on a previous draft of this paper. The financial support by CNR I is gratefully acknowledged.

1 Henceforth, I shall indicate the two streams with the acronyms NKEric and NKEiai, respectively. The acronym NKEric emphasizes that the East Coast stream treats the rigidities

synthesizing the analytical contents of the two strains of NKE, but shall attempt to show why the results obtained from new Keynesian economics with market imperfections due to asymmetric information (NKEiai) are more promising than those from new Keynesian economics with rigidities due to non-competitive markets (NKEric).

To this end, I begin by examining the main problems of the old Keynesian model that drew criticism from NCM (section 2). Then I review those aspects of NKEric which attempt to overcome this kind of criticism and, as a consequence, lead to (Keynesian) results that are of particular interest for the opening of new perspectives in macroeconomic theory (section 3). From this point of view, however, the contribution of NKEric appears less bountiful than that of NKEiai (section 4). This does not mean that the NKEiai framework is without limits. The reinterpretation of these limits, often ascribed to the fact that NKEiai uses partial analysis instead of general analysis, enables us to bring to the surface the important role that must be reserved for NKE in the renewal of macroeconomics (section 5). In the Conclusions, I summarize the results obtained, and mention some of the perspectives of research that are still to be developed.

2. THE LIMITS OF THE KEYNESIAN LEGACY

It is superfluous here to point out the reasons why the *General Theory* represented a milestone in the construction of modern macroeconomics. It is, however, less obvious to underline what the unsolved analytical points of that great work are that enabled the affirmation of macroeconomic orthodoxy centered on the combination of the 'neoclassical synthesis' (NCS) and the Phillips curve. In this regard, I consider that the main limits of Keynes' macroeconomic legacy (1936) can be synthesized as follows:

1. the insufficient specification of the relationships between flexible nominal wages, changes in the expectations of entrepreneurs and wealth-owners, persistence of involuntary unemployment;
2. the non-perception of the incompatibility between the exogenously given nominal supply of money and the mechanism of transmission centered on the causal link between a purely monetary interest rate and the amount of investment.
3. the incongruity between the cyclical dynamics of price variables and, markedly, real wages, which derives from Keynes' framework, and the

as the consequence of the 'first principle' represented by non-competitive markets (imperfect competition); and the acronym NKEiai emphasizes that the West Coast stream establishes incomplete and imperfect information (information asymmetries) as the 'first principle' of imperfections in capital markets.

cyclical dynamics of these same variables that emerges from empirical evidence.

Point 1 refers in particular to Chapter 19 of the *General Theory*. After assuming the rigidity of money wages in the first eighteen chapters (see Keynes, 1936, p. 257), Keynes shows that the downward flexibility of these wages does not eliminate involuntary unemployment, in that it can worsen the expectations of entrepreneurs and wealth-owners. Nevertheless, since Keynes does not endogenously specify the formation of the expectations, he has to justify their worsening by introducing hypotheses which, although empirically plausible, are *ad hoc* from an analytical point of view.

Point 2 refers to the fact that, if the nominal money supply is exogenously given by the central bank (see for example Keynes, 1936, pp. 166-174), the typical Keynesian mechanism of monetary transmission must be integrated by the links between the level of income, the demand for money and the interest rate. Thus, if it remains true that the 'real' aspects depend on monetary aspects, it becomes also true that the monetary aspects depend on 'real' aspects. This means that, as well as being directly determined by the supply of and the demand for money, and as well as constraining the equilibrium level of income by means of its influence on investment decisions, the Keynesian interest rate is also indirectly determined by savings and investment decisions through the influence that both variables have on the level of monetary income (see also Messori, 1991).

Point 3 refers to the empirical evidence that changes in real wages are at least moderately pro-cyclical. Given the maximizing behavior of entrepreneurs and the traditional production function assumed in the *General Theory*, Keynes' analysis determines, on the other hand, an anti-cyclical change in real wages: with the growth of employment in the expansionary phases of the cycle, labour marginal productivity decreases and, consequently, so do the equilibrium real wages. The traditional application of the full cost principle does not eliminate the incongruity.

The NCS, which finds full expression in the works of Modigliani (1944, 1963), elaborates a theoretical answer to problems 1 and 2; the Phillips curve (1958) offers a descriptive answer to sub-problem 3.

Regarding point 1, the NCS model clarifies at least three aspects. First of all, it shows that flexibility in the prices of goods and labour does not lead to a full employment equilibrium only if there are rigidities in the return to financial activities (see Hicks, 1937) or in the function of the investment demand (see Klein, 1947) such as to eliminate the so-called 'Keynes effect', that is, the stimuli to investment decisions exercised by the increase in the real supply of money induced by the decrease in the nominal prices of goods which, in turn, is due to a fall in money wages and to the relative increase in the demand for labour units. The subsequent refinements of the NCS prove, however, that the 'Pigou effect' (or wealth effect) can supplement the 'Keynes effect' as a

107

proper mechanism for ensuring the full employment equilibrium. In particular, when the downward rigidity of the interest rate or the rigidity in the investment demand prevent the working of the 'Keynes effect', one can assume, on the basis of the 'Pigou effect', that the consumption function also depends on the real wealth of purchasers; thus, if a decrease in the nominal prices of goods does not have positive effects on investments, it will at least determine an increase in the amount of 'real' wealth and hence an increase in the demand for consumption (see Patinkin, 1948).[2]

Thus, the conclusion is reached that the NCS model can incorporate the Keynesian result of unemployment equilibrium only by assuming rigidities in money wages (see Modigliani, 1944). As this author points out, this assumption leaves room for expectations and guarantees the effectiveness of the monetary policy.[3] The typical demand shock introduced by the NCS to generate a situation of unemployment, in fact consists of an exogenous worsening of (entrepreneurial) expectations that causes a decrease in the marginal efficiency of capital. The consequent downward shift of the investment demand curve implies a decrease in the aggregate demand which, due to the rigidity in money wages, gives rise to adjustments in quantities, and not only in the goods price. The decrease in aggregate demand could be reabsorbed without changes in the quantity of goods produced only by means of a monetary policy sufficiently expansive to ensure that there is a new proportion between nominal supply of money and money wages which is compatible with full employment equilibrium.

Regarding point 2, the NCS at first confirms the purely monetary determination of the interest rate. Although the application of 'Walras law' to the capital market renders the liquidity preference theory equivalent to the Robertsonian theory of loanable funds,[4] Hicks (1939, pp. 147-9 and 165-6) maintains that: (a) the Keynesian long-term interest rate is equal to the average

---

[2]   It is worth noting that these statements do not query the empirical importance of the Pigou effect and, therefore, the speed of adjustment of the aggregate demand at a level compatible with full employment equilibrium. The critics of the Pigou effect have concentrated precisely on these questions (see for example Tobin 1980). In particular, they have insisted on the fact that a deflation not only increases the purchasing power of wealth-holders but also the insolvency of debtors. It is known that the typical debtors of the economic system are entrepreneurs. Thus, their higher default risk negatively affects the marginal efficiency of capital and increases the wealth-holders preference for liquidity. Both these factors determine a fall in the investment demand (a leftward shifting, respectively, of and along the investment curve), which can more than compensate for the increase in the consumption demand.

[3]   It must be noted that, according to Hicks' model (1937), in 'liquidity trap' the only effective economic policy is the fiscal one; changes in the nominal supply of money have no effects even on the general price level.

[4]   See Hicks (1936, 1937). It should be remembered, however, that just as Hicks (1980-1) offers a partial self-criticism of his own model of 1937, Hicks (1989, p. 351) denounces the superficiality of his former application of the Walras law to the capital market (see also Messori, 1995b, section 6).

of the current short-term interest rate and expected short-term future rates, increased by a constant risk premium; (b) short-term interest rates are purely monetary. Hicks's position, however, is not included in the subsequent NCS models. Modigliani's more general contribution (1944, 1963) ends up, in fact, implying that the interest rate performs the double function of bringing capital markets (monetary and financial) as well as investment and savings decisions into equilibrium. This conclusion of the NCS derives from the fact that the monetary transmission mechanism gives rise to the 'real' retroaction mentioned above. It therefore appears tightly bound to the assumption, peculiar to the *General Theory*, of an exogenously given nominal supply of money.[5]

The answers the NCS provides for points 1 and 2, deal with the aggregate demand side. *Per se*, they do not offer an univocal contribution with regard to the aggregate supply side, which in the NCS models can assume at least three characterizations. The aggregate supply can conform to the *General Theory* framework with the effect that real wages decrease as employment increases, it can be determined by the labour demand, or it can be reduced to a 45 degree line with the effect that the prices of goods are given until the full employment production level is reached. None of these specifications of the aggregate supply, however, offers an answer to the problem sub 3. In this regard, it is necessary to refer to the Phillips curve (1958) which *describes* an inverse relationship between the rate of unemployment and the rate of change in money wages and which can, therefore, account for the dynamics in the price of goods and for the stable or moderately pro-cyclical change in real wages. This stresses that the Phillips curve performs an important function of complementarity with regard to the NCS. Thus, it is not surprising that various attempts have been made to give a theoretical justification for the shape of this curve (see for example Lipsey, 1960). Here, it is not of importance to assess the robustness of these attempts. It is, however, necessary to bear in mind that the combination of Modigliani's model with rigidity in money wages and in the nominal prices of goods and the Phillips curve, constitutes the core of the NCS. In the Sixties the model, that can be called the Modigliani-Phillips model, gained such wide consensus among economists as to rise to the status of macroeconomic orthodoxy. It is, however, a macroeconomic orthodoxy without ties to the traditional microeconomic analysis elaborated by the Neo-Walrasian research program (see for example Arrow and Hahn, 1971).[6]

---

[5] The reference to the own rates of own interest (see Keynes, 1936, chapter 17) allows for a monetary determination of the Keynesian interest rate in the presence of an exogenously given nominal supply of money. The analytical cost is, however, to reduce money as a particular type of *good* (see in this regard Messori, 1995a).

[6] It is evident that, also during the Sixties, not all macroeconomists adhered to the Modigliani-Phillips model. Apart from the heterodox authors represented by the post-Keynesian Americans (for example Weintraub) and by Keynes's followers in Cambridge (Kahn, Kaldor and Robinson), at least two lines of research should be recalled: that elaborated by Patinkin

The debate of the Seventies pitilessly bared the weaknesses of this Keynesian 'orthodoxy'. The first bastion to collapse under Friedman's (1968) and Phelps' (1967) onslaughts was the Phillips curve (see on this subject Laidler 1995). The attack weapons monetarists used can be narrowed down to three: the treatment of expected inflation rates as one of the determinants of changes in money wages; the definition of a given unemployment rate, compatible with stability in the growth rate of the nominal prices of goods, known as natural rate of unemployment; the elimination of workers' long-term 'monetary illusion'. These elements imply that every expansionary shock on the aggregate demand side has the sole stable effect of a proportional increase in money wages and in the nominal prices of goods. Thus, in the long-run, the Phillips curve becomes perfectly rigid at the natural rate of unemployment and the monetary policy becomes neutral.

Similar conclusions, which characterize Friedman's monetarism, are in obvious contrast with the crucial results of the Modigliani-Phillips model. It is, however, a widely held opinion that monetarist criticisms have a less explosive theoretical reach than at first could appear. Two orders of reasons can be adduced which, at least in part, support this opinion. In the first place, although modifying the working of the NCS model and the costs and benefits of the monetary policy, these criticisms admit that economic policy has real effects in the short term. In the second place, the main differences between the NCS models and those of monetarism, although deriving from divergences in the assumptions or in the analysis, ultimately depend on the different values attributed to the parameters. In this regard, the long-term Phillips curve provides a good example. If the value of the parameter in the function that ties the wage dynamics to the expected rate of inflation is positive but less than one, the assumption of workers' 'money illusion', criticized by monetarists (see above), is revived. Given this value of the parameter, if the related function is linearized, an inverse relationship between the unemployment rate and changes in money wages is also revived. Although not without a certain strain, this suggests two statements:[7] the greater elasticity attributed to the above-mentioned function by the Modigliani—Phillips model, depends on the fact that the parameter under consideration is implicitly posited as equal to zero; the rigidity of this same function in Friedman's model depends on the fact that the parameter under consideration is stated as equal to one (see also Gordon, 1976).

(1965).[2] and that elaborated by Clower (1965, 1967) and by Leijonhufvud (1968). Beyond the differences, both these lines sought microeconomic foundations for their macroeconomic results. Furthermore, especially Clower and Leijonhufvud anticipated problems crucial to NKEiai: the former emphasizes the importance of timing in firms' financial constraint, the latter insists on market imperfections owing to lack of information.

[7] As will be specified further on (see section 2), the strain is to be found in the fact that the surreptitious introduction of workers 'monetary illusion' satisfies criteria of realism but does not fit with the substantial rationality of individual behavior which is also assumed by the NCS model.

The tendency to downgrade the theoretical differences between the NCS and Friedman's monetarism to a disagreement over the empirically relevant values of a set of parameters finds confirmation in the position taken by Modigliani (1977). Although stressing that this disagreement has important implications with regard to the theory of economic policy, with particular reference to the effectiveness of long-term monetary policy and the related benefits of its discretionary management, Modigliani concludes that NCS and monetarists macroeconomics can still be merged under the common label of 'Keynesianism' (see also Friedman, 1977). The Modigliani–Friedman model, putting itself forward as a modernized form of NCS, candidates itself for the role of macroeconomic orthodoxy.

This candidature was, however, soon undermined by Lucas and Sargent (1978). Taking advantage of the flaws opened up by monetarist criticisms on the aggregate supply side of the NCS model and—especially—referring to the results of their previous analyses (for example: Lucas-Rapping 1969; Lucas 1972, 1973; Sargent 1973; Sargent-Wallace 1975), these two authors and - more generally- the NCM attacked the new Keynesian orthodoxy by means of two criticisms aimed at destroying the analytical roots of the Modigliani and Friedman model and, even more so, the framework of the *General Theory*:

1. agents' behaviour and the nominal rigidities, that prevent the realization of optimal equilibria on the different markets in the short or the long term, are incompatible with the analyses of Walrasian microeconomics and are not based on adequate alternative microeconomic foundations;
2. the formation of expectations, which the Keynesian and monetarist frameworks use to justify the unfulfilled or delayed adjustment to exogenous shocks, is not compatible with the assumption of agents' rational and maximizing behavior, which is shared by the Keynesians.

NCM aims to overcome point 1 by microfounding macroeconomic analysis on an Arrow–Debreu model of general equilibrium with perfectly flexible nominal prices but with incomplete markets. NCM stresses, furthermore, that the incompleteness of markets does not hinder the realization of optimal intertemporal equilibria if the incongruities of point 2 are removed with the introduction of 'rational expectations', that is, by means of the assumption that every agent knows the working 'model' of the economy and uses this knowledge to best advantage to form her/his own expectations. The analytical aspect, characterizing NCM, thus lies in the fact that in every point in time, prices guarantee the optimal equilibrium of markets and the absence of involuntary unemployment, that is, of unemployed persons ready to supply labour units at the existing real wage. Monetary policy can have temporary 'real', but in any case distortionary effects, only if it is not anticipated by agents because it deviates from the optimal working model of the economic system.

The season that saw the supremacy of the theoretical NCM models was short-lived. There is no point here in lingering over the causes that brought about its rapid demise. It is sufficient to bear in mind that, according to Hahn (for example 1982), the most important weaknesses of NCM depend on the too free-handed use of the apparatus of general equilibrium and on the institution of too direct ties between the microeconomic level and the macroeconomic aggregates. In the first chapter of this book it is maintained, instead, that the crisis of the NCM research programme can be ascribed to a defect in origin: the incompatibility between Walrasian microfoundations and the assumption of incomplete markets. Complementing this kind of observation, I would only add that NCM refers to a microeconomics which, in the course of the Seventies, was disputed by new lines of analysis such as, for example, contract theory, the game theory, neo-institutionalism and the economics of information.[8] The NKE apparatus, in particular the NKEiai strain, incorporates the key concepts that characterize some of these new lines of research. Thus, it is not surprising that NKE was able to accept the challenge presented by NCM, overcoming the basic limits of Keynesian orthodoxy while reviving important Keynesian results at the same time.

3. THE MICROFOUNDATIONS OF RIGIDITIES

The main aim of NKEric is to obtain the crucial results already reached by the NCS by means of microfounded models with rational expectations. This aim has been pursued by the following passages: (i) on the basis of the NKEric assumptions, agents realize maximizing behavior in an (almost) rational way; (ii) in the presence of nominal and real microfounded rigidities, these individual behaviours tend to determine sub-optimal macroeconomic equilibria with involuntary unemployment, that is, to generate negative macroeconomic externalities;[9] (iii) since (ii) implies that the shocks on the aggregate demand and supply side affect the employment level and equilibrium income, at least over a short-term period, monetary policy comes to have real effects once more (see also Gordon, 1990). Points (i)-(iii) show that in order to be able to confirm the conclusions typical of Keynesian 'orthodoxy', and at the same time to

---

[8]   Some of the recent microeconomic developments question whether agents' rationality should coincide with maximizing behavior. This implies that the necessary congruency between agents' rational behavior and the formation of rational expectations, underlined by the NCM to criticize the NCS (see above, point 2), fails. In what follows, we do not deal with the problem, as neither Keynesian orthodoxy nor the streams of NKE here analyzed radically bring the maximizing behavior of the agents under discussion.

[9]   It is worth noting that nominal rigidities indicate obstacles in the adjustment of monetary prices following exogenous changes in the quantities, whereas real rigidities indicate obstacles in the adjustment of relative prices, typically in the adjustment of monetary wages with regard to the nominal prices of goods.

accept the challenge of NCM, NKEric must first of all prove the validity of point (ii) given (i). This means, in particular, to prove that microfounded rigidities can prevent the immediate realization of full employment equilibria even if each agent maximizes her/his own expected utility and has rational expectations. The NKEric strain proves this result starting from the 'first principle' of non-competitive markets structure: bilateral negotiations or degrees of monopoly in the labour market and imperfect competition in the goods market.[10]

The first attempts in this direction concern the justification of nominal rigidities in the labour market and in the goods market. In particular, although incorporating many typical assumptions of NCM (such as rational expectations), the models of Fischer (1977) and Taylor (1979, 1980) obtain equilibria with involuntary unemployment by referring to staggered wage contracts; and the Phelps-Taylor model (1977; see also Taylor, 1985) implies that the aggregate supply can differ from that compatible with full employment whenever the price of goods is fixed in advance by one period and equals the expected aggregate demand and supply. Since this form of wage contracts or this rule for prices formation imply that money wages and the price of goods can change less rapidly than other variables, it follows that a negative shock on the supply or the demand side determines, until renewal of the pre-existing wage contracts or until the new definition of the price of goods, quantity rather than price adjustments. As a short-term result, monetary policy interventions subsequent to this shock have effects on the 'real' variables even if they are fully expected in the current period by agents with rational expectations. Conversely, in the long term, the adjustment of expiring wage contracts or new prices of goods to modified data in the economy imply the reinstatement of optimal equilibria and the neutrality of monetary policy. Taylor (1980) on the other hand, shows that if workers with expiring contracts stipulate their new money wages, relatively to the wages of other workers, the suboptimality of the equilibria and the non-neutrality of monetary policy can become persistent in that the obstacles to price adjustments persist over time.[11]

The models with 'staggered' contracts, or with the price of goods fixed in advance by one period, denote various limits. The most evident limit is analogous to that characterizing the NCS framework which is emphasized by NCM: even though the models under consideration render the rigidity of wages, or of the price of goods, empirically plausible, they are not capable of microfounding this rigidity from an analytical point of view. The numerous

---

[10] The view that the market structure is the 'first principle' will be briefly discussed at the end of this section.

[11] It is interesting to note that, given the definitions of fn. 9, Taylor's further hypothesis is equivalent to introducing real rigidities into the model. It will become clearer below that the combination of nominal and real rigidities reinforces the Keynesian results in all the NKEric models examined here.

contributions, aimed at proving that 'staggered' wage contracts are advantageous to both entrepreneurs and workers, weaken but do not overcome this limit since they do not succeed in rigorously demonstrating that the equilibria with 'staggered' contracts dominate those with nominal flexible prices. Moreover, the models of Fischer (1977) and Taylor (1979, 1980) do not explain why, although safeguarding the advantages deriving from the asynchronicity, these contracts are not perfectly indexed.

Leaving aside the limits mentioned above, the approach initiated by Fischer, Taylor and Phelps is of great interest in that it indicates the path NKEric has followed to microfound the nominal rigidities in prices. The NKEric shows that, for the single agent, the price adjustment can have costs greater than the profit possibly unrealized because of unchanged prices. A set of models achieves this result in the second half of the Eighties (Akerlof and Yellen, 1985; Mankiw, 1985; Parkin, 1986; Blanchard and Kiyotaki, 1987; and for a review Rotemberg, 1987; Mankiw and Romer, 1991). The mentioned models are notably different from each other. Here, it is sufficient to point out that they are characterized by a core of homogeneous assumptions and results. A common and fundamental assumption is that firms operate in imperfect competitive markets, so that they set the nominal price of the goods produced also on the basis of the elasticity of their negatively sloped demand curve. This is sufficient to prove that, in the presence of a negative shock on the demand side, the unfulfilled price adjustment at the new equilibrium level causes a 'second-order' decrease in the expected profit of the single firm.

This statement can be specified. *Ceteris paribus*, the unfulfilled price adjustment determines a decrease in the expected profit of the single firm which is smaller the greater (a) the elasticity of the (increasing) curve of marginal costs and (b) the negative difference between the expected elasticity of the new demand curve and the elasticity of the old curve at the unchanged nominal price.[12] The elasticity of the marginal costs curve of the single firm depends, apart from technical-productive factors, on the market structure and the trend in real wages. The market imperfections and the stickiness of real wages increase this elasticity in the sense that they make the relative curve flatter. Difference sub (b) depends, apart from 'income effects', on the expectations the single firm has regarding the price reactions adopted by the firms operating in contiguous sections of the market: if the expectation is that other firms also prefer to undergo quantity adjustments rather than proceed to price adjustments, the single firm expects that, like the case of the kinked demand curve, the new demand curve will be less elastic at the unchanged price (at least) in its right hand side.

---

[12] To have an intuition of point (a) and (b) it is enough to draw a graphic representation of the old and the new demand curve, of the curves of marginal costs and expected proceeds, and of the area of expected profits of any imperfectly competitive firm.

According to Akerlof and Yellen (1985), these observations are sufficient to explain the rigidity in the nominal prices of goods when there are negative shocks on the demand side. If single firms act according to a model of 'near-rationality', they do not adjust prices in order to avoid a 'second-order' decrease in profits. Conversely, assuming maximizing behaviors and rational expectations of agents, Mankiw (1985) and Blanchard and Kiyotaki (1987) stress that the single firm will not find it advantageous to respond to negative demand shocks by lowering the nominal price of the goods produced if the costs of price adjustments ('small menu' costs) are greater than the 'second-order' decrease in expected profits, taken as an absolute value. The preceding points (a) and (b) make it clear that, if the 'small menu' costs are exogenously given, it is more probable that each firm will find it advantageous not to reduce the nominal price of its own goods since the higher is the elasticity of its marginal costs curve and the lower is the elasticity on the right side of the new demand curve, at the unchanged price, relative to the elasticity of the old demand curve. Apart from whether the unfulfilled price adjustments are, from the microeconomic point of view, near-rational or optimal, all the models under consideration concur on an important point: if the unfulfilled price adjustments extend to a sufficiently large number of firms, they have 'first-order' negative effects at the macroeconomic level. Microeconomic optimality thus generates negative macroeconomic externalities level (in particular, involuntary unemployment); and policies in support of aggregate demand, including expansionary monetary policies, have real effects.

Satisfying the standards imposed by NCM and reviving the essential conclusions of the NCS (see section 2), these results seem to realize the objectives set by the NKEric research program (see above, points 2 and 3): nominal rigidities, if they can still be called such, are microfounded and have real macroeconomic effects. The models examined, however, reveal analytical failures that can be traced to the fact that small menu costs are exogenously given. A first failure is that price adjustments become profitable in the long run also from the microeconomic point of view, since the given and unchanged amount of small menu costs must be compared with the increasing sum total of the losses in expected profit that would derive from the unfulfilled price adjustments through time. As a consequence, in the long run, involuntary unemployment disappears and money and monetary policy become neutral once more. A second failure consists of the fact that the greater the demand shock, the greater the 'second-order' decrease in profits and the probability that this decrease exceeds, in absolute value, the exogenously given costs of price adjustment. The consequence is obvious but paradoxical: if negative demand shocks are too great, nominal rigidities do not prevent price adjustments and thus do not have macroeconomic effects even in the short run (see Ball, Mankiw and Romer, 1988).

Analogous to the case of 'staggered' wage contracts (cf. n. 11), NKEric has attempted to overcome the two weaknesses examined by associating 'real' rigidities with nominal ones. It is evident that the real rigidities alone do not prevent the creation of optimal equilibria; however, it is still true that the combination of rigidities of nominal prices and rigidity of relative prices can render suboptimal equilibria with involuntary unemployment persistent, also in the presence of substantial demand shocks (Ball and Romer, 1990). A typical example is offered by the case of nominal rigidities in the goods market and real rigidities in the labour market. Let me firstly assume that, given the amount of small menu costs and given the presence of only nominal rigidities, a negative demand shock would be strong enough to make it advantageous for a given firm to lower the nominal price of the goods produced to a level compatible with an equilibrium without involuntary unemployment. Let me now assume that there is also a rigidity in the real wage. The new real rigidity can strengthen the impact of the nominal rigidities to such an extent that it eliminates the advantage in price adjustment instead of quantity adjustment for at least two reasons: as has been noted above, it makes the curve of marginal costs of the single firm more elastic; and above all, it creates a binding constraint to the firm's labour demand. Note that this constraint can also eliminate incentives to increase the long-term labour demand, that derive from the fact that quantity adjustments determine involuntary unemployment and drive the money wage down.

These results not only overcome the NKEric weaknesses mentioned above, but they also enable an articulated answer to the objection repeatedly forwarded by Greenwald and Stiglitz (1989, 1993b). This objection regards the fact that small menu costs should not be simply compared to the decrease in expected profit but to the sum of the absolute value of this decrease and the cost of quantity adjustments. Hargreaves Heap (1992, pp. 111-12) provides a first answer to this objection: the single firm, given the expectation that firms operating in contiguous sections of the market will adjust quantities and not prices (see above), expects it will, in any case, have to bear the costs of quantity adjustments in the future, but that it will be able to avoid the costs of price adjustment; thus, it is justified to neglect *unavoidable* quantity adjustment costs to compare *avoidable* small menu costs with the decrease in expected profit. In the case just examined with a combination of nominal and real rigidities, the Hargreaves Heap argument can be integrated by interpreting the real rigidities in the labour market as an indicator of quantity adjustment costs. Therefore, it is not surprising that Mankiw and Romer (1991) maintain that the crucial aspect of NKEric is the interaction between nominal and real rigidities.

Given that the most important real rigidities occur in the labour market,[13]

---

[13] If one assumes that the purchasers are not able to asses the qualitative aspects of transactions, another important case of real rigidities derives from the dependence of the quality of the goods or services exchanged on their price (see Stiglitz, 1987a). This dependency implies that, also apart from the level of production costs, the suppliers of given goods or services, whether they

Mankiw and Romer's conclusion raises a new question: how can the rigidity in real wages be explained? In recent years labour economy has put forward various answers, which range from models with 'implicit' contracts to those with 'efficiency wages', and from insider–outsider models to union ones (on this matter: see Weiss, 1990; Lindbeck, 1992). The space at my disposal here does not allow me to discuss these models (see the second part of this book), or to compare their different degree of realism with respect to the institutional organization of the labour market of a specific economic system (for example, the European one). It is enough for me to state here that, with regard to the theoretical problems under consideration, the most interesting justifications of rigidity in real wages are offered by:

1. that sub-set of efficiency wages models which, assuming information asymmetries between workers and firms, identifies the determination of real wages at a level incompatible with full employment as an instrument that the single firms use to stimulate the efforts of the labour units, or to limit the adverse selection of workers with different abilities and skills (see for example: Akerlof and Yellen, 1986; Weiss, 1990) and thereby minimizing the cost of labour per unit of product;

2. the efficiency wages models *à la* Shapiro and Stiglitz, 1984; (see also Bowles and Gintis, 1993) which, still based on information asymmetries, make it advantageous for firms to fix real wages higher than those compatible with full employment with the aim at increasing the costliness of dismissal for workers, thereby discouraging labour shrinking to an extent that minimizes the cost of labour per unit of product.

3. the sub-set of insider–outsider models that attributes old employees with a power of monopoly, and consequently a power to fix their real wages, based on the capacity of the old employees to constrain the training and the productivity of new potential employees (see Lindbeck and Snower, 1988; Lindbeck, 1992).

The models sub 1-3 reveal deficiencies regarding both the analytical tools and the empirical evidence. What has to be stressed here is, however, that these models explain rigidities in the real wage using information asymmetries and designing incentive and self-selection contracts. Thus, these models incorporate many of the tools and results obtained by the 'principal-agent' approach and the economics of information (see section 2). This is not so for the NKEric models which often use 'game theory' but which, unlike the NKEiai models (see below, section 4), base their microfoundations neither on information

---

are of high or low quality, do not bring down their relative price. High quality suppliers do not have any advantage in sending out a signal of bad quality by means of a too low relative price; and low quality suppliers take advantage of imitating the behavior of high quality ones. Such a case of real rigidities is based, however, on purchasers' smaller information with regard to suppliers (asymmetry of information) and is modelled by means of the principal-agent theory. Hence, as will shortly become clear, it is to be referred to as the NKEiai strain rather than to the NKEric one.

asymmetries nor on the definition of specific contracts. Consequently, the analysis of nominal rigidities in the goods market, put forward by NKEric, appears homogeneous with the already mentioned models with 'staggered' wage contracts or with simple efficiency wages models that postulate a direct link between the level of the real wage and the effort supplied by workers (see for example Solow, 1979), rather than with the subsequent and more articulated models based on incentive and self-selection contractual mechanisms.

These considerations do not mean that NKEric microfoundations cannot be made compatible with labour market models sub 1-3. In this regard, it could be maintained that the NKEric models would achieve an interesting combination since they would apply game theory and competitive imperfections to spot markets, such as the goods markets, the contract theory and imperfect information to customer markets, such as labour markets. The point is that, as far as I can see, none of the NKEric models has explicitly addressed the analytical problems raised in this perspective. Thus, it seems legitimate to draw a first conclusion: NKEric has not yet elaborated a unitary framework capable of satisfactorily microfounding the combination between nominal and real rigidities.

This first conclusion weakens NKEric results regarding the persistence of suboptimal equilibria with involuntary unemployment and the real long-term effects of monetary policy. It also raises a more fundamental problem. As has been mentioned already, the NKEric results are based on the assumption that firms operate in imperfect competitive markets. Differing from what is suggested by traditional microeconomics, I maintain that this assumption is not at all more restrictive than that of perfect competition. Nevertheless, if NKEric aimed at constructing a framework directed at incorporating the various contributions of new microeconomic approaches, it would have to treat the imperfection in the markets structure as an endogenous variable and not as the 'first principle' of its own analytical model. Although with a different emphasis and with often conflicting results, the theory of 'contestable markets' (Baumol and Panzar and Willig 1982), the information theory (Stiglitz, 1987b) and the theory of 'property rights' (Hart and Moore 1990), have tried to endogenously determine markets structure; and, unlike NKEric, NKEiai has absorbed the results of some of these attempts. Apart from the criticism levelled at Baumol and Panzar and Willig, (Stiglitz, 1987c), the NKEiai models incorporate, for example, an aspect drawn from the theory of contestable markets: although setting the price as in the traditional imperfect competitive markets, in the capital markets lenders have zero expected profits as in the traditional perfect competitive markets.

These considerations can be summarized in three points: (i) in order to overcome the weaknesses revealed by the Keynesian results of NKEric, the nominal and real rigidities should be combined in a unitary framework; (ii) given the features of the more articulated models that explain rigidity in the real wages, this framework would have to incorporate concepts of recent microeconomics which are neglected by NKEric (for example: principal-agent relationships, asymmetric information); (iii) if point (ii) were fulfilled, NKEric's essential reference to imperfect competition would no longer be interpretable as a 'first principle' but could be microfounded. Points (i)-(iii) show that, in spite of the results obtained and the perspectives of research opened, NKEric is not able to offer a fully satisfactory microfoundation of nominal rigidities and real rigidities.

4. IMPERFECTIONS IN THE CAPITAL MARKET

The conclusions drawn at the end of the previous section should not be seen as a negative appraisal of the possible evolution of NKEric. On the contrary, they are aimed at stressing the necessity to expand its lines of research in order to obtain a more robust justification of the existence of nominal rigidities compatible with the maximizing behaviour of economic agents. Nevertheless it is still apparent that NKEric reveals other important deficiencies regarding the treatment of monetary aspects. Like the NCS, NKEric shows that money influences real variables only in the presence of the rigidities examined above. It also neglects the analysis of credit and other financial instruments. By contrast, in the NKEiai models the monetary aspects play a crucial role. In these models, suboptimal equilibria with involuntary unemployment and cyclical fluctuations are realized due, in particular, to the inefficient working of the various sections of the capital market and the consequent financial constraints that bear upon firms' productive decisions.[14] It should also be borne in mind that these Keynesian results require the presence of real rigidities, which especially concern the labour market, and are founded on efficiency wages and asymmetric information models (see section 3 and n. 13), but they do not require the presence of nominal rigidities.[15] This is not surprising since, by concentrating the analysis on the limited availability of financing flows in the capital market and referring to efficiency wages fixed by the firms in the labour market, NKEiai favours the supply side over the demand side in the goods market.

---

[14] In the previous analysis of NKEric models the problem of the cycle was not dealt with because it is of little interest. In fact, in most of the NKEric models, the economic fluctuations are the result of negative demand shocks which have real short term effects and become neutral again in the long term. Conversely, many NKEiai models are dedicated to the endogenous explanation of economic cyclical trends (see for example Greenwald and Stiglitz, 1988 and 1993a).

[15] The most noted exponents of NKEiai go as far as to sustain, with Keynes (1936, chapter 19; also: Tobin 1993), that the nominal flexibility of prices would worsen markets imperfections and the instability of the economic system (see for example Greenwald and Stiglitz, 1993b).

The leading reference to the capital market and the supply side of the goods market, and the elimination of nominal rigidities imply, with regard to NKEric, that the NKEiai strain has looser ties with the NCS and assumes NCM as its more explicit critical reference.[16] A similar orientation is confirmed in the microeconomic framework. Unlike NKEric and like NCM, NKEiai attributes great importance to the incompleteness of markets and to imperfect information; nevertheless, while NCM tries to include these aspects in the Arrow-Debreu framework, NKEiai uses and homogenizes the main microeconomic results of the asymmetric information theories (Akerlof, 1970; Rothschild and Stiglitz, 1976; Jaffee and Russell, 1976; Jensen and Meckling, 1976; also Stiglitz, 1987a) and of the contract theory (Hart and Holmstrom, 1987; Sappington, 1991; also: Stiglitz and Weiss, 1991; Stiglitz, 1992b) into its own framework.

These microeconomic references lay the foundations for the NKEiai analysis regarding the imperfections of three markets: the credit market (Stiglitz and Weiss 1981, 1992), the equities market (for example: Greenwald and Stiglitz and Weiss 1984; Gale and Stiglitz 1989) and the labour market (for example Greenwald, 1986; Weiss, 1990). I maintain that, in order to account for the constraints that the two imperfections in the capital market put on production, a time sequence must be specified. This sequence is either undervalued or neglected in the NKEiai models. A time lag should be assumed between the purchase of inputs and the subsequent sale of outputs in order to stress the crucial role of production financing (Hicks, 1956). This justifies the thesis of NKEiai, according to which the constraints faced by single firms depend on two factors: (a) the amount of self-financing; (b) the quantity or price rationing in the flows of finance for the realization of their productive decisions. Note that point (a) implies that the firms' supply of goods is a direct function of the amount of self-financing due to the increasing bankruptcy costs that they bear as the quantity produced rises, or, similarly, due to their bankruptcy risk aversion (Greenwald and Kohn and Stiglitz, 1990; Greenwald and Stiglitz, 1992). Together with imperfections in the labour market that generate the real rigidities mentioned above, the constraints on the production side sub (a) and (b) make involuntary unemployment possible. Financial constraints on the realization of firms' productive decisions would explain, then, the cyclical behaviour of the economy (Stiglitz, 1992a; Greenwald and Stiglitz 1993a).

The above enables a more precise comparison between the results of

---

16 The distance from NCS has been stressed since the presentation of the NKEiai research programme (Greenwald and Stiglitz, 1987) and also emerges in works that take it explicitly as the point of departure (see for example: Greenwald and Stiglitz, 1991). On the other hand, the relationship with the NCM clearly emerges in all of the NKEiai's attempts to build a model of the economic system as a whole (for example Stiglitz, 1992a; Greenwald and Kohn and Stiglitz, 1990; Greenwald and Stiglitz, 1993a). An evaluation of the differences and the analogies between the NCM and the NKEiai is offered in the second chapter of this book.

NKEric, NKEiai and NCM. Like in NCM, in NKEiai there are no binding constraints on the aggregate demand side.[17] Nevertheless, as in NKEric models without nominal rigidities, in NKEiai the increasing supply of goods with regard to the firms' self-financing (see above, point a) is a sufficient condition to determine suboptimal equilibria but not involuntary unemployment. Furthermore, since the margins of self-financing are, in turn, a function of the level of activity, this supply curve causes cyclical fluctuations in the economic system. As a result, there is room for stabilization policies. Similarly to NCM, however, in the absence of quantity or price rationing in the flows of finance for the realization of firms' productive decisions (above, point b), in NKEiai monetary policy can have real effects only if it is not anticipated by agents and thus affects the margins of self-financing.

These observations lead to the following conclusions: (i) the essential differences between NKEiai and NCM can be reduced to the quantity rationing in the capital market and to the increasing bankruptcy costs or the bankruptcy risk aversion of firms; (ii) the complementarity between NKEiai and NKEric derives from the fact that the first strain concentrates its analysis on the links between financing flows and the supply of goods while the second strain expands the analysis of the ties between demand constraints and price adjustment; (iii) the analogy between NKEiai and NKEric derives from the fact that, in both lines of research, involuntary unemployment requires the use of real rigidities. Points (i)-(iii) bring out the limits and the partiality of the different NKE models and indicate that, in order to overcome the more evident of these limits, and to counter the framework of NCM by means of more robust Keynesian results, it would be useful to re-interpret the NKEiai and NKEric models within a unitary framework capable of bringing out the complementarities. The aim of this paper, however, is another. It is to point out the reasons that lead me to prefer NKEiai models to those of NKEric. This should enable me to devote space to aspects of NKEiai that tend to be sacrificed in the attempt to reinforce its ties with the other strain of the NKE. Above all, this aim does not lead me to build a model of general equilibrium, but to bring out the analyses of the single markets or, in other words, to choose a partial analysis.

In order to illustrate these points, I shall refer to the time lag between the inputs purchase and the output sale (Hicks, 1956; Amendola and Gaffard 1988; see also Graziani, 1989) that I have mentioned above and which is not developed, or is neglected altogether, in the NKEiai models. Moreover, I dwell on the contribution these models have made to the debates regarding credit

---

[17] Greenwald and Stiglitz (1993a) weaken such an implication in their model emphasizing the interdependency between demand and supply shocks. Stiglitz (1987a; also n. 13), furthermore, remembers that the dependency of quality on price makes the functions of supply and demand for goods interdependent. As will emerge in relation to the problem of investment (see section 4), it is still true that the models of the NKEiai do not deepen the determinants of aggregate demand.

rationing and equity rationing;[18] and I examine the impact these forms of rationing can have on the productive decisions of firms, on their labour demand and on the effectiveness of monetary policy. The time lag is essential for justifying the fact that single firms must finance the setting in motion of their productive processes through the use of profits stocked in the past, the borrowing from banks or wealth-owners, or the issue of new equities.[19] If the production and sale of outputs were instantaneous firms would in fact be able, as a rule, to purchase the desired productive inputs by means of the use (of a part) of the proceeds from the sale of their outputs. This is confirmed by the contractual arrangement typical of one of the more usual sources of financing: debt. Debt contracts differ from ordinary market transactions precisely because they have to define the terms of exchange for two semi-transactions that are separate in time; the lender offers 'money today' against 'future money' thus running the risk that, on the expiry date of the contract, (a part of) the borrowers will default. The interests must at least compensate the lender not only for his/ her intertemporal preference (the case of savers) or for the credit supply costs (the case of banks) but also for borrowers' default risk.[20] This means that, if there were no time lag between lending and repayment and if, consequently, there were neither default risks nor positive interest rates, there would be no reasons for stipulating debt contracts to finance firms' productive decisions. The credit flows would be limited to the sub-set of firms that sustain losses (that is, with proceeds lower than the inputs cost) but are not turned out of the market. The credit flows would function as the link between the different points in time in which the market exchanges take place, and therefore would not have the crucial importance that NKEiai attributes to them.

By creating a tie between sources of financing and the realization of productive decisions, the time lag between the purchase of inputs and the sale of outputs has an even more general consequence that NKEiai neglects in the representation of the working of the economic system. This lag calls for a substitution of the general equilibrium models with a sequential analysis characterized by the point in time in which the period begins, and the point in time in which the same period ends. Note that, in this Hicksian sequence, there is a time lag also between the opening of the different markets (see Messori and Tamborini, 1995). The credit market, the equity market and the labour market open at the beginning of the period; while the labour market closes definitively

---

[18] Some critical evaluation on this matter have been deferred to section 5.

[19] The NKEiai models do not operate any difference between the demand for bank credit and the issue of other financial securities. It should be noted, in this respect, that unlike securities and in spite of recent financial innovations (securitization), bank credit cannot be directly exchanged on well-organized secondary markets.

[20] For simplicity, we assume that the cost of the credit supply depends on the intertemporal preference of savers (interest rates on deposits) and on the default risk of the banks themselves (discount rate fixed by the central bank).

in at the same point time, the credit market closes temporarily and the equities market stays open throughout the period. Conversely, the goods markets open and the credit market re-opens at the end of the period.

The time lags in the opening of the markets that characterize sequential analysis bring out the contribution made by NKEiai regarding the problems of credit rationing and equity rationing. With regard to credit rationing, it should be mentioned at once that—together with Keeton's contribution (1979, Chapter III)—the Stiglitz-Weiss model (1981) offers the first rigorous demonstration of the phenomenon: a bank, faced with a sub-set of borrowers, with projects of different riskiness but ex-ante indistinguishable due to information asymmetries, may find it advantageous to set an equilibrium interest rate at which it totally satisfies the credit demand of a randomly chosen part of this sub-set, and it does not grant any credit to the remaining part[21].

In the Stiglitz-Weiss model (1981) the asymmetry of information works in such a way that, at the moment of defining debt contracts, banks are not able to perfectly differentiate the productive projects of their potential borrowers according to the different default risks. Furthermore, the conditions of credit supply established by the banks influence the riskiness of the projects financed. High interest rates on credit weigh more heavily on a low-risk borrower who has a high probability of being solvent, that is, of returning the 'principal' with interest on the expiry date of the contract, than on a high-risk borrower, who has a high probability of defaulting. This means that every increase in the interest rates, set by a given bank, has a double consequence for this bank. On one hand, this increase induces an obvious 'positive incentive effect' in that it increases the proceeds obtained by the bank in the case of solvency of its borrowers. On the other, it negatively modifies the sub-set of projects (ex-ante indistinguishable) financed by the bank, in that it drives the low-risk borrowers to leave the credit market ('adverse selection effect') or it drives the borrowers to choose increasingly risky projects from those at their disposal ('adverse incentive effect'). This raises the effective weight of insolvency and thereby reduces the effective proceeds of the bank. Stiglitz and Weiss prove that, above certain levels of interest rates (r^*), the 'adverse selection' effects and/or the 'negative incentive' effects dominate the 'positive incentive' effects. Thus, both the unitary returns expected by the bank and its relative credit supply are not an increasing monotonic function of the interest rate, but reach a maximum in correspondence with r^*.

Stiglitz and Weiss (1981) conclude that, if the bank costs of financing are increasing, the non-monotonicity of the credit supply curve can lead to 'type

---

[21] The situation illustrated describes the so-called type II credit rationing. There is a type I credit rationing when, at the equilibrium interest rate, a given bank finds it advantageous to offer to all (or a part of) the firms of the sub-set under consideration an amount of financing that is less than that requested. It is of interest to note that, before Milde and Riley (1988), the models with type I rationing did not obtain any rigorous result.

II' credit rationing. This rationing result has given rise to numerous critical comments. One of the most recurring criticisms is that, if there are ex-ante information asymmetries, the introduction of 'non-price' variables in debt contracts (that is, collaterals) would enable the banks to better screen the borrowers with different default risks and, hence, to supply different debt contracts that would lead to the realization of separating equilibria without credit rationing (see Bester, 1985 and 1987). A recent and refined Stiglitz and Weiss model (1992) demonstrates the weakness of this criticism. It is enough for the ex-ante information asymmetries to apply to some supplementary characteristics of borrowers or of borrowers' projects to prevent that a more complex debt contract leads to a perfect screening of borrowers. In the case under consideration, Stiglitz and Weiss (1992) assume that ex-ante indistinguishable borrowers, as well as being able to undertake projects with different riskiness, have a different store of wealth, and prove that this makes (type II) credit rationing possible with both pooling and separating equilibria, in that richer firms tend to activate riskier projects.

Even if, for now, we leave aside the unsolved problems in the Stiglitz and Weiss analysis and the possible indexing of debt contracts (see below section 5), what has been said is not sufficient to show that credit rationing has macroeconomic effects on the activity level. In principle, that part of the borrowers which undergoes credit rationing could finance production with stocked profits (self-financing) or by the issue of equities. The first of these two alternatives is, however, to be discarded. Given increasing bankruptcy costs or bankruptcy risk aversion, any firm would prefer to self-finance rather than stipulate a debt contract; thus, it is certain that firms that have required credit and have been rationed do not have sufficient self-financing margins. The alternative of issuing equities can also be discarded in that the information asymmetry assimilates the working of the equity market to Akerlof's market for 'lemons' (1970; also Greenwald, Stiglitz and Weiss 1984). Not being able to evaluate the actual value of each firm and its prospective profits, savers are willing to underwrite equities at an intermediate price between that of the 'good' equities and that of the 'bad' equities; these demand prices trigger 'adverse selection' or 'adverse incentive' effects which determine, in turn, increasingly lower demand prices. This process leaves new equities of worse firms on the market. In the presence of some restrictive assumptions, this leads the demand for new equities to zero and introduces equity rationing in the extreme form of the elimination of the market itself; even if this extreme case does not come about, the fact remains that the costs of equity financing are very high.

The 'lemon' problem implies that the highest quality firms could place their new equities only at prices lower than the right value. It is not advantageous for firms of this kind to bear the supplementary costs of equity financing, which these conditions of placement imply. This means that every issue of equities from a given firm sends negative signals to potential purchasers regarding its quality. Hence it is not advantageous for even the lowest quality firms to issue equities because they would self-select through the negative signal sent out. The conclusion is that, if lacking in sufficient self-financing margins, firms of every type prefer to finance the purchase of the decided inputs by using the credit rather than the equity market.[22] The only firms for which it is advantageous to finance their productive decisions in the equity market, tend to be firms previously rationed in the credit market. This is common knowledge. Thus, instead of constituting an effective alternative to credit rationing, the supply of new equities generates another form of rationing: equity rationing

These considerations show that, if the assumptions of the NKEiai models hold true (in particular, the presence of real rigidities but not of nominal rigidities), then quantity rationing in the capital market can have a macroeconomic impact on the firms' productive decisions and on their labour demand. In the presence of rationing, firms do not have sufficient means of payment to purchase all the inputs necessary for the realization of full employment.

This makes room for economic policy interventions; expansionary monetary policies, in particular, can have real effects even if they are perfectly predicted by economic agents. The problem is, as Stiglitz and Weiss (1992) point out, that credit rationing and equity rationing work in such a way that monetary policy is effective only if it follows channels different from the usual ones. The effectiveness of monetary policy is ensured by the credit channel instead of the traditional monetary channel. Given credit rationing, an expansion in the money supply has an impact on real variables only if, decreasing the cost credit and thus weakening the adverse selection or the adverse incentive effects, it can increase the maximum amount of credit offered by the single banks.

5. PARTIAL AND SEQUENCE ANALYSIS

The previous analysis of the imperfections in the capital market and labour market has various implications, both microeconomic and macroeconomic. At the microeconomic level, it especially stresses that, in the presence of information asymmetries, prices must combine the traditional allocative function with an information function regarding the 'quality' of agents and/or of the object of the transactions. This supplementary prices function, that

---

[22] The financial hierarchy ('pecking order') between self-financing, bank credit and the issue of equities has been pointed out by several authors (see for example: Myers and Majluf, 1984; Fazzari and Hubbard and Petersen, 1988) and is now commonly accepted. In particular, Greenwald and Stiglitz, (1993b) recognize that the bankruptcy costs, inherent to debt contracts, are not normally high enough to overturn the hierarchy between debt and equities.

Stiglitz (1987a) summarizes with the phrase 'quality depends on price', is often performed in a distortionary way. As has just been shown, it can determine equilibria with credit rationing and equity rationing that are not constrained to be Pareto efficient; it also contributes to determining employment rationing in the labour market. Thus, at the macroeconomic level, market failures imply suboptimal levels of activity and involuntary unemployment. It is worth noting here that these macroeconomic implications are inferred from the examination of the working of single markets rather than from a general analysis of the economic system. In the partial analysis of the labour market, firms' productive decisions are constrained by the influence real rigidities have on the demand for labour. The partial analysis of the capital market constrains the realization of these productive decisions and the relative labour demand by means of quantity rationing. It follows that the analysis of goods markets is concentrated on the supply side and has a residual character, in that it is forced to absorb the results obtained from partial analysis of the labour market and the capital market.

According to the most authoritative exponents of NKEiai, the absence of a general macroeconomic model represents a problem to be solved. Stiglitz, for example, has repeatedly maintained that his research program aims at elaborating a *new* model of *general equilibrium*. The fundamental role that NKEiai attributes to information asymmetries and market failures, would exclude any positive reference to 'general equilibrium' *à la* Arrow-Debreu. Information asymmetries and market failures require the definition of different groups of agents, thus preventing the transformation of individual demand and supply curves into aggregate curves as well as the adoption of the 'representative agent' concept (see Stiglitz, 1991; Greenwald and Stiglitz 1993b).[23] NKEiai exponents, however, do not seem to have any doubt regarding the fact that Keynesian macroeconomics should abandon the study of single markets and, safeguarding the heterogeneity of the agents, should evolve toward the general and simultaneous analysis of the different markets that characterize the working of the economic system.

As I have already premised (see section 3), in the following I make some suggestions that aim at opening a different line of research: the partial analysis of the single markets can be a strong, instead of a weak point of NKEiai.[24] In

---

[23] The thesis, sustained in the first chapter of this book, is that NKEiai does not completely overcome the problems raised by the representative agent in that Greenwald and Stiglitz (1993b), although admitting the presence of 'composition effects', do not build a model able to examine these effects and to asses their macroeconomic impact. The conclusion, drawn from this thesis, is that the building of a new general equilibrium model is impeded by analytical deficiencies of the NKEiai such as the non-specification of the determinants of the aggregate demand and, above all, of investments.

[24] This does not mean that the NKEiai framework is free of the many analytical deficiencies indicated in the first chapter of this book. As will be shown shortly, the NKEiai models are not able to examine investment in fixed capital.

order for such a possibility to be realized, the two conditions, touched upon but not elaborated by Stiglitz (1991), must be satisfied. (1) The partial analyses of different markets must fulfil a minimum degree of homogeneity that guarantees their ex-post coherence [25]. (2) Reference to the representative agent must be replaced with the maximum level of aggregation compatible with the minimum elements of differentiation necessary for the information asymmetries to have their effects on the various markets under consideration. The realization of points (1) and (2) would enable compliance with a commitment 'economizing' in analysis, and would give rise to gradual and flexible theoretical building blocks of the working of the economic system which could be linked in different ways in more advanced stages of elaboration.

At least two elements show that the reinterpretation of NKEiai proposed here is able to satisfy points (1) and (2). Regarding point (1), the sequential analysis, based on the time lag between inputs purchase and outputs sale, and the consequent time lags between the openings of the various markets make the assumption of a partial equilibrium view possible and enhances the ex-ante homogeneity requirements that must be satisfied to guarantee an ex-post coherence of the results thus obtained (see section 4). The common analytical basis that characterizes NKEiai models of the labour market and the capital market, satisfies the high degree of homogeneity required for the partial analysis of these markets, which open simultaneously at the beginning of the period, and facilitates their subsequent linking. Vice versa, the time lag between the opening of these two markets at the beginning of the period and the opening of the goods markets at the end of the period, does not require equally tight ex-ante homogeneity or ex-post link. At a first appraisal, this enables the goods markets to be treated as subordinate to the capital and labour markets.

Regarding point (2), the use NKEiai makes of the principal-agent relationship is important. Generally, this enables a reference to a 'representative principal' but, at the sametime, safeguards the heterogeneity of operators and markets by means of the analysis of different groups of agents. For example, in NKEiai the analysis of the credit market is characterized by the assumption of a 'representative' bank (the 'principal') and by heterogeneous groups of borrowing firms. The study of each of these groups is based on a specific ex-ante 'representative firm' which determines at least two sub-groups,

[25] Stiglitz (1992a) touches on condition (1) when he stigmatizes the scarce generality of the NKEric models. In fact, he bases his criticism on the non-homogeneity between the explanation of efficiency wages, the theory of small menu costs and the nature of exogenous shocks from the demand side (see also, section 2). In disagreement with the declared NKEiai aspiration of elaborating a model of general equilibrium, this seems to suggest that the generality of a given approach should not be evaluated on the basis of the traditional Marshallian distinction between partial analysis and general analysis, but on the basis of the ex-post degree of coherence between the different partial analyses.

characterized by different access to bank financing and randomly defined. Similarly, the analysis of the equity market refers to a 'representative' wealth-owner, who acts as 'principal' and as possible purchaser, and to heterogeneous firms (agents) which are the possible suppliers. Lastly, the analysis of the labour market assumes a 'representative' firm (the 'principal') and heterogeneous groups of workers (agents); in each of these groups a 'representative worker' can be isolated in terms similar to those already specified for the credit market. The plurality of operators that thus emerges, strengthens the consequences of information asymmetries and makes the market failures significant. On the other hand, the parallel re-statement of a 'weak' version of the 'representative' agent concept satisfies the criterion, proposed by Stiglitz, of minimizing the complexity of the analytical framework under the constraint of attaining a model that is sufficiently articulated to account for the information asymmetries and market failures.

With these considerations I do not intend to imply that NKEiai is free of unsolved problems. On the contrary, I believe that NKEiai does not capture crucial aspects of sequence analysis; as a consequence, its partial analyses of both the labour market and the credit market reveal some specific but important deficiencies. Consider firstly the main unsolved problem in the labour market.

As has been noted above (section 4), according to NKEiai the working of this market is characterized by rigidity in real wages. If transferred to a sequential framework, this rigidity would require that employees are able to negotiate with firms or, at least, to know not only their money wages but also their real wages at the beginning of every period. The problem is that (a) if the firms set the price of goods at the beginning of the period and cannot modify it in the course of the period (fix- price markets), the denominator of real wages—that is, a price index of consumption goods–depends on the autonomous and private decisions of the various producers; (b) if the market of consumption goods is instead a flex-price market, the real wage denominator is set only at the end of each period, that is at the opening of the goods markets. In both cases, workers are not able to negotiate the level of this denominator at the beginning of the period; therefore they are in a condition to directly control the money wage but not the real wage.[26]

There are at least three ways to get round the problem. First, it can be assumed that both wage contracts and financial contracts are perfectly indexed;

---

[26] It is noteworthy that, if in the system analysed prices are not set by firms at the beginning of the period and if they do not remain unchanged for the rest of it, the real wages are not even determined by the firms but depend on the aggregate demand for goods. The flawed analysis on the demand side, which characterizes the NKEiai models, thus makes it more difficult to solve the question under consideration. It could be sustained that, unlike the *General Theory*, NKEiai is not able to examine the ties between goods markets and the labour market. This point will be shortly developed below.

it cannot, however, be immediately established whether, in the presence of
the indexation of all contracts stipulated at the beginning of the period,
quantity rationing in the capital market persists unchanged and is still able
to impose binding constraints on the realization of the firms' productive
decisions.[27] Second, it can be assumed that the workers consume (the desired
part of) their money wages at the very moment in which they receive them,
in that at the beginning of every period they have access to goods produced
by the firms in the previous period; the introduction of such a 'delay' is,
however, an *ad hoc* assumption which revives the traditional tie between
savings decisions and investment decisions and which—above all—eliminates
the sequence into the single period. In turn, the elimination of the intraperiod
sequence makes the bank finance for the realization of the productive
decisions of firms inessential (see also section 4): the firms' purchase of
productive inputs instantaneously generates an expenditure flow and a
savings flow that are, as a sum total, of equal amount; thus, the total financing
must be equal only to the savings flow and can be guaranteed by this flow.
Third, it can be assumed that workers and firms negotiate the (expected) real
wage at the beginning of each period on the basis of an expected price index
of consumption goods.

If real rigidities in the labour market are to be safeguarded without
altering other fundamental aspects of the model under consideration, the only
possible alternatives are the first and the third. As has been mentioned (see fn.
27), the first alternative requires however a specific analysis that lies outside
the aims of this paper. Hence there is no choice but to follow the third
alternative. It is sufficient to specify that, depending on the assumptions on the
formation of expectations (realized expectations, rational expectations, adaptive
expectations, and so on), the prices expected by workers can, or cannot,
coincide with the prices decided by firms (fix-price markets), or the prices
expected by workers and the prices expected by firms can, or cannot, coincide
with those set by markets (flex-price markets); and the possible differences can
relate to both the price index and—especially—the relative prices (see also
Greenwald-Stiglitz 1993a). In any case price expectations, as well as making
possible ties between the level of money wages and the price of goods into
account, are based—directly or indirectly—on expectations regarding the
level and the composition of the aggregate demand. This reintroduces those
constraints placed by the demand for goods which, as has been repeatedly
pointed out, are undervalued in NKEiai. My previous assertion that NKEiai
can treat the goods markets as subordinate to the capital and labour markets,

---

[27] This question is so important that it merits *ad hoc* treatment. One could argue that the
indexation of contracts eliminates the suboptimality of the NKEiai equilibria. It is sufficient
to assume, in this regard, that the supply function of goods is constrained by the self-financing
margins of the firms but not by credit rationing. If the possibility of credit rationing is re-
introduced, the last statement will remain correct only in the case of lenders' monetary illusion.

is thus qualified; an efficiency wages theories must be revised, since they have to be based on expected and not on actual real wages.

There are at least two major problems which characterize the partial analysis of the credit market. The first regards the implicit and arbitrary generalization of Stiglitz's and Weiss' rationing results mentioned above proposed by Stiglitz himself. Stiglitz (for example 1992a) and Greenwald and Stiglitz (1988) treat credit rationing as an essential component of their cyclical models, which are devoted to analyze changes in the supply of goods brought about by the firms; by contrast, the proof of the possibility of type II credit rationing which is offered by Stiglitz and Weiss (1981, 1992), *only* applies to the financing of indivisible projects, that is projects with a given and unchanging size. Various authors (in particular Milde and Riley, 1988) maintain that the divisibility of projects—that is projects with variable size—strongly reduces bank's advantage to screen its borrowers by means of quantity rationing since the amount of financing requested by every single firm is an important signal regarding its default risk. For example, many models with divisible projects end up subordinating the possibility of credit rationing to the presence of specific forms of production functions.[28] It follows that, in order to support the centrality of credit rationing in the NKEiai models, these results must be overcome and the persistence of credit rationing also in the presence of divisible projects must be shown. A first step in this direction is taken in chapter 4 of this book, which generalizes and extends the cases of rationing elaborated in Milde and Riley.

The second problem to be solved in the partial analysis of the credit market concerns the form of debt contract. Taking into account only indivisible projects, Stiglitz and Weiss (1981) are not able to endogenously determine the optimal form of the debt contract and limit themselves to assuming that banks and firms stipulate standard debt contracts [29]. Thus, it could be maintained that Stiglitz-Weiss' credit rationing is not only due to information asymmetries regarding the riskiness of the project to be financed, but it is also and especially due to the choice of a suboptimal form of the debt contract. Also this problem must be overcome; in particular, it must be proved that an endogenous determination of the optimal debt contract does not eliminate quantity rationing.

The Gale-Hellwig model (1985; also Townsend, 1979; Wiliamson, 1986) enables a first, although not decisive, step forward in this direction. It substitutes the *ex-ante* information asymmetry regarding the riskiness of the project to be financed with an *ex-post* information asymmetry regarding the

---

[28] These models also impose the substitution of type I for type II credit rationing.

[29] It is worth mentioning that a standard debt contract implies that the single firm is solvent if, on the agreed expiry date, it returns the predetermined sum (principal and interests) to the lending bank; in the opposite case, the firm defaults and must transfer to the bank the entire proceeds of the financed project as well as the possible amount of collaterals (see Gale and Hellwig 1985).

realized results of the project; and shows that, in this case, the standard debt contract is optimal in that it minimizes the costs that every bank must sustain to verify the results of the projects financed. The limit of Gale and Hellwig's result is that NKEiai models are mainly based on ex-ante information asymmetries. Only recently, Innes (1993) was able to demonstrate, under not particularly restrictive conditions, that the standard debt contract is optimal, even with ex-ante information asymmetries. The interesting point is that Innes' model (1990, 1993) is compatible with the generalization of the Milde-Riley model (1988), that is, with the generalization of the results of type I credit rationing in the financing of divisible projects (see also chapter 4 in this book).

The previous considerations stress that it is possible to overcome the unsolved problems in the partial analysis of the labour and capital markets, and thus to utilize these two theoretical 'building- blocks' of NKEiai in a sequence analysis. A similar positive conclusion does not apply to the second category of problems, which remain unsolved and can be attributed to NKEiai's neglect of essential aspects of sequence analysis. This new category of problems has its roots in two important subjects: investment and money.

The NKEiai models incorporate only circulating capital and thus are not able to elaborate a satisfactory investment theory. This remains true for one of the most recent and complete models of Greenwald and Stiglitz (1993a). The introduction of production functions with fixed capital and of the related investment demand into this model causes an ambiguous tie between firms' uncertainty with regard to goods market prices and their investment decisions (see Saltari, 1996). The intensification of this uncertainty increases firms' risk of bankruptcy, and thus has a negative influence on their investment decisions; nevertheless it also generates an increase in the investments expected net yield, and therefore stimulates their demand. This ambiguity affects firms' self-financing margins and the rationing choices of the possible lenders, that is, the variables that determine the level of activity and its cyclical changes. As a consequence, it threatens to undermine the cycle theory advanced by NKEiai.

The limits of investment analysis prevent NKEiai from attaining an adequate aggregate demand function and constrain its analysis to a single-period sequence. It is important to stress here the last point since it shows that, as well as being a component of the aggregate demand, the investments flow in fixed capital represents an increase in the relative stock (see also Amendola and Gaffard, 1992). This flow thus plays a fundamental role in the analysis of the sequence: it determines the possibilities (quantitative and qualitative) of future productions and, on this basis, acts as a link between periods. The conclusion to be drawn is that the failures denoted by the NKEiai investments theory, also prevent the elaboration of a sequential analysis and the utilization of the results obtained in the partial analyses of the labour and capital markets.

This conclusion finds confirmation in the other limit which prevents NKEiai from elaborating a sequence analysis: its conception of money. As has

131

been already mentioned (see section 4), the NKEiai monetary theory marks notable progress with regard to the Keynesian tradition to which the monetary approach of NKEric remains largely subordinated. Nevertheless, NKEiai neglects the classic microeconomic focus of monetary theory: the explanation of the reasons that induce rational economic agents to use money, devoid of intrinsic value, as a means of payment and as a store of value (see Messori and Tamborini, 1995). In the NKEiai models this problem is neglected in that credit and new financial assets tend to replace money (Blinder and Stiglitz 1983; Stiglitz 1988; Greenwald and Stiglitz 1991). The result is that the NKEiai monetary theory concentrates on the flow analysis and eliminates the stock analysis. Paraphrasing the passage of Robertson's (1940) in which the Keynes of the *General Theory* is accused of having insisted so much on the fact that one can ask for money in order to hold it that he overlooks the obvious fact that normally one asks for money in order to spend it, it could be argued that NKEiai insists so much on flows of bank money to spend that it completely forgets the stocks of money to be held.

This 'oversight' weighs negatively on the sequence analysis of NKEiai. Together with the stock of fixed capital, the stock of money is essential for linking the decisions assumed by the various groups of economic agents at the beginning of every period with their behaviours brought about and realized at the end of the same period and for linking the events of the various periods (Hicks 1956, 1967). The attempt at justifying a precautionary demand for liquid assets thus aims at filling an effective gap in the NKEiai monetary theory. The justification put forward here (see also Messori and Tamborini 1995), is that the holding of precautionary money is necessary to the different agents in order to minimize their default risks as well as the divergence between their decided and their realizable expenditures, that is, to minimize their 'fallibility' which is often dependent on an unexpected state of illiquidity. This means that the precautionary money stock influences the possible future expenditures and, on this basis, acts as a link between periods. Thus, as in the case of investments in fixed capital, the lack of a money stock theory in NKEiai prevents the elaboration of a sequence analysis of the results obtained in the partial analyses of the labour and capital markets.

6. CONCLUSIONS

In the previous pages I have tried to suggest a new key of interpretation in order to develop the NKE contributions: instead of referring to a possible general model of NKE, I have highlighted the potential value of its partial analyses. Based on a sketchy reconstruction of its two main strains, I have argued that NKEiai offers the more interesting partial analyses. I have especially referred to the analyses of the capital market and I have made some mention of those analyses of the labour market. This has emphasized that the analytical framework of NKEiai can also be utilized to develop a sequence analysis, where the price signals are not merely limited to the traditional allocative function, and where the quantity constraints become dominant. It is enough to remember, in this last regard, that credit rationing and equity rationing can prevent the realization of a part of the production decisions in that they constrain the financing of these decisions.

These elements lead me to the conclusion that NKEiai offers an important contribution for the construction of a new macroeconomic method. As I have pointed out, this does not mean that NKEiai is without problems. Beyond the relevant but specific deficiencies that impinge on the examination of the real rigidities in the labour market and on credit rationing models, the fundamental problem remains: NKEiai does not capture essential aspects of the sequence analysis, which should be called to play a crucial role in linking the partial analyses of the single markets. In this regard, the failures of NKEiai can be ascribed to two analytical deficiencies: the lack of a theory of investment in fixed capital and the lack of a monetary theory complementary to the credit theory.

BIBLIOGRAPHY

Akerlof, G.A. (1970), 'The market for 'lemons': Quality uncertainty and the market mechanism', *Quarterly Journal of* Economics, 84, 488-500.

Akerlof, G.A. and J.L. Yellen, (1985), 'A near-rational model of the business cycle, with wage and price inertia', *Quarterly Journal of Economics*, 100, 823-38.

Akerlof, G.A. and J.L. Yellen, (1986), 'Introduction', in *Efficiency wage models of the labour market*, edited by G.A. Akerlof and J.L. Yellen, Cambridge: Cambridge University Press.

Amendola, M. and J.L. Gaffard,(1988), *The Innovative choice. An economic analysis of the dynamics of technology*, Oxford: Basil Blackwell.

Amendola, M. and J.L. Gaffard, (1992), 'Towards an 'out of equilibrium' theory of the firm', *Metroeconomica*, 43, 267-88.

Arrow, K.J. and F.H. Hahn, (1971), *General competitive analysis*, Amsterdam: North Holland.

Ball, L. and D. Romer, (1990), 'Real rigidities and the non-neutrality of money', *Review of Economic Studies*, 57, 183-203.

Ball, L., N.G. Mankiw, and D. Romer, (1988), 'The new Keynesian economics and the output-inflation trade-off', *Brookings Papers on Economic Activity*, n.1, 1-65.

Baumol, W.J., J.C. Panzar, and R.D. Willig, (1982), *Contestable markets and the theory of industry structure*, New York: Harcourt Brace Jovanovich.

Bester, H. (1985), 'Screening vs. rationing in credit markets with imperfect information', *American Economic Review*, 75, 850-55.

Bester, H. (1987), 'The role of collateral in credit markets with imperfect information', *European Economic Review*, 31, 887-99.

Blanchard, O.J. (1990), 'Why does money affect output?', in *Handbook of monetary economics*, edited by B.M. Friedman and F.H. Hahn, Amsterdam: North Holland.

Blanchard, O.J. and N. Kiyotaki, (1987), 'Monopolistic competition and the effects of aggregate demand', *American Economic Review*, 77, 647-66.

Blinder, A.S. and J.E. Stiglitz, (1983), 'Money, credit constraints and economic activity', *American Economic Review*, 73, 297-302.

Bowles, S. and H. Gintis, (1993), 'The revenge of homo economicus: Contested exchange and the revival of political economy', *Journal of Economic Perspectives*, 7, 83-102.

Clower, R.W. (1965), 'The Keynesian counter-revolution: A theoretical appraisal', in *The theory of interest rates*, edited by F.H. Hahn and F.P.R. Brechling, London: Macmillan.

Clower, R.W. (1967), 'A reconsideration of the microfoundations of monetary theory, *Western Economic Journal*, 6, 1-8

Fazzari, S.M., R.G. Hubbard, and B.C. Petersen, (1988), 'Financing constraints and corporate investment', *Brookings Papers on Economic Activity*, n.1, 141-95.

Fischer, S. (1977), 'Long-term contracts, rational expectations, and the optimal money supply rule', *Journal of Political Economy*, 85, 191-205.

Friedman, M. (1968), 'The role of monetary policy', *American Economic Review*, 58, 1-17.

Friedman, M. (1977), 'Inflation and unemployment', *Journal of Political Economy*, 85, 451-72.

Gale, D. and M. Hellwig, (1985), 'Incentive-compatible debt contracts: The one-period problem', *Review of Economic Studies*, 52, 647-63.

Gale, I. and Stiglitz, J.E. (1989), 'The informational content of initial public offerings', *Journal of Finance*, 44, 469-77.

Gordon, R.J. (1976), 'Recent developments in the theory of inflation and unemployment' *Journal of Monetary Economics*, 2, 185-219.

Gordon, R.J. (1990), 'What is new Keynesian economics?', *Journal of Economic Literature*, 28, 1115-71.

Graziani, A. (1989), 'The theory of the monetary circuit', *Thames Papers in Political Economy*, spring.

Greenwald, B.C. (1986), 'Adverse selection in the labour market', *Review of Economic Studies*, 53, 325-47.

Greenwald, B.C., M. Kohn, and J.E. Stiglitz, (1990), 'Financial market imperfections and productivity growth', *Journal of Economic Behavior and Organization*, 13, 321-45.

Greenwald, B.C. and J.E. Stiglitz, (1987), 'Keynesian, new Keynesian and new classical economics', *Oxford Economic Papers*, 39, 119-32.

Greenwald, B.C. and Stiglitz, J.E. (1988), 'Imperfect information, finance constraints and business fluctuations', in *Finance constraints, expectations, and macroeconomics*, a cura di M. Kohn and S.C. Tsiang, Oxford: Oxford University Press.

Greenwald, B.C. and J.E. Stiglitz, (1989), 'Toward a theory of rigidities', *American Economic Review*, 79, 364-69.

Greenwald, B.C. and J.E. Stiglitz, (1991), 'Towards a reformulation of monetary theory', *Caffé Lectures*, Roma.

Greenwald, B.C. and J.E. Stiglitz, (1992), 'Imperfect information and macroeconomic analysis', *mimeo*.

Greenwald, B.C. and J.E. Stiglitz, (1993a), 'Financial market imperfections and business cycles', *Quarterly Journal of Economics*, 108, 77-113.

Greenwald, B.C. and J.E. Stiglitz, (1993b), 'New and old Keynesians', *Journal of Economic Pespectives*, 7, 23-44.

Greenwald, B.C., J.E. Stiglitz, and A. Weiss, (1984), 'Informational imperfections in the capital market and macroeconomic fluctuations', *American Economic Review*, 74, 194-99.

Hahn, F.H. (1982), *Money and inflation*, Oxford: Basil Blackwell.

Hargreaves Heap, S.P. (1992), *The new Keynesian macroeconomics. Time, belief and social interdependence*, Aldershot: Edward Elgar.

Hart, O. and B. Holmstrom, (1987), 'The theory of contracts', in *Advances in economic theory*, edited by T.F. Bewley, Cambridge: Cambridge University Press.

Hart, O. and J. Moore, (1990), 'Property rights and the nature of the firm', *Journal of Political Economy*, 98, 1119-58.

Hicks, J.R. (1936), 'Mr Keynes's theory of employment', *Economic Journal*, 46. Reprinted as: 'The General Theory: A first impression', in J.R. Hicks, (1982).

Hicks, J.R. (1937), 'Mr Keynes and the classics', *Econometrica*, 6. Reprinted in J.R. Hicks, (1982).

Hicks, J.R. (1939) *Value and capital*, Oxford: Clarendon Press, 1946.

Hicks, J.R. (1956), 'Method of dynamic analysis', in *25 economic essays in English, German and Scandinavian languages*. Reprinted in J.R. Hicks, (1982).

Hicks, J.R. (1967), 'The two triads', in J.R. Hicks, *Critical essays in monetary theory*. Oxford: Clarendon Press.

Hicks, J.R. (1980-1), 'IS-LM: An explanation', *Journal of Post Keynesian Economics*, Winter. Reprinted in J.R. Hicks, (1982).

Hicks, J.R. (1982), *Money, interest and wages*. Cambridge Ma.: Harvard University Press.

Hicks, J.R. (1989), 'LF and LP', in Tsiang, S.C., *Finance constraints and the theory of money. Selected papers*, edited by M. Kohn, San Diego: Academic Press.

Innes, R. (1990), 'Limited liability and incentive contracting with ex-ante action choices', *Journal of Economic Theory*, 52, 45-67.

Innes, R. (1993), 'Financial contracting under risk neutrality, limited liability and *ex ante* asymmetric information', *Economica*, 60, 27-40.

Jaffee, D.M. and T. Russell, (1976), 'Imperfect information, uncertainty, and credit rationing', *Quarterly Journal of Economics*, 90, 651-66.

Jensen, M.C. and W.H. Meckling, (1976), 'Theory of the firm: Managerial behavior, agency costs and ownership structure', *Journal of Financial Economics*, 3, 305-60.

Keeton, W.R. (1979), *Equilibrium credit rationing*, New York: Garland Press.

Keynes, J.M. (1936), *The general theory of employment, interest and money*, London: Macmillan.

Klein, L.R. (1947), *The Keynesian revolution*, New York: Macmillan.

Laidler, D. (1995), 'The emergence of the Phillips curve as a policy menu', *mimeo*.

Leijonhufvud, A. (1968), *On Keynesian economics and the economics of Keynes*, London: Oxford University Press.

Lindbeck, A. (1992), 'Macroeconomic theory and the labour market', *European Economic Review*, 36, 209-35.

Lindbeck, A. and D.J. Snower, (1988), *The insider-outsider theory of employment and unemployment*, Cambridge Ma.: MIT Press.

Lipsey, R.G. (1960), 'The relation between unemployment and the rate of change of money wage rates in the United Kingdom, 1861-1957: A further analysis', *Economica*, 27, 1-31.

Lucas, R.E. (1972), 'Expectations and the neutrality of money', *Journal of Economic Theory*, 4, 103-24.

Lucas, R.E. (1973), 'Some international evidence on output-inflation tradeoffs', *American Economic Review*, 63, 326-34.

Lucas, R.E. and L.A. Rapping, (1969), 'Real wages, employment and inflation', *Journal of Political Economy*, 77, 721-54.

Lucas, R.E. and T.J. Sargent, (1978), 'After Keynesian macroeconomics', in *After the Phillips curve: Persistence of high inflation and high unemployment*, Conference Series n.19, Boston Ma.: Federal Reserve Bank of Boston.

Mankiw, N.G. (1985), 'Small menu costs and large business cycles: A macroeconomic model of monopoly', *Quarterly Journal of Economics*, 100, 529-39.

Mankiw, N.G. and D. Romer, (1991), 'Introduction', in *New Keynesian economics*, edited by N.G. Mankiw and D. Romer, Cambridge Ma.: MIT Press.

Messori, M. (1991), 'Keynes' *General Theory* and the endogenous money supply', *Economie appliquée*, 44, 115-42.

Messori, M. (1995a), 'Own rate of own interest and the liquidity preference', *Economic Notes*, n. 4.

Messori, M. (1995b), 'Keynesians, new Keynesians and the loanable funds theory', in *Money, financial institutions and macroeconomics*, edited by A. Cohen, H. Hagemann and J. Smithin, Boston: Kluwer (forthcoming)

Messori, M. and R. Tamborini, (1995), 'Fallibility, precautionary behaviour and the new Keynesian monetary theory', *Scottish Journal of Political Economy*, 42, 443-64.

Milde, H. and J.C. Riley, (1988), 'Signaling in credit markets', *Quarterly Journal of Economics*, 103, 101-29.

Modigliani, F. (1944), 'Liquidity preference and the theory of interest and money', *Econometrica*, 12, 45-88.

Modigliani, F. (1963), 'The monetary mechanism and its interaction with real phenomena', *Review of Economics and Statistics*, 45, 79-107.

Modigliani, F. (1977), 'The monetarist controversy, or should we forsake stabilization policies?', *American Economic Review*, 67, 1-19

Myers, S.C. and N.S. Majluf, (1984), 'Corporate financing amd investment decisions when firms have information that investors do not have', *Journal of Financial Economics*, 13, 187-221.

Parkin, M. (1986), 'The output-inflation trade-off when prices are costly to change', *Journal of Political Economy*, 94, 200-24.

Patinkin, D. (1948), 'Price flexibility and full employment', *American Economic Review*, 38, 543-64.

Patinkin, D. (1965), *Money, interest and prices: An integration of monetary and value theory*, New York: Harper and Row, 2a ed..

Phelps, E.S. (1967), 'Phillips curves, expectations of inflation and optimal unemployment over time', *Economica*, 34, 254-81.

Phelps, E.S. and J.B. Taylor, (1977), 'Stabilizing powers of monetary policy under rational expectations', *Journal of Political Economy*, 85, 163-90.

Phillips, A.W. (1958), 'The relation between unemployment and the rate of change of money wage rates in the United Kingdom, 1861-1957', *Economica*, 25, 283-99.

Robertson, D.H. (1940), 'Mr. Keynes and the rate of interest', in D.H. Robertson, *Essays in monetary theory*, London: Staples.

Rotemberg, J.J. (1987), 'The new Keynesian microfoundations', in *NBER Macroeconomics Annuals*, 2, 69-104.

Rothschild, M. and J.E. Stiglitz, (1976), 'Equilibrium in competitive insurance markets: An essay on the economics of imperfect information', *Quarterly Journal of Economics*, 90, 629-49.

Saltari, E. (1996), 'Razionamento azionario, offerta effettiva e fluttuazioni cicliche', in *La nuova economia keynesiana*, edited by M. Messori, Bologna: il Mulino.

Sappington, D.E.M. (1991), 'Incentives in principal-agent relationships', *Journal of Economic Perspectives*, 5, pp.45-66.

Sargent, T.J. (1973), 'Rational expectations, the real rate of interest and the natural rate of unemployment', *Brookings Papers on Economic Activity*, 2, 429-72.

Sargent, T.J. and N. Wallace, (1975), 'Rational expectations, the optimal monetary instrument and the optimal money supply rule', *Journal of Political Economy*, 83, 241-54.

Shapiro, C. and J.E. Stiglitz, (1984), 'Equilibrium unemployment as a worker discipline device', *American Economic Review*, 74, 433-44.

Solow, R. (1979), 'Another possible source of wage stickiness', *Journal of Macroeconomics*, 1, 79-82.

Stiglitz, J.E. (1987a), 'The causes and consequences of the dependence of quality on price', *Journal of Economic Literature*, 25, 1-48.

Stiglitz, J.E. (1987b), 'Competition and the number of firms in a market: Are duopolies more competitive than atomistic markets?', *Journal of Political Economy*, 95, 1041-61.

Stiglitz, J.E. (1987c), 'Technological change, sunk costs, and competition', *Brookings Papers on Economic Activity*, n.3, 883-937.

Stiglitz, J.E. (1988), 'Money, credit, and business fluctuations'. *Economic Record*, 64, 307-22.

Stiglitz, J.E. (1991), 'Alternative approaches to macroeconomics: Methodological issues and the new Keynesian economics', *NBER Working Paper*, n.3580.

Stiglitz, J.E. (1992a), 'Capital markets and income fluctuations in capitalist economy', *European Economic Review*, 36, 269-306.

Stiglitz, J.E. (1992b), 'Contract theory and macroeconomic fluctuations', in *Contract economics*, edited by L. Werin and H. Wijkander, Oxford: Basil Blackwell.

Stiglitz, J.E. and A. Weiss, (1981), 'Credit rationing in markets with imperfect information'. *American Economic Review*, 71, 393-410.

Stiglitz, J.E. and A. Weiss, (1991), 'Contract theory and macro-economic fluctuations', *mimeo*.

Stiglitz, J.E. and A. Weiss, (1992), 'Asymmetric information in credit markets and its implications for macroeconomics', *Oxford Economic Papers*, 44, 694-724.

Taylor, J.B. (1979), 'Staggered wage setting in a macro model', *American Economic Review*, 69, 108-13.

Taylor, J.B. (1980), 'Aggregate dynamics and staggered contracts', *Journal of Political Economy*, 88, 1-23.

Taylor, J.B. (1985), 'Rational expectations models in macroeconomics', in *Frontiers of Economics*, edited by K.J. Arrow and S. Honkapohja, Oxford: Basil Blackwell.

Tobin, J. (1980), *Asset accumulation and economic activity*, Oxford: Basil Blackwell.

Tobin, J. (1993), 'Price flexibility and output stability: An old Keynesian view', *Journal of Economic Perspectives*, 7, 45-65.

Townsend, R. (1979), 'Optimal contracts and competitive markets with costly state verification'. *Journal of Economic Theory*, 21, 265-93.

Weintraub, S. (1966), *Keynes and the monetarists and other essays*, New Brunswick: Rutgers University Press.

Weiss, A. (1990), *Efficiency wages. Models of unemployment, layoffs, and wage dispersion*, Princeton: Princeton University Press.

Williamson, S.D. (1986), 'Costly monitoring, financial intermediation, and equilibrium credit rationing'. *Journal of Monetary Economics*, 18, 159-79.

4. Credit Rationing with Loans of Variable Size*

Pier Giorgio Ardeni

Marcello Messori

1. INTRODUCTION

In this paper we analyze the optimizing behaviour of risk-neutral firms and banks in a competitive credit market under conditions of imperfect and asymmetric information. Firms choose projects that vary in size and quality and whose final return is stochastic. This implies that firms have a heterogeneous endowment of *quality* and of the production *technology*. Since we assume that each profit-maximizing firm has a null wealth endowment, projects must be financed out of loans, the firm must borrow from banks. Ex-ante uncertainty about project returns generates an incomplete-information problem for both the firms and the banks. Conversely, each firm knows the quality of its project which is unobservable by banks; hence, ex-ante uncertainty about project quality also generates an asymmetric information problem on the side of the lenders. Our model only refers to such an *ex-ante* asymmetry of information, since banks can observe firms' end-of-period returns at no costs, and this asymmetry is sufficient to prevent banks from designing debt contracts contingent on the quality of the projects. Moreover, given that firms have limited liability, debt contracts cannot compel firm owners to pay to the bank more than the *ex-post* return of the project chosen. Asymmetric information

---

* This paper draws on previous works by the two authors, particularly: Ardeni, P.G. (1992), 'Investment and Debt Contracting Under Asymmetric Information. I: The Static Case', *Working Paper*, Istituto di Scienze Economiche, Università di Urbino, *Quaderni di Economia, Matematica e Statistica*, no. 15, February; Ardeni, P.G. and Messori, M. (1994), 'Loan Size and Credit Rationing Under Asymmetric Information', *Working Paper*, Dipartimento di Scienze Economiche, Università di Bologna, *Collana Rapporti Scientifici*, no. 195, April. We thank all the people who provided us with their comments and suggestions, as well as all the participants to conferences and seminars where our works have been presented. Financial support from CNR and MURST is acknowledged.

and limited liability imply that lenders face adverse selection and/or moral hazard problems (but here we do not deal with the latter problem). Our aim is to show that, under these assumptions and a Wilson construction of the contracting game between the firm and the bank, either separating or pooling contracts obtain, allowing for a rich set of over- and under-financing or credit-rationing equilibria in the credit market.

Several models of credit-market equilibria with asymmetric information have been proposed in the past, starting with Jaffee and Russell (1976) and followed by Stiglitz and Weiss (1981) (henceforth S-W), Stiglitz and Weiss (1992), De Meza and Webb (1987) (D-W), Milde and Riley (1988) (M-R), Innes (1991). S-W analysed banks' financing of loans of fixed size with equal expected firm returns but different riskiness across firms in accordance with the *mean preserving spread* principle (Rothschild and Stiglitz, 1970), and obtained pooling equilibria with type-II credit rationing. D-W, too, referred to the case of fixed size loans for firms of different quality. They considered the case of loans given to firms whose expected returns are equal and actual returns differ, which replicated the results reached by S-W, and the case of loans given to firms whose returns are equal and the probability of success are different, which leads to a pooling equilibrium with over-financing of higher quality firms. Conversely, M-R and Innes (1991) considered loans of variable size and standard debt contracts contingent on realized firm returns. In their models, the variable size of the loan allows for borrowers' signalling, thus generating self-selection and separating equilibria for firms of different but unobservable quality. While Innes (1991) also obtains pooling equilibria with over- and under-financing, both signaling and separating equilibria weaken the occurrence of type-I credit rationing.

As the latter models highlight, when the size of the loan is allowed to vary, differences in firms' returns can be due both to differences in firms' quality and to differences in the loan size. Moreover, the variable loan size can imply the non-existence of Nash equilibria and the consequent reference to other concepts of equilibrium (for example Riley or Wilson equilibria). In M-R, for instance, each firm is endowed with a production function which depends on the amount of the loan and on a firm-specific quality parameter unobservable by lenders, and firms' returns are increasing in quality. Borrowers' signalling stems from the relation between quality, loan size and output. M-R depict three different cases based either on different production technologies, which are known to both the firms and the banks, or on different orderings of the random returns. In the first case, the production function is multiplicative in the quality parameter so that the loan size is increasing in quality, and hence higher quality firms can signal their type by demanding larger loans; in the second case, the production function is additive in the quality parameter so that the loan size is invariant to quality, and hence higher quality firms can signal their type by accepting smaller loans because of their lower default risk[1]; in the third case, firms projects have different riskiness but the same expected return, for any given amount of loan, so that lower quality firms with higher returns in case of success require larger loans. Under a Riley equilibrium construction, given asymmetric information, the latter two cases imply under-financing whereas the former case implies over-financing of firms of higher quality, and separating second-best equilibria.

The main limits of M-R's analysis are that their three models are unrelated to each other and assume what would have to be explained. In this paper we aim to overcome these two limitations by referring to a unified setting in which output depends not only on an unobservable quality parameter but also on an observable technological parameter. More precisely, we consider how different ways of organizing production activities can have different implications in terms of firms' quality and can lead, in a three-stage Wilson contracting game, to a set of equilibria which is richer than those deriving from M-R's cases.

For this purpose, as quality is not observable, we assume that firm realized returns have the *monotone likelihood ratio property* (MLRP) with respect to *quality*, in the sense of Milgrom (1981). The rationale for assuming this MLRP for the firm profit densities is that of exploiting the monotonicity property implied by the definition of quality. In the literature on credit rationing, two different quality definitions are used. With the first definition, higher quality implies a better profit distribution in the sense of first order stochastic dominance (for example Chan and Kanatas, 1985, Besanko and Thakor (1987)). With the second, lower quality implies a mean preserving spread or higher risk in the sense of second order stochastic dominance (for example Stiglitz and Weiss, 1981, 1986, Bester, 1985). In both cases *higher* quality means *better* outcomes, which is what matters for the monotonicity property of the definition of quality we need. However, these two definitions of quality imply different relations between quality and the amount of loans, so that, as M-R have shown in their models, we have to specify these relations on an a-priori basis. In this paper we argue that this basis can be given by the way we look at how firms organize their production activities. Hence, we say that if *internal* economies of scale and/or *transaction* costs prevail, a larger size of the loan demanded will signal a higher firm quality, while if *external* economies of scale and/or *organizational* costs prevail, a larger size of the loan demanded will signal a lower firm quality.

---

[1] Innes (1991), too, refers to these first two cases which, however, are stated as assumption and not derived from specific production functions (he only models the first case, anyway). Moreover, differently from M-R, Innes (1991) does not refer to a Riley but to a Wilson equilibrium, as we will see Innes' (1990, 1993) contribution is important with respect to the determination of the optimal form of the debt contract. Even if this is not at issue in our paper, we will be able to replicate Innes' results by using the monotone likelihood ratio property.

The above 'institutional' setting (that is technological in a wide sense) allows the strengthening of the credit-rationing results. The present paper shows that credit rationing is still a possible outcome once the loan size is allowed to vary and, hence, signalling is permitted, but pooling equilibria are not ruled out by the equilibrium-game construction. More precisely, by allowing banks to choose both the repayment schedule and the loan size, we allow for the possibility of banks to use the loan contract as a screening device. However, we prove that, while some quality-types are under-financed, some others will be over-financed so that some applicants do not get the amount of credit they would be willing to borrow. Furthermore, we prove that credit rationing is compatible with pooling as well as separating equilibria. This means that our paper entails a robust possibility of 'type-I credit rationing': all quality-types get financed, but some quality-types will obtain a smaller amount of loan than that desired at the market interest rates. Conversely, and differently from S-W, our reference to projects of varying loan size rules out the possibility of 'type-II credit rationing': no quality-type will ever be denied credit, even on a random basis.

The remainder of this paper is organized as follows. In sections 2.1 and 2.2, we characterize the main features of borrowers and lenders in order to specify the debt contract. The latter specification requiring the definition of a three-stage pure strategy game between banks and entrepreneurs which leads to Wilson equilibria (Section 2.3). Together with the entrepreneurs' indifference curves and the banks iso-profit curves, we can thus specify the set of contracts designed by banks and chosen by entrepreneurs (Section 2.4). The introduction of the assumption that firm realized profits have the MLRP with respect to quality completes the setting of the model and allows for the determination of the set of equilibria which can arise when either internal or external economies of scale prevail (sections 3.1 and 3.2). Our results are robust to the extension to the general case in which the technological parameter becomes a continuous variable (section 3.3). We then show that these results are actually more general than those reached by the previous literature on credit rationing by comparing the characteristics of our orderings of random variables with those of other models, and in particular with S-W and D-W (Sections 4.1, 4.2 and 4.3). In the final section we sum up the main results of the paper and we stress a number of problems which still remain unsolved.

2. THE SETTING OF THE MODEL

2.1. The firms

We consider a competitive market for a single homogeneous good and an arbitrarily large population of risk neutral entrepreneurs with a null individual wealth endowment, so that the production of each firm must be financed by outside sources, that is bank *loans*. Each firm has a production function $\pi=\pi(L,q,H,\theta)$, where p is firm's output in nominal terms, L is the amount of loan received and coincides with the amount of firm's production input in nominal terms[2], q is a *quality* parameter which is firm's private information, H is a technological parameter which is common knowledge, and q is a random shock which is i.i.d. across firms. Here we assume that entrepreneurs can only have two types of endowment of quality, either *low* or *high*, so that the *quality* parameter $q \in [q_l, q_h]$.[3] The relative frequency of the two different quality types is such that $\text{PROB}(q = q_h) = p$, and $\text{PROB}(q = q_l) = 1 - p$, and it is common knowledge.

As M-R have shown, when the size of the loan is allowed to vary, differences in the level of output can be due both to differences in quality and to differences in the amount of loan received. Depending on the relation between quality, loan size and output, a larger amount of loan demanded does not necessarily indicate better quality: the amount of 'working capital' used can be either increasing or decreasing in quality, so that firms of better quality will be willing to accept either larger or smaller changes in loans than those accepted by firms of lower quality, for given changes in the interest rate. In this paper we aim to generalize M-R's approach by couching their two different (and unrelated) cases based on different production functions within a unitary analytical framework. This can be achieved by considering that the relation between loan size and quality ultimately depends on the technological parameter of the firm.

In order to clarify this point, let us refer to two ideal and opposite ways of organizing production activities: firm A&A is vertically integrated and organized in various departments so that its intermediate output flows into one or more final goods by passing through several internal production phases;

---

[2]   We could refer to a population of entrepreneurs with positive wealth endowments, so that L would become the amount of firm's input financed through external funds. Since no debt contracting with outside private investors is allowed in this model, following Leland and Pyle (1977), it can be shown that in such a case all entrepreneurs will invest all of their wealth in the firm before raising any fund from outside sources (see also De Meza and Webb, 1987, p.289, Innes', 1992, p. 1430). Hence, signalling through wealth (as well as through any other instrument, for example collaterals) would still be impossible, and the assumption of positive wealth would not affect our conclusions.

[3]   In the following we use 'firm quality' and 'entrepreneur quality' interchangeably: each firm is owned by only one entrepreneur.

firm B&B is specialized in a particular activity which is not suitable to be organized in mass production. According to the neo-institutionalist parlance (for example Coase, 1937, Grossman and Hart, 1986), the organization of firm A&A is substituting entrepreneurial co-ordination and hierarchical relations for market exchanges, whereas the organization of firm B&B gives large room to market exchanges. The rationale for these different institutional settings is that -for every given loan size- firm A&A has *large internal economies of scale, high transaction* (or bargaining) *costs*, and *small organizational* (or influence) *costs* whereas firm B&B has *large external economies of scale, high organizational* (or influence) *costs,* and *small transaction* (or bargaining) *costs.*[4]

On the basis of the above example we can define *technological/ organizational* parameter, H, which we assume for the moment as taking on two values: either I, meaning that internal economies of scale and/or transaction costs are prevailing, or E, meaning that external economies of scale and/or organizational costs are prevailing. Obviously, there can be many different technological 'settings', each with a varying degree of *internalization* or *externalization* of economies of scale. In any case, by parametrizing the relations between loan size and firm quality, we can unambiguously state that, given the banks' supply function, when $H=I$, output and quality will be positively related, so that high-quality entrepreneurs will be willing to choose larger loans than low-quality entrepreneurs; whereas, when $H=E$, output and quality will be unrelated, so that high-quality entrepreneurs will be willing to choose relatively smaller loans to low-quality entrepreneurs due to their lower default probabilities. Thus, *in the case of $H=I$, larger loans will signal higher firm quality*, while *in the case of $H=E$, larger loans will signal lower firm quality*. This implies that the non-random component of the relation between the amount of 'working capital' L (the loan of size L) and the firm output, π, is not unique, depending on two parameters: the *technological* parameter, H, and the *quality* parameter, q. Since we assume that firms' technological and organizational setting is publicly observable, banks face two separate groups of applicants and are able to elicit either separating or pooling equilibria between low and high-quality firms within each of these two groups.

The end-of-period return for each firm, π, that is nominal output 'sold in the market', has a stochastic component due to the random shock θ (for

---

[4]   It must be noted that it should not be terribly controversial to assume that the characteristics of each firm that we define as 'technological' or 'organizational' can be *observable* by outside lenders, in the sense that they may be gathered from the known 'identity card' of the borrowers (industrial sector, market structure, firm size, number of employees, internal organization, and so forth) which is obviously common knowledge. In fact, we may think of the *technological setting* as, for instance, the degree of vertical integration, the size of the firm (in terms of plants and machinery), the number of people employed, and so on: something which is, in any case, publicly observable.

example a demand shock) which has a positive support on $[0, \theta]$. Hence, given L, q and H, θ gives rise to the probability density and distribution functions for π, $f(\pi \mid L,q,H)$ and $F(\pi \mid L,q,H)$, respectively. The function $f(\cdot)$ is assumed to be continuously differentiable on $[0,K(L,q,H)]$, where $K(\cdot) > 0$ whenever $L > 0$. In addition, we assume that larger loan sizes produce 'better' net worth distributions in the sense of first-order stochastic dominance:

ASSUMPTION.[5] For all $\pi \in [0, K(L,q,H)]$:

(A1) $F_L(\pi) \leq 0.$

Defining the firm expected return, which is indexed by *quality* and *technology*, as:

$$\bar{\pi}(L \mid q,H) \equiv \int_0^{K(L,q,H)} \pi f(\pi(L \mid q,H))\, d\pi \tag{1}$$

then condition (A1) implies that $\bar{\pi}_L(L \mid q,H) > 0$. We will also assume that $\bar{\pi}_{LL} < 0$, $\bar{\pi}_L(L \mid q,H) = \infty$ as $L \to 0$ and $\bar{\pi}_L(L \mid q,H) = 0$ as $L \to \infty$. The latter constraints ensure positive and finite equilibrium loan sizes for any quality and technology type.

2.2.   The banks

Banks are assumed to be competitive and risk neutral. On each loan, banks require an expected unit return of at least $(1+\rho)$, where ρ is the return on a risk-free bond,[6] that is, banks only offer those contracts which are expected to earn them a non-negative mean profit. This return is obtained by ex-post firm payments that satisfy limited liability and which depend on the observable π, as specified in the financial contract defined below. Perfect competition in the loan market ensures that each bank satisfies a zero-profit condition.

2.3.   The debt contract and the definition of equilibrium

The financial contract signed by the entrepreneur with the bank prescribes the size of the loan, L, and the amount of money which the bank is to be paid at the

---

[5]   Subscripts denote partial derivatives.
[6]   We simply assume that banks pay depositors the 'safe' rate of interest ρ.

end of the period. Despite the fact that each bank would be willing to sign different contracts with different applicants, that is different quality types, it does not know on an *ex-ante* basis 'who is who' as information about firms quality is asymmetric. Moreover, banks cannot observe *ex-post* the 'state of nature', θ, nor the firm's quality q; they can only observe the firm's return, π, at no cost of monitoring. Thus, in our model, the financial contract will set, beside L and independently of the optimality of its form, the bank's payoff $B(\pi)$, that is the amount to be paid back by the firm; in other words, it will be a *debt contract* contingent on the firm's technology and return. It must be noted that the bank's payoff $B(\pi)$ is constrained by π since limited liability implies that $B(\pi) \leq \pi$, that is, the firms cannot be compelled to pay more than the available return.[7]

It has already been shown (Innes, 1993) that, with a fixed and homogeneous loan size across firms, a Nash equilibrium exists. A set of debt contracts is a Nash equilibrium if all contracts in the set earn banks an expected unit return of at least $(1+\rho)$, and there is no other set of contracts that, when offered in addition to the equilibrium set, earn banks an expected unit return greater than $(1+\rho)$. In that case, each quality-type class of borrowers subscribes a single *pooling* contract which leads to a *pooling* equilibrium. Normally (for example S-W 1981) it is exogenously assumed that this contract takes a *standard* debt form, namely, $B(\pi) = \min(\pi,z)$, with z representing the *fixed and predetermined loan payment*. The problem is that, when the size of the loan is allowed to vary and thereby to serve as a screening device, a Nash equilibrium will often fail to exist (as in Rothschild and Stiglitz, 1976). Thus, a number of studies have suggested alternative concepts of equilibrium, including Miyazaki (1977), Wilson (1977), and Riley (1979). At first, these concepts have been justified by assumptions on an uninformed agent's (that is a bank's) expectations about the plausible responses of the competitors (that is competing banks) to his actions. More recently, they have obtained game-theoretic foundations by Hellwig (1987) and Cho and Kreps (1987).

Following the latter approach (see also De Meza and Webb, 1989 and Innes, 1991) we define a three-stage pure strategy game between banks and entrepreneurs, as this game structure has at least one Nash equilibrium overall (Kreps and Wilson, 1982). The extensive form of the game could be as follows:
Stage 1. The uninformed lenders (banks) move first and propose a menu of contracts. A contract specifies the repayment schedule and the size of the loan.
Stage 2. Each borrower chooses a contract within the offered menu.

---

[7] For analytical purposes, some weak restrictions are placed on the forms which this function can take: $B(\pi)$ must be differentiable from the right, with positive first derivative for all $\pi > 0$. Also, we assume $B(\pi)$ is monotonically nondecreasing, like De Meza and Webb (1987) (see below, equation (2b)).

Stage 3. After observing the application choices, lenders decide whether to accept or reject each application, and either sign or withdraw contracts.

Such a game structure can have many 'sequential' Nash equilibria. A *variable loan size equilibrium* is defined by the set of contracts $\{B(\pi \mid q,H), L(q,H)\}$ that maximizes the utility of the higher quality entrepreneur subject to three constraints:

(E1) *Incentive compatibility*: lower-quality entrepreneurs weakly prefer their own contract to any of the contracts designed for higher-quality.

(E2) *Low-quality rationality*: lower-quality entrepreneurs expected profit is at least as high as on a perfect-information contract, that is, for this quality-type of borrowers the perfect-information contract is the 'benchmark' which earns lenders zero expected profits.

(E3) *Non-negativity of lenders profits*: lenders earn an expected unit return of at least $(1+\rho)$ on each distinct contract.

The latter constraint characterizes a Wilson allocation.[8] Given the game structure posited above, the resulting equilibrium is thus a *Wilson equilibrium*. This is not the only possible outcome. M-R refer, for instance, to a *reactive Riley equilibrium*. The main difference between these two alternative concepts of equilibrium is that Riley's equilibrium elicits complete separation, whereby all agents reveal their type by their contract choice, whereas Wilson's equilibrium admits pooling contracts that are shared by different quality-type borrowers, even when separating allocations are possible. Thus, a Wilson allocation can flow into either separating or pooling equilibria, and Wilson's and Riley's equilibria diverge only when the Wilson allocation is pooling. It is important to stress that, in the latter case, the Wilson allocation Pareto dominates the Riley equilibrium. This means that the reference to Riley's concept of equilibrium eliminates, by construction, the most favourable cases of credit rationing.[9] Hence, as we are mainly interested in analysing the possibilities of credit rationing, the Wilson construction seems more promising.[10]

As shown by Innes (1993), under asymmetric information the optimal form of any variable loan size contract is the standard debt form, provided the

---

[8]   If (E3) were replaced with the assumption that banks earn an expected unit return of at least $(1+\rho)$ on *all contracts taken together*, that would be a Miyazaki allocation, while if (E3) was replaced with the assumption that banks earn an expected return of at least $(1+\rho)$ on *each entrepreneur*, that would be a Riley allocation (see also note below). This means that a Riley allocation requires the informed borrowers move first, that is at Stage 1 of the game.

[9]   Several authors (for example Bester (1987)) maintain that separating equilibria eliminate the possibility of credit rationing. However, Besanko and Thakor (1987) have built a model with separating equilibria and credit rationing.

[10] We maintain that the weak rationing results obtained by M-R largely depend on their arbitrary choice of a Riley allocation. Wilson's allocation has been criticized because it implies passive reactions by competing agents. However, the game-theoretic foundation of this allocation is able to weaken this problem.

lender's payoff is monotonic.[11] Thus, even for the Wilson equilibrium, the bank's payoff function must be here compatible with the *standard* debt form, namely $B(\pi) = \min(\pi, z)$, with $z=z(q,H)$ representing the *promised loan payment*, which depends on the unobservable quality parameter, q, and on the observable technology parameter, H. In essence, given H, debt contracts maximize banks' payoffs with respect to low-quality profit distributions: since high-quality entrepreneurs, by signing a debt contract, can minimize the low-quality type incentive to 'masquerade', a contract can be completely described by the pair (z, L).

2.4. Choices of the loan size

Given H, the quality q entrepreneur's choice problem can be formally written as:

$$\frac{\max}{L} V(L|q,H) = E\{\pi - B(\pi)|q,H\} \tag{2}$$

$$s.t. = E\{B(\pi)|q,H\} \geq (1+\rho)L \tag{2a}$$

$$B(\pi) \leq \pi, \ B_\pi(\pi) \geq \forall \pi \in [0, K(L,q,H) \tag{2b}$$

where V is the expected profit of the quality-q entrepreneur of a firm H for a loan of size L. Condition (2a) gives the minimum bank return requirement, while (2b) gives the limited liability and monotonicity constraints on the contract firm. The entrepreneur's limited liability, together with the possibility of zero-output levels, make any contract with payments that are invariant to the firm's returns (including the fixed-payment contract), unfeasible.[12] Thus, in (2), $B(\pi) = \min(\pi, z)$.

The expected profit V of the quality-q entrepreneur of a firm H for a loan of size L is thus given by:

$$(L,q,H) = E\big(\max[\pi(L,q,H) - z(q,H), 0]\big) \tag{3}$$

Equation (3) implies that, if the firm is 'successful', then $V(\cdot)$ is equal to the positive difference between the firm return π and the promised loan payment z, whereas, if the firm is 'unsuccessful', and then $\pi < z$, $V(\cdot)$ is 0. Since the

[11] Recall also that Innes (1990) specifies under which conditions the optimal form of any fixed loan size contract is the standard debt form.
[12] In the absence of the limited liability constraint, the solution to (2) would be the fixed-payment debt contract, $B(\cdot)=(1+\rho)L$, that yields 'perfect information' choices of L (Shavell, 1979), for given q and H.

entrepreneur is risk-neutral, he maximizes $V(L\,|\,q,H)$ in (2). Hence, given (1), (2) can be rewritten as:

$$\max_L V(L,q,H) = \int_{\pi_0}^{K(L,q,H)} [\pi(L,q,H) - z(q,H)]f(\pi L,q,h)d\pi \qquad (4)$$

where π_0 satisfies:

$$\pi_0 - z\,(q,H) = 0 \qquad (5)$$

Basically, $V(\cdot)$ is the profit of a firm when successful times the probability of a 'success'.[13] The probability of a 'success' is given by the integral of the density function of π for $\pi \in [\pi_0, K(L,q,H)]$.[14] In order to solve equation (4), it is necessary to specify condition (2a) above, that is bank expected profits. Bank expected profits are defined as:

$$R(L,z|q,H) = E[\min(\pi,z)|L,q,H] - (1+\rho)L, \qquad (6)$$

that is, as:

$$R(L,z|q,H) = z(q,H) - (1+\rho)L + \int_0^{\pi_0} [\pi(L,q,H) - z(q,H)]f(\pi|L,q,H)d\pi \qquad (7)$$

Substituting (7) for (2a) and (4) for (2), we can formally solve the choice problem of the entrepreneur of quality q. The easiest way to handle this problem is to refer to entrepreneurs' *indifference* curves and banks' *supply* curves.

An entrepreneur's *indifference curve* is a set of (z, L) contracts yielding a common expected profit level.[15] Since entrepreneurs are always better off

---

[13]   Thus, $z(q\,|\,\pi \geq \pi_0) > (1+\rho)L > \pi(q\,|\,\pi \leq \pi_0)$. De Meza and Webb (1987) define R^s as the return of a successful project and R^f as the return of an unsuccessful project. They thus assume that $R^s > (1+\rho)L > R^f$.

[14]   As we have seen above, the density function of π, given L, q and H, depends on θ, which is i.i.d. across firms. Hence (4) could also be written as:

$$\underset{(L)}{Max}\, V(L|q,H) = \int_{\theta_0}^{K(L,q,H)} [\pi(L,q,H,\theta) - z(q,H)]f(\theta)L,q,H)d\theta,$$

where θ_0 is such that:

$$\pi(L,\,q,\,H,\,\theta_0) = z(q,\,H).$$

[15]   Since we assumed that both banks and entrepreneurs are risk neutral, we can obviously refer to 'indifference' or 'iso-profit' curves. Indifference curves (a more general concept) imply that the set of contracts must yield a common expected utility level.

with a lower promised payment, z, given the loan size, L, lower indifference curves correspond to higher expected profit levels for firms. Formally, entrepreneurs' indifference curves are defined as:

$$(L,z|q,H) = \int_{z}^{K(L,q,H)} [\pi(L,q,H) - z(q,H)]f(\pi|L,q,H)d\pi = \overline{V}(q,H), \tag{8}$$

a constant. Regardless of firm quality, indifference curves are *upward sloping*, as:

$$\frac{\partial V(L,z|q,H)}{\partial L} \equiv - \int_{z}^{K(L,q,H)} F_L(\pi|L,q,H,)d\pi > 0, \tag{9a}$$

$$\frac{\partial V(L,z|q,H)}{\partial L} \equiv -(1 - F(\pi|L,q,H)) > 0. \tag{9b}$$

Intuitively, larger loan sizes, given z, increase an entrepreneur's expected profit. Hence, to preserve the latter profit, an increase in L must be accompanied by an increase in the debt obligation, z. Because entrepreneurs 'like' any increase in L, and 'dislike' any increase in payments to banks, z, indifference curves are upward-sloping (and lower curves correspond to higher firm profits).[16]

Banks' isoprofit curves are defined as the locus where banks expected profits, $R(L,z \mid q,H)$, are constant, that is:

$$R(L,z|q,H) = E[\min(\pi,z)|L,q,H] - (1+\rho)L = \overline{R}(L,z|q,H). \tag{10}$$

Banks' isoprofit curves are *upward sloping* and *convex*, with slope greater than $(1+\rho)$. The reason is that, given the increasing default risk of bank loans, when a bank commits an additional dollar of funds to loans, the increase in the promised loan payment z must be increasingly greater than $(1+\rho)$ dollars in order to satisfy the non-negative condition of the bank expected profit.[17] Thanks to perfect competition in the loan market, we can limit our attention to banks iso-profit curves from loans to quality-q entrepreneurs, which imply:

$$\overline{R}(L,z|q,H) = 0 \tag{11}$$

---

[16] Notice also that the second derivative with respect to L is negative, implying that indifference curves are concave.

[17] The increase in the promised loan payment, z, needed to satisfy the bank's expected zero-profit condition, will be higher the lower the quality of the applicant entrepreneur, because of the latter higher default risk. Hence, banks' iso-profit curves are not only upward sloping and convex, but their slope is decreasing with quality.

The latter iso-profit curves will coincide with banks' *supply* curves.

Whenever a bank is able to offer different contracts to borrowers of different quality, *separating* supply curves prevail, whereas if a bank cannot discriminate between borrowers of different quality, a *pooling* supply curve obtains.

Banks' *separating* supply curves are defined as the locus where:

$$E[\min(\pi, z)|L, q, H] = (1+\rho)L, \tag{12}$$

that is, making use of (7):

$$z(q, H) - (1+\rho)L + \int_0^z (\pi - z)f(\pi|L, q, H)d\pi = 0 \tag{13}$$

Using equations (1) and (8) we can rewrite this expression as:

$$\bar{\pi}(L|q, H) - V(L|q, H) - (1+\rho)L = 0. \tag{14}$$

or:

$$\bar{\pi}(L|q_l, H) - V(L|q_l, H) = (1+\rho)L, \tag{15a}$$

$$\bar{\pi}(L|q_h, H) - V(L|q_h, H) = (1+\rho)L. \tag{15b}$$

Only by having a different supply curve for each quality type we can have firm signaling (self-selection).

Similarly, banks' *pooling* supply curves are such that:

$$\{E[\min(\pi, z)|L, H, q_l] - (1+\rho)L\}(1-p) + \{E[\min(\pi, z)|L, H, q_h] - (1+\rho)L\}p = 0 \tag{16}$$

that is

$$\begin{bmatrix} z(q_l, H) - (1+\rho)L + \int_0^z (\pi - z)f(L, q_l, H)d\pi \end{bmatrix}(1-p)$$
$$+ \begin{bmatrix} z(q_h, H) - (1+\rho)L + \int_0^z (\pi - z)f(\pi|L, q_h, H)d\pi \end{bmatrix}p = 0 \tag{17}$$

Using equations (15a,b) we can rewrite this as:

$$[\bar{\pi}(L, q_l, H) - V(L|q_l, H)](1-p) + [\bar{\pi}(L|q_h, H) - V(L|q_h, H)]p = (1+\rho)L. \tag{18}$$

This implies that the bank set of contracts offered will lie somewhere between the separating supply curve to the low-quality types and that to the high-quality ones. In other words, a bank pooling supply curve is the supply curve to the 'average' quality-q entrepreneur, given H.

Each entrepreneur will solve his optimal choice problem by signing the debt contract which coincides with the tangency point between the bank supply curve and his lowest iso-profit curve.

3. EQUILIBRIUM OUTCOMES

As M-R have shown, when the size of the loan is allowed to vary, the entrepreneur's choice of the contract becomes crucial.[18] A bank offers an entrepreneur a menu of contracts, each specifying both the loan size and the repayment schedule, with the aim of financing a *specific firm* whose *specific return* will be due to the combination of the size of the loan actually obtained by this firm, its stochastic return, its 'technological setting' and its quality-type. Since in general there is a relation between the loan size obtained and the return expected by the firm, the entrepreneur's contract choice could signal his quality which is not directly observable by the lender because of the ex-ante asymmetry of information. The limits to this signalling derive from the fact that, as shown above, the relation between loan size and firm marginal returns is specific to the firm, in the sense that it can be either increasing or non-increasing in the quality parameter. This implies that the relation between firm's quality and its loan size can be either a positive or a negative one. If marginal returns are increasing in quality, the quality and size of the loan will be *positively related*; and, since the bank knows this relation (by observing that $H=I$), 'better' firms can signal their higher quality by agreeing on a higher loan interest rate, thus signing contracts based on loans of larger size. On the other hand, if firm marginal returns are non-increasing in quality, quality and size of the loan will be *negatively related*; and, since the bank knows this relation (by observing that $H=E$), 'worse' firms agree on a higher loan interest rate, thus signing contracts based on loans of larger size (see also Innes, 1991, p. 359).

This means that, from the lender's perspective, ordering loan applicants on the basis of their expected marginal returns would not be sufficient to discriminate between borrowers of different quality.[19] The assumption that the

---

[18] It must be recalled that we are abstracting from moral-hazard problems and referring to adverse-selection problems only.

[19] This would also apply to models with loans of fixed size across firms. In the S-W model, the various projects are classified within groups of observationally equal riskiness, that is, by the equality of their expected returns. However, the subset of projects with greater mean return is not necessarily the less (or the more) risky one. The same holds true for the D-W model: a higher 'successful' return is not univocally related to a higher (or a lower) p.

technological parameter of each firms is common knowledge allows the bank to exploit the borrowers' signaling through their choice of the loan size. Therefore, when receiving applications for the menu of loans offered, the bank finds it convenient to screen first the borrowers off according to their observable 'technology'. The bank will initially group all applicant firms according to their observable value of H (either $H=I$ or $H=E$). Once firms have been split into these two groups, we will see that either separating or pooling equilibria (between low and high quality firms within each group) will obtain, depending on the relative slope of the indifference curves of the firms.

An *optimal* equilibrium contract obtains whenever the indifference curve of a given quality-q firm and the bank's supply curve to that quality-q type are tangent at:

$$\frac{\partial V(L,z,H)}{\partial L} = \frac{\partial \bar{\pi}(L|q,H))}{\partial L} - (1-\rho), \tag{19}$$

given H.

For given values of (z, L), these are the points where expected profits of a quality-q entrepreneur are maximized, subject to the non-negativity of bank's expected profits from loans to that entrepreneur, given H. Such equilibrium contracts will be *first-best* (perfect information) contracts if they satisfy the feasibility constraints of a Wilson equilibrium, as defined above (see (E1), (E2) and (E3)). We have thus the following proposition:

PROPOSITION 1. In a world of asymmetric information, only a *separating equilibrium* can be a *first-best* equilibrium.

It must be noticed that, if an optimal separating equilibrium cannot obtain, a sub-optimal separating equilibrium can still obtain, where the high quality firms elicit a 'second-best' contract which implies a loan size either higher (when $H=I$) or lower (when $H=E$) than the optimal one. Conversely, a pooling equilibrium attains.

3.1. Internal economies of scale prevailing: $H = I$.

Consider first the case of $H=I$. Given the feature of this 'technological' parameter, we have that marginal project returns are higher the higher the quality of the firms. Moreover, we can exploit a suitable assumption of monotonicity of the loan size with respect to quality by comparing signals in terms of relative favourableness, using the so-called *monotone likelihood ratio property* (MLRP) (Milgrom, 1981).

The MLRP states that, if a signal x is *more favourable than* another signal y about a random parameter Φ, and if Φ takes on two particular values ϕ_1 and

ϕ_2, with $\phi_1 > \phi_2$, then

$$f(\chi|\phi_1)f(y|\phi_2) > f(\chi|\phi_2)f(y|\phi_1)$$

As shown by Milgrom, this is a necessary and sufficient condition for x to be more favourable than y both in the sense of first-order and second-order stochastic dominance, for every increasing concave function $U(\Phi)$ and nondegenerate prior distributions $G_1(\Phi)$ and $G_2(\Phi)$.[20]

Therefore, in the case of $H = I$ we can assume that higher quality produces 'better' net worth distributions in the sense of statistical 'good news' (Milgrom, 1981):

ASSUMPTION. For all $\pi \in [0, K(L,q,H)]$, if $H = I$, then:

$$\frac{\partial}{\partial \pi}\left(\frac{f_q(\pi|L,q,H)}{f(\pi|L,q,H)} \right) > 0 \qquad (A2)$$

This assumption implies that the posterior distribution $G(\Phi|\pi_1)$ dominates the posterior distribution $G(\Phi|\pi_2)$ both in the sense of FOSD and in the sense of SOSD, and that any signal U_1 is *more favourable than* U_2 in either senses. Given a stochastic environment which yields uncertain returns, the rationale for assuming a MLRP with respect to quality for firms profit densities is that of exploiting the monotonicity property implied by assumption (A1), so that higher loans will give rise to higher returns.

Given (A1), condition (A2) implies that:

$$F_{Lq}(\pi) < 0, \qquad (20)$$

where the negative cross-partial derivative shows that higher quality yields first order stochastically dominant returns from marginal loans, that is, higher quality is associated with 'better' *marginal* returns.[21] Then:

$$\frac{\partial}{\partial q}\left(\frac{\partial \pi(L,q,H)}{\partial L} \right) > 0. \qquad (21)$$

This implies that the marginal rate of substitution between L and z is greater, and the steeper the indifference curve, the higher the entrepreneurs' quality. That is, in each and every point in the space (z, L) where the high- and the low-quality indifference curves cross, the former are steeper than the latter ones,

---

[20] In Milgrom's words, 'a signal x is *more favourable than* another signal y if for every nondegenerate prior distribution G for f, the posterior distribution G($\cdot$|x) dominates the posterior distribution G($\cdot$|y) in the sense of strict FOSD' (1981, p.382).

[21] Notice that our results partially coincide with those obtained by M-R in the case where the firm production function has a multiplicative form (with respect to the quality parameter).

that is $\text{MRS}(z,L|q_h) > \text{MRS}(z,L|q_l)$. It must also be noted that the increase in the promised loan payment, z, needed to satisfy the bank's expected zero-profit condition, will be higher the lower the quality of the entrepreneur, because of the latter higher default risk. Hence, banks isoprofit curves are upward sloping, with slope decreasing with quality. Formally, (20), (9a), and (9b) together imply:

$$\frac{\partial \, dz}{\partial q \, dL}\bigg|_{\overline{V}} \frac{\partial}{\partial q} \left(\frac{\dfrac{\partial V(L,z|q,H)}{\partial L}}{\dfrac{\partial V(L,z|q,H)}{\partial z}} \right) > 0 \tag{22}$$

Similarly to M-R, we can restate this by saying that the marginal increase in promised loan payment that a borrower is willing to accept in order to receive a marginal increase in the loan size is greater the higher firm quality.

Suppose that two entrepreneurs, a low-quality and a high-quality one, choose the two different contracts $\{zO_{(l},{}^{*}), LO_{(l},{}^{*})\}$ and $\{zO_{(h},{}^{*}), LO_{(h},{}^{*})\}$, respectively (see Figure 4.1, points A and C). The conditions for the two contracts to be a *separating* equilibrium are that:

(i) each lies on a bank's separating supply curve (S^q (I); $q=l, h$);

(ii) the low-quality contract is weakly preferred by the low-quality entrepreneur.

Condition (i) is necessary but not sufficient to have a separating equilibrium. For instance, the contract $\{zO_{(h},{}^{*}), LO_{(h},{}^{*})\}$ chosen by the high-quality entrepreneur (C in Figures 4.1, 4.2, and 4.3) can lie below the low-quality indifference curve which yields the low-quality preferred contract $\{zO_{(l},{}^{*}), LO_{(l},{}^{*})\}$ (A in Figures 4.1, 4.2, and 4.3). If this was the case, as in Figures 4.2 and 4.3, condition (ii) would not be satisfied for this contract. Thus, the entrepreneurs' optimal choice elicits *a first-best* equilibrium (a *separating equilibrium* with firm signaling) only if the high-quality *optimal* contracts lie *on* the high-quality preferred indifference curve, $V^{*}(q_h, H=I)$ (the one that is tangent to the supply curve to the high-quality types) and *above* the low-quality preferred indifference curve, $V^{*}(q_l, H=I)$. In Figure 4.1 we see that a separating optimal equilibrium (contracts A and C) obtains since the indifference curves are such that the high-quality firm chooses contract C from the offered menu of contracts without having the low-quality firm choose the same contract.[22]

The converse of Proposition 1 is not true, however, in the sense that we can have separating equilibria which are not 'first-best' (see Figure 4.2).

---

[22] This happens exactly as the tangency point between the high-quality preferred indifference curve $V^{*}(q_h, I)$ and the supply curve to the high-quality type, point C, lies above the intersection point between the low-quality preferred indifference curve $V^{*}(q_l, I)$ and the supply curve to the high-quality type (point B).

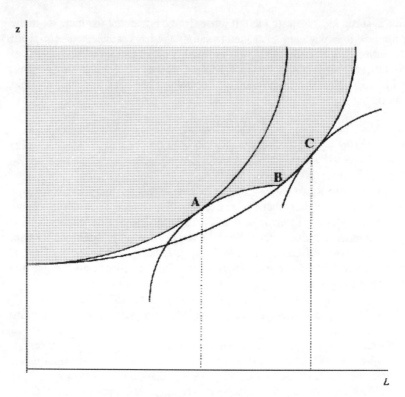

Figure 4.1 Optimal separating equilibrium (H=I)

Suppose that the high-quality preferred contract lies below the intersection between the low-quality preferred indifference curve and the bank supply curve to the high-quality types, thus attracting low-quality entrepreneurs, so that an optimal equilibrium is not feasible. The consequent equilibrium will be separating if the high-quality indifference curve $V^p(q_h, I)$, that is tangent to the bank pooling supply curve,[23] crosses the bank supply curve to the high-quality types, at a point (D) higher than the intersection between the low-quality preferred indifference curve, $V^*(q_b, I)$, and the bank supply curve to the high-quality type (point B). Since the latter point of intersection (point B) will be the contract chosen by the high-quality types, it allows for their signaling and avoids the possibility of a bank's negative expected profits on loans to low-quality entrepreneurs. Thus, low-quality entrepreneurs will choose their 'first-best' contract $\{zO(_l, ^*), LO(_l, ^*)\}$, point A, whereas high-quality entrepreneurs

---

[23] Recall that, since a borrower can be low-quality with probability $(1-p)$ and high-quality with probability p, the pooling supply curve is determined by equation (17) above.

158

will choose their 'second-best' contract (z_B, L_B), point B. The resulting equilibrium will be a *suboptimal separating equilibrium*. Notice that under this contract, high-quality firms get a loan *larger* than what they would have like to: thus, when a suboptimal separating equilibrium attains, we have *over-financing* of high-quality firms.

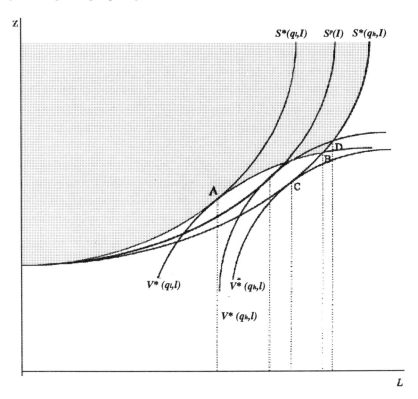

Figure 4.2 - Sub-optimal separating equilibrium (H=I)

Our conclusion shows that we can have separating equilibria that are *suboptimal* (that is 'second-best') since they allow costly signaling of the high-quality firms. With a given contract menu offer, whether we get an optimal or a suboptimal separating equilibrium depends on the slope of the indifference curves of the different types of borrowers. Given that the low-quality firms choose their first-best contract (points A in Figures 4.1, 4.2, and 4.3), all depends on the shape and the curvature of the indifference curves of the high-quality types as opposed to the low-quality preferred indifference curve. Notice that the $V(q_{lo}, I)$ curves are less steep in Figure 4.2 than in Figure 4.1: the slope of $V^*(q_h,I)$ in C is smaller in Figure 4.2 than in Figure 4.1[24]. In other words, since with $H=I$, for any given z or L, $\mathrm{MRS}(z,L|q_h) > \mathrm{MRS}(z,L|q_l)$, the closer $\mathrm{MRS}(z,L|q_h)$ is to $\mathrm{MRS}(z,L|q_l)$ the more unlikely it becomes for an optimal separating equilibrium to obtain.

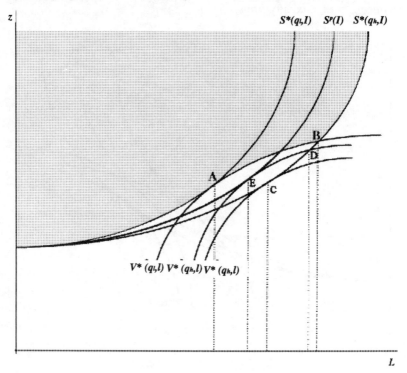

Figure 4.3 - Pooling equilibrium (H=I)

The closeness of $\mathrm{MRS}(z,L|q_h)$ to $\mathrm{MRS}(z,L|q_l)$ can imply that, while condition (i) above is satisfied, condition (ii) is not. In this case no separating equilibrium obtains, either optimal or suboptimal. To see this, consider the contract pair $\{z_E,L_E\}$ determined by the tangency point between bank's pooling supply curve, and the high-quality indifference curve, $V^p(q_h,I)$ (point E, Figure 4.3). The breaking down of condition (ii) above implies that this latter indifference curve would cross on the right the bank supply curve to the high-quality types, at a point (D) lower than the intersection between the low-quality preferred

---

[24] If the $V(q_h,I)$ curves are such as those in Figure 4.2, then the high-quality types can elicit their first best choice, C (it lies above $V^*(q_l,I)$). Conversely, if the $V(q_h,I)$'s are such as those in Figure 4.3, then the high-quality types cannot elicit their first best choice, C (it lies below $V^*(q_l,I)$ and it would attract the low-quality, too).

indifference curve, $V^*(q_h, I)$, and bank supply curve to the high-quality type (point B). In this case, the high-quality first-best contract $\{zO_{(h}{}^*), LO_{(h}{}^*)\}$ (point C) would be clearly unfeasible, as it would attract low-quality entrepreneurs, whereas the $\{z_B, L_B\}$ contract (point B) would not be chosen by high-quality entrepreneurs with respect to $\{z_E, L_E\}$ or $\{z_D, L_D\}$. On the other hand, low-quality entrepreneurs would prefer a contract like point E to that in point A (it lies on a lower indifference curve). Hence, since high-quality entrepreneurs would be indifferent between point D and point E and low-quality entrepreneurs would prefer point E to point A, both quality-types of entrepreneurs would choose the $\{z_E, L_E\}$ *pooling* contract (point E, Figure 3).

Intuitively, a pooling equilibrium occurs when not only indifference curves of high and low quality types are similar but also bank's separating supply curves are far apart.[25] Banks' separating supply curves are far apart whenever there are large differences in default risks between different quality-type firms, whereas indifference curves of different types are similar whenever the differences in marginal firm returns are small and offset differential default risks to produce similar tradeoffs between L and z. In these conditions, while the bank is not able to exploit the differences in the shapes of entrepreneurs' indifference maps, the high-quality firms find it too costly to signal their type, so that a pooling equilibrium emerges. Now, when a pooling equilibrium attains, we have that low-quality firms will obtain loan amounts *larger* than their first-best levels, while high-quality firms will obtain loan amounts *smaller* than their first-best level (see Figure 4.3). In other words, the 'better' firms subsidize the 'worse' ones: high-quality firms are under-financed, in the sense that they get less than what they would like to.

Can we say that this under-financing is equivalent to *type I credit rationing* of high-quality firms? Independently of the specific case analysed, it is possible to distinguish between credit rationing *strictu senso* and under-financing. We say that under-financing and type I credit rationing coincide whenever an entrepreneur obtains an amount of loan smaller than the amount desired, even if he is willing to sign a debt contract with the bank prescribing a larger loan amount; and we say that under-financing does not imply type I credit rationing whenever an entrepreneur obtains an amount of loan smaller than the amount desired, but he is not willing to sign alternative debt contracts prescribing a larger loan amount.[26] It follows from these two definitions that,

---

[25] In the extreme case, we can have a pooling equilibrium where indifference curves are strictly convex functions of z as q changes ($\mathrm{MRS}(z, L|q_h) = \mathrm{MRS}(z, L|q_l)$). In such case, both the cross-partial derivative in equation (20) and the derivative in equation (21) would be zero. However, indifference curves need not be strictly convex in z (different quality types may have indifference curves that intersect somewhere). Moreover both (20) and (21) can keep holding and yet we can have a pooling equilibrium.

[26] It can be given several justifications to this behavior: maybe our entrepreneur considers the alternative debt contracts either too costly or Pareto dominated by the under-financing

in the case analysed above, we have under-financing *but not* credit rationing of high-quality firms, for the latter choose to sign an under-financing contract (point E, Figure 4.3) in order to avoid the cost of signalling their quality-type to the lending bank (point B, Figure 4.3).

It must be noticed that while a Riley construction of the game structure would lead to the same results as the Wilson construction we have adopted here in the cases where separating equilibria occur, it would not do so when a Wilson construction leads to a pooling equilibrium. In the Riley construction, firms move first so that a pooling contract is not viable, as there is no pooling supply curve offered by banks. While assumptions (A1) and (A2) keep holding, the incentive compatibility constraint and the low-quality rationality constraint ensure that in Figures 4.1, 4.2, and 4.3, either the two contracts A and C will attain a separating optimal equilibrium, or the two contracts A and B will attain a separating sub-optimal equilibrium. In a Riley construction, in fact, no indifference curve crossing $S^h(I)$ at D can be preferred by the high-quality entrepreneur, it not being tangent to any supply curve (as there is no pooling supply curve in this case). In other words, contract D would never be proposed in the first place, and hence would never be chosen, even if indifference curves were such as those in Figure 4.3. In this latter case, as in the case of Figure 4.2, low-quality firms get their first-best loan size (which is less than the 'pooling level') and high-quality firms get more than their first-best (and obviously more than the 'pooling level').

This stresses that the sequence of moves in the structure of the contracting game is very important since, before an equilibrium is reached, all the feasibility constraints must be satisfied. Thus, when the bank first starts by offering a contract menu, if some applicants choose A while others choose C, implying that indifference curves are like those in Figure 4.1, then an optimal separating equilibrium obtains (low-quality applicants choose their first-best contract A, while high-quality applicants choose their first-best contract C), as the bank will earn non-negative expected profits on both contracts. If some applicants choose A while others choose B, implying that indifference curves are like those in Figure 4.2, then a suboptimal separating equilibrium obtains (low-quality are better off, while high-quality applicants can signal their quality by being over-financed). Finally, suppose some applicants prefer C (most probably the high-quality ones) and this attracts all other applicants. Then the high-quality ones would shift to D, which is preferred to B. If that is the case, it means that indifference curves are as in Figure 4.3. Then the low-quality applicants would shift to E, and so would the high-quality who are

---

equilibrium. In any case, as it will become clearer below, under-financing, as opposed to type-I credit rationing, is characterized either by the firm's willingness to 'signal' its quality-type or by the firm's willingness to avoid the signalling cost. On the other hand, under-financing coincides with credit rationing in all the situations where the rationed firm has no alternative choices to overcome its quantity constraint.

indifferent between D and E. Hence, a pooling equilibrium would obtain. Firm signalling in such a case would be inconvenient for high-quality firms.

To conclude, we can state the following propositions.

PROPOSITION 2. When $H = I$, under conditions (A1) and (A2) the equilibrium set of separating contracts has the properties:

(i) the lowest-quality firm that is financed gets a *first-best* contract;
(ii) each contract breaks even for the bank;
(iii) the loan size for each contract $\{z_q, L_q\}$ is increasing in q: if $\{z_{q+1}, L_{q+1}\} > \{zO_{(q,}{}^*)_{+1}, LO_{(q,}{}^*)_{+1}\}$ (the first-best contract for the quality-$(q+1)$ entrepreneur), then we have a suboptimal separating contract, otherwise we have a first-best separating contract.

PROPOSITION 3. When $H = I$, under conditions (A1) and (A2), the equilibrium pooling contract has the properties:

(i) no single contract breaks even for the bank but the average contract does;
(ii) no firm that is financed gets a first-best contract: 'lower-than-average' quality firms are over-financed whereas 'higher-than-average' quality firms are under-financed.

3.2. External economies of scale prevailing: $H = E$.

Consider now the case of prevailing external economies of scale ($H=E$). Given the feature of this 'technological' parameter, we have that larger loans signal lower quality (better quality needs smaller loans). However, we can continue to exploit an assumption of monotonicity of the loan size with respect to quality by using the MLRP (see above). Therefore, in the case of $H = E$ we can assume that lower quality produces 'better' net worth distributions in the sense of statistical 'good news':

ASSUMPTION. For all $\pi \in [0, K(L,q,H)]$, if $H = E$, then:

$$\frac{\partial}{\partial \pi} \left(\frac{f_q(\pi | L,q,H)}{f(\pi | L,q,H)} \right) < 0 \tag{A3}$$

Given (A1), condition (A3) implies:

$$F_{Lq}(\pi) > 0, \tag{23}$$

where the positive cross-partial derivative now ensures that lower quality is associated with higher *marginal* project returns.[27] Then:

$$\frac{\partial}{\partial q}\left(\frac{\partial \pi(L|q,H)}{\partial L}\right) < 0. \tag{24}$$

This implies that the marginal rate of substitution between L and z is greater, and the steeper the indifference curve, the lower the entrepreneurs' quality. That is, in each and every point in the space (z, L) where low-quality and high-quality indifference curves cross, the former are steeper than the latter curves, that is $\text{MRS}(z,L|q_h) < \text{MRS}(z,L|q_l)$.[28] Formally, (23), (9a), and (9b) together imply:

$$\frac{\partial \, dz}{\partial q \, dL}\bigg|_{\overline{V}} = \frac{\partial}{\partial q}\left(\frac{\frac{\partial V(L,z|q,H)}{\partial L}}{\frac{\partial V(L,z|q,H)}{\partial z}}\right) < 0. \tag{25}$$

Similarly to M-R, we can restate this by saying that the marginal increase in promised loan payment that a borrower is willing to accept in order to receive a marginal increase in the loan size is greater the lower firm quality.

The equilibrium conditions in the case of $H = E$ mirror the conditions derived above for $H = I$. In particular, Proposition 1 still holds, in the sense that we will have a *separating* set of first-best equilibria if:
(i) each lies on a separating supply curve ($S^q(E); q=l, h$);
(ii) the low-quality contract is weakly preferred by the low-quality entrepreneur. Condition (i) is necessary but not sufficient to have an optimal separating equilibrium. It is also necessary that the high-quality optimal contract (point A, Figure 4.4) lies above the low-quality optimal indifference curve (point C, Figure 4.4). In this case, the entrepreneurs' optimal choice elicits a 'first-best' equilibrium. However, the high-quality contract $\{zO_{(h}{}^*), LO_{(h}{}^*)\}$, point A, can lie below the low-quality indifference curve which yields the low-quality preferred contract $\{zO_{(l}{}^*), LO_{(l}{}^*)\}$ (point C, Figure 4.5). In this case, condition (ii) would not be satisfied for this contract.

The latter possibility points out that, again, the converse of Proposition 1 is not true, in the sense that we can have separating equilibria which are not 'first best'. Suppose that the high-quality preferred contract (point A, Figure 4.5) attracts the low-quality firms, lying on a low-quality indifference curve which is below the low-quality preferred indifference curve, so that an optimal equilibrium would not be feasible. The consequent 'suboptimal' equilibrium will be separating if the high-quality indifference curve which is tangent to the

---

[27] Notice that our results partially coincide with those obtained by M-R in the case where the firm production function has an additive form (with respect to the quality parameter).

[28] Notice that either the MLRP of firm returns with respect to quality (A2) and the negative cross-partial derivative (equation (20)) or the MLRP of firm returns with respect to quality (A3) and the negative cross-partial derivative (equation (23)) together imply SOSD with respect to the loan size, provided returns are not only increasing but also concave in quality.

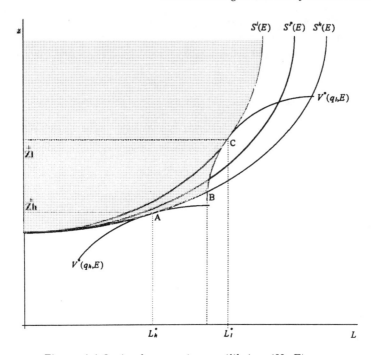

Figure 4.4 Optimal separating equilibrium (H=E)

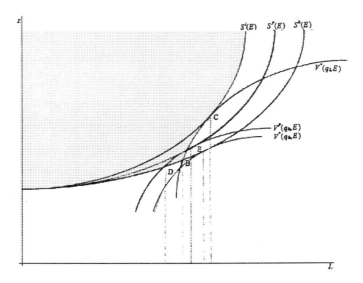

Figure 4.5 Sub-optimal separating equilibrium (H=E)

bank pooling supply curve, lies above the high-quality indifference curve passing through the point of intersection between the low-quality preferred indifference curve and bank supply curve to the high-quality types (point B, Figure 4.5). In the case of Figure 4.5, the latter condition is satisfied and the point of intersection B is the high-quality contract. This contract allows for the signalling of high-quality firms, and avoids the possibility of bank's negative expected profits on loans to low-quality firms. Thus, low-quality entrepreneurs will choose their 'first best' contract $\{zO(_l,^*), LO(_l,^*)\}$, point C, whereas high-quality entrepreneurs will choose their 'second best' contract $\{z_h, L_h\}$, point B. The resulting equilibrium will be a *suboptimal separating equilibrium*. Notice that under this contract, high-quality firms will be under-financed. However, according to our previous definitions, this under-financing *does not imply* type I credit rationing: high-quality firms choose to sign an underfinancing contract in order to signal their quality-type to the lending bank.

As with $H=I$, we can still have that condition (i) above is satisfied while condition (ii) is not. In this case no separating equilibrium obtains, either optimal or suboptimal (see Figure 4.6).

To see this, consider the $\{z_E, L_E\}$ contract determined by the tangency point between the bank pooling supply curve and the high-quality indifference curve (point E). The breaking down of condition (ii) above is implied by the fact that this latter indifference curve lies below the low-quality preferred indifference curve and the high-quality indifference curve which pass through point B.

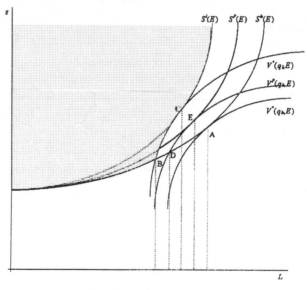

Figure 4.6 Pooling equilibrium (H=E)

In this case, the high-quality 'first best' contract $\{zO_{(h,}{}^{*}), LO_{(h,}{}^{*})\}$, point A, is clearly unfeasible, as it would attract low-quality entrepreneurs; moreover the high-quality entrepreneurs are indifferent between D and E, which are preferred to B. On the other hand, low-quality entrepreneurs prefer contract E to contract C. Hence, both quality-types of entrepreneurs will choose the *pooling contract* $\{z_E, L_E\}$ (point E, Figure 4.6).[29] When a pooling equilibrium attains and $H=E$, we have that low-quality firms will obtain loan amounts *smaller* than their first-best levels, while high-quality firms will obtain loan amounts *larger* than their first-best level (see Figure 4.6). In other words, 'worse' firms get less than what they would like to since they subsidize 'better' firms. According to our previous definitions, this under-financing of low-quality firms coincides with type-I credit rationing: low-quality firms would be ready to sign a debt contract for a larger loan amount, but they have no alternative choice to overcome their quantity constraint.

Notice also that, like in the case of $H=I$, with $H=E$ a Riley construction of the game structure would lead to the same results as the Wilson construction we have adopted here in the cases where separating equilibria occur, but it would not do so when a Wilson construction leads to a pooling equilibrium. Even if indifference curves were such as those in Figure 4.6, in Riley construction, contract D would not even appear, and the choice would again be the separating couplets of contract C and B. In that case, while low-quality firms get their first-best loan size (which is more than the 'pooling level'), high-quality firms get less than their first-best (and obviously even less than the 'pooling level'). Hence, under-financing does occur in a Riley construction for the high-quality types.

This stresses once more that the sequence of moves in the structure of the contracting game is very important since, before an equilibrium is reached, all the feasibility constraints must be satisfied. Thus, when the bank first starts by offering a contract menu, if some applicants choose A while others choose C, implying that indifference curves are like those in Figure 4.4, then an optimal separating equilibrium obtains (low-quality applicants choose their first-best contract C, while high-quality applicants choose their first-best contract A), as the bank will earn non-negative expected profits on both contracts. If some applicants choose A while others choose B, implying that indifference curves are like those in Figure 4.5, then a suboptimal separating equilibrium obtains (low-quality are better off, while high-quality applicants can signal their quality by being under-financed). Finally, suppose some applicants prefer A

---

[29] As in the case of $H=I$, with $H=E$ we can have a pooling equilibrium where indifference curves are strictly convex functions of z as q changes ($\text{MRS}(z,L|q_h) = \text{MRS}(z,L|q_l)$). In such a case, both the cross-partial derivative in equation (23) and the derivative in equation (24) would be zero. However, indifference curves need not be strictly convex in z (different quality types may have indifference curves that intersect somewhere). Moreover both (23) and (24) can keep holding and yet we can have a pooling equilibrium.

(most probably the high-quality ones) and this attracts all other applicants. Then the high-quality ones would shift to D, which is preferred to B. If that is the case, this means that indifference curves are as in Figure 4.6. Then the low-quality applicants would shift to E, and so would the high-quality ones who are indifferent between D and E. Hence, a pooling equilibrium would obtain. Firm signalling in such a case would not be convenient for the high-quality firms.

To conclude, we can state the following propositions.

PROPOSITION 4. When $H = E$ and is common knowledge, under conditions (A1) and (A3), the equilibrium set of separating contracts has the properties:

(i) the firm of lowest quality that is financed gets a 'first best' contract;
(ii) each contract breaks even for the bank;
(iii) the loan size for each contract (z_q, I_q) is decreasing in q: if $(z_{q+1}, I_{q+1}) < (z^*_{q+1}, I^*_{q+1})$ (the 'first-best' contract for the quality-$(q+1)$ entrepreneur), then we have a suboptimal separating contract, otherwise we have a 'first-best' separating contract.

PROPOSITION 5. When $H = E$ and is common knowledge, under conditions (A1) and (A3), the equilibrium pooling contract has the properties:

(i) no single contract breaks even for the bank but the average contract does;
(ii) no firm that is financed gets a 'first best' contract: 'lower-than-average' quality firms undergo an under-financing, which implies type I credit rationing, whereas 'higher-than-average' quality firms are over-financed.

3.3. The technological parameter as a continuous variable

As we have mentioned above, the assumption that H is a discrete binary variable is a rather strict one. Yet, letting H be a continuous variable makes the problem increasingly more complex to analyse. In this sub-section we suggest that these technical complications do not alter our main results.

The treatment of H as a binary variable has basically allowed us to state that if internal economies of scale and/or transaction costs prevail, then the sign of the MLRP of project returns with respect to quality is positive, while if external economies of scale and/or organizational costs prevail, then the sign of this MLRP is negative. Consequently, the cross-partial derivative of profit densities with respect to loan size and quality is negative in the former case ($H = I$) and positive in the latter ($H = E$). We have also seen that, when $H = I$, the higher is project quality, the greater is the marginal rate of substitution between I and z (that is high-quality indifference curves are steeper), while, when $H = E$, the higher is project quality, the smaller is the marginal rate of substitution between L and z (that is low-quality indifference curves are steeper). Moreover, we have seen that a sufficient condition for a pooling equilibrium is that indifference curves are convex, which implies that the marginal rates of substitution between L and z are equal in their correspondence to the parallel tangency points.

These elements explain the specific features of both our pooling and separating equilibria when either $H = I$ or $H = E$. As we have seen above, a separating equilibrium will emerge (i) if banks' separating supply curves are not so far apart, that is, if there are small inter-quality differences in default risks, and (ii) if the indifference curves of low- and high-quality entrepreneurs are dissimilar, that is, if inter-quality differences in projects' marginal returns do not offset different default risks to produce different tradeoffs between loan size and repayment. As banks' separating supply curves shift farther apart, that is, inter-quality differences in default risks get larger, and indifference curves of different types gets more similar, that is, inter-quality differences in projects marginal returns offset differential default risks to produce similar tradeoffs between loan size and repayment, a pooling equilibrium emerges.

It can thus be shown, at least on an intuitive ground, that if the 'technological' variable H takes more than two values, or even a continuum of values in a defined range, the features of the different emerging equilibria are not substantially altered. So, it is apparent that, if continuous, H can take a value by which the MLRP of returns with respect to quality will be zero, so that the cross-partial derivative of return densities with respect to loan size and quality will be zero too. Then, *a fortiori*, this must hold true even if H is a discrete (binary) variable, in the sense that it becomes equal to I whenever it is lower than some arbitrarily given value ϕ, and equal to E whenever it is higher than that same value ϕ; for there will be a point $H = \phi$ at which $H \neq I, E$. In both these cases, larger loans *do not* signal either higher or lower quality: they would be simply invariant to quality. This happens when the two indifference maps of low-quality and high-quality borrowers are the same, or at least when these maps coincide in the relevant range of contracts offered by the bank. A pooling contract will be the only possibility for the bank in this case.

This result perfectly fits with the equilibrium features as stated by (i) and (ii) above. Let us compare Figure 4.1 where $H = I$ and Figure 4.4 where $H = E$. As H changes, the two figures depict two opposite 'extreme' situations: the low-quality indifference map shifts from the left-bottom part north-westward along the bank supply curve to the low-quality types, while the high-quality indifference map shifts from the right-top part south-eastward along the bank supply curve to the high-quality types. Hence, we may presume that as H changes from I to E the two indifference maps of the two quality types shift in opposite directions becoming more and more similar and the bank supply curves get farther apart as far as H reaches a given value. In the neighbourhood of this value, H is neither equal to I nor to E, the bank supply curves are the farthest apart, and the indifference maps of the two quality types coincide. In this interval, a pooling equilibrium emerges. On the other hand, at the two extremes ($H = I$ or $H = E$), we can think of no differences in inter-quality default risks and of large difference in projects marginal returns. In this case one single supply curve will be sufficient for the bank to elicit a separating equilibrium at two points lying on the same curve.

4. A COMPARISON WITH PREVIOUS MODEL SETTINGS

In the previous sections we have often claimed that our paper offers a more general and unifying framework for the definition of credit market equilibria. However, the comparison with other models has until now been limited to a rather quick critical analysis of the assumptions and of the equilibria characterizing the M-R model. For the sake of completeness, it seems necessary to extend this comparison to other models, and in particular to the S-W and D-W ones.

There are several key issues that make this comparison actually rather difficult. Although the main purpose of the S-W, D-W, and M-R models as well as ours is quite similar (to show the possibility of credit rationing in competitive credit markets), the setting of each of these models is rather different. In the first place, different models allow for projects either of fixed size or of variable size. Secondly, different models resort to different variables in order to gather projects of different 'natures' within homogenous pools, which are thus determined and ordered according to different dominance criteria. The direct comparison between non-homogeneous ordering variables or dominance criteria is unfeasible in raw terms. At this aim, it seems necessary to define a common framework by which to relate the realized outcomes of different projects in the different models, as well as a principle of generalization. In this section we deepen our focus with respect to two key issues: the comparison between the *quality* and the *riskiness* of a given project, and the comparison between FOSD, SOSD, MPS and MLRP.

4.1. Low-risk versus high-risk loans

In all the cases described above, we had that larger loans implied higher firm expected returns, while higher quality implied higher firm expected returns when $H = I$ and lower firm expected return when $H = E$. As we already mentioned, in the S-W model, projects are different in riskiness, which is unobservable to lenders. In particular, 'the bank is able to distinguish projects

170

with *different mean returns*' (p. 395). It follows that all the projects in the same risk pool have the same expected return but some are riskier than others in the sense of mean-preserving spread (MPS). In the notation of the present paper we can say that $q_i < q_j$ indicates that projects of quality q_i are riskier than those of quality q_j, so that a decrease in q represents an increase in riskiness. As is well known, S-W considered projects of fixed loan size, whilst we apply their case to loans of variable size, and show that S-W analysis gets to results similar to ours.

Consider a population of firms of different increasing riskiness, indexed by ϕ. We say that if, for a nondegenerate prior distribution G for ϕ, the posterior distribution $G(\cdot \mid \phi_2)$ dominates the posterior distribution $G(\cdot \mid \phi_1)$ in the sense of MPS, then ϕ_1 is *riskier* than ϕ_2. This is the definition of a MPS increasing risk which implies but it is not implied by SOSD.[30] Thus, if a signal ϕ_1 is *less favorable (riskier)* than ϕ_2, then it follows that the conditional densities $\{f(\cdot \mid q)\}$ have the MLRP for every $\phi_1 < \phi_2$. In other words, we restrict our attention to the case of two firms i and j ($i<j$) whose expected profit is the same, but whose riskiness is different. Suppose, for instance, that firm i is riskier (it has a 'fatter right tail') than firm j.[31] For the same given level of expected profits, an increase in risk (a decrease in quality) will induce an increase in the demand for loans. Hence, we are back to the case of $H = E$ in our model above, and condition (A3) will keep holding. Also, for the profit distribution to be a MPS risk increasing it must be that equation (23) holds, as the cross-partial derivative of the cumulative profit distribution function with respect to L and q has to be positive (higher q means lower risk, that is lower ϕ). We can thus parallel the conditions of the S-W model, as, for profit densities characterized by MPS differential riskiness, the MLRP implies SOSD (and thus MPS), while assumption (A3) and equation (23) will ensure that increases in risk and loan size be positively related.

Hence, similarly to the case of $H = E$ described above, we have that applicants with riskier projects are willing to pay a larger z for a larger loan. Applicants with riskier projects are bound to signal their quality type by accepting a larger rather than a smaller loan. This implies that the marginal rate of substitution between L and z is higher, the riskier is the project. Formally, assumption (A3) still holds, where q now stands for 'risk' rather than 'quality'. Similarly to M-R, we can restate this by saying that the marginal decrease in promised loan payment that a loan applicant requires in order to accept a smaller loan is lower the riskier the project. Therefore, all the equilibrium

[30] When two cumulative density functions have the same mean, second-order stochastic dominance is equivalent to a mean-preserving spread (one has a wider spread than the other). Conversely, we may have a mean-preserving spread of a density function which is not dominated in the sense of SOSD.

[31] And hence, it has lower quality. Quality and riskiness are inversely related: the higher is riskiness, the lower is quality and vice versa.

conditions are thus similar to those depicted above for the case of $H = E$, once we replace the concept of 'lower quality' of a project with that of 'higher risk' of a project.

The extension of the above results to the case of Q quality types is straightforward. We can thus state the following Propositions, paralleling Propositions 4 and 5 above.

PROPOSITION 6. Under conditions (A1) and (A3) the equilibrium set of separating contracts has the properties:
(i) the riskiest project that is financed gets a 'first best' contract;
(ii) each contract breaks even for the bank;
(iii) each contract $(z_q, L_q,)$ is increasing in riskiness: if $(z_{q+1}, L_{q+1}) < (z^*_{q+1}, L^*_{q+1})$ (the 'first-best' contract for the quality-$(q+1)$ entrepreneur), then we have a suboptimal separating contract, otherwise we have a 'first-best' separating contract.

PROPOSITION 7. Under conditions (A1) and (A3), the equilibrium pooling contract has the properties:

(i) no single contract breaks even for the bank but the average contract does;
(ii) no project that is financed gets a 'first best' contract: projects of 'lower-than-average' risk are over-financed whereas projects of 'higher-than-average' risk are under-financed.

4.2. Features of the MLRP

The claim that our model offers a more general and unifying framework to study credit rationing equilibria in the market for loans is not sufficient to prove that the S-W model leads to results analogous to ours. The S-W model itself features key differences with respect to other models such as the D-W one. In this last respect, it suffices noticing that, even if both these models assume a fixed loan size, they widely differ with respect to the variables explaining how projects are pooled within homogeneous groups and to the related dominance criteria.

We just recalled that, in S-W, all projects in the same pool have the same expected return but different riskiness. On the other hand, D-W assume that all projects in the same pool 'yield *the same return R^S if successful and R^f if not.* [...] What distinguishes projects is the probability of success' p. 282). This means that projects in the same pool have *different mean returns* in D-W, while projects in the same pool have *different returns if successful* in S-W. As a consequence, we can single out the main elements which can be held as given in a simplified version of the two models. In S-W the bank screens out projects according to their *average* return, while in D-W the bank distinguishes projects according to their return *in the case of success*. In both cases, the probability of success is unknown to the lender. Hence, in S-W the bank pools together all projects with the same average return, R, *for a given* return in the case of a failure, R^f (often equalized to zero), whereas in D-W the bank pools together all projects with the same return in the case of success, R^s, *and* the same return in the case of a failure, R^f. Thus, the expected return of a project is *decreasing* in p, the probability of success, in the first case, and it is *increasing* in p in the second one.[32] Therefore, all projects in the same pool have the same mean and can be ranked according to their *dispersion* (the MPS criterion) in the S-W case, while they can be ranked according to their *different mean* (the FOSD criterion) in the D-W case.

All this makes clear that, to compare the S-W and the D-W models, it would be necessary to subsume the two different projects' orderings across pools resulting from the different criteria of project ranking under a unique sorting criterion. However, the rankings implied by the MPS and the FOSD criteria are not directly comparable, as the former only applies when the latter cannot be conclusive (two distributions with the same mean cannot be ranked according to the FOSD criterion, as the latter holds if and only if two distributions have different means).

We can elaborate on these differences as follows. Consider the S-W model: by dropping the assumption that all projects yield the same R^f, if a *higher p* implies a *higher R^s* (a lower R^f), then the expected return of a project will be *increasing* in p. Conversely, consider the D-W model: by dropping the assumption that projects yield the same R^f, if a *higher p* is still associated with the same *mean return R* (and thus higher R^s and lower R^f), then the expected return of a project will be *decreasing* in p. Hence, the expected return could be increasing in p, and rising as p rises across projects for given levels of R^s, in both the S-W and the D-W models.[33] Therefore, the problem has three 'dimensions': R^s, R^f, and p. Suppose two projects have the same R^f: then a higher p could either imply the same R^s, and the expected return will be rising (D-W), or a lower R^s, and the expected return will be the same (S-W). Thus, for given levels of R^f and R^s, a *higher* expected return implies either a higher p (D-W) or a lower p (S-W). Clearly, for given values of p and R^s, a lower R^f implies a higher expected return, but if R^f is not the same across projects this

---

[32] Consider two projects of different quality/riskiness grouped *within the same pool*. In the S-W setting, this implies that the two projects yield the *same* mean return: hence, a *higher* probability of success means a *lower* return in the case of success (the mean must be the same). In the D-W setting, this implies that the same two projects yield the *same* return in case of success: hence, a *higher* probability of success implies a *higher* return in the case of success (the mean does not have to be the same) or, equivalently, the *same* return in the case of success implies a *higher mean* return.

[33] If projects were pooled according to their return in case of success, R^s, the problem then would become how to compare projects with *different* returns in the case of success.

will no longer be true.[34] As we have seen, we can always associate higher returns in case of success R^s with equal or higher p's, and, provided R^f is equal or lower, we will have higher expected returns or equal expected returns, respectively. While the former case implies first-order stochastic dominance (FOSD), the latter implies a mean-preserving increase in dispersion (MPS). This means that, even if the two models remain characterized by their original dominance criteria (MPS in S-W and FOSD in D-W), they could deliver comparable *signals*.[35]

The above conclusion is important, since the presence of comparable signals allows a comparison between different dominance criteria according to their degree of generality. As we have seen in section 2, the MLRP is implied by FOSD in the case of two-point distributions, like in the case we are dealing with now, but also by MPS, provided the increase in skewness is monotonic. As Milgrom (1981) points out, this is not always true: with discrete multinomial or continuous distributions, the MLRP is not implied by FOSD (and, *a fortiori*, not even by MPS). The converse is true, however, as we will state in the following propositions. The MRLP is suited for comparing two *signals* and is a necessary and sufficient condition for a signal x to be *more favourable than* a signal y both in the sense of FOSD and SOSD for every increasing concave function of a parameter τ, $U(\tau)$, and non-degenerate prior distributions $G_1(\tau)$ and $G_2(\tau)$. Thus, the MLRP is useful when we have a continuum of values for an observable variable (for example a project return) with associated probabilities of occurrence.

Let G be a prior distribution for the random variable τ that assigns probabilities $g(\tau_1)$ and $g(\tau_2)$ to two possible values τ_1 and τ_2 of τ. Let the densities $\{f(\cdot\,|\,\tau)\}$ have the MLRP for every $x > y$ and $\tau_1 > \tau_2$, so that:

$$f(x\,|\,\tau_1)\,f(y\,|\,\tau_2) > f(x\,|\,\tau_2)\,f(y\,|\,\tau_1). \tag{26}$$

Then, the following propositions hold.

PROPOSITION 8. If the densities $\{f(\cdot\,|\,\tau)\}$ have the MLRP for every $x > y$ and $\tau_1 > \tau_2$, so that equation (26) holds, then $G(\tau\,|\,x)$ dominates $G(\tau\,|\,y)$ in the sense of FOSD.

PROOF. By Bayes' theorem, (26) implies that:

$$\frac{g(\tau_1|\chi)}{g(\tau_2|\chi)} = \frac{g(\tau_1)f(\chi|\tau_1)}{g(\tau_2)f(\chi|\tau_2)} > \frac{g(\tau_1)f(y|\tau_1)}{g(\tau_2)f(y|\tau_2)} = \frac{g(\tau_1|y)}{g(\tau_2|y)}, \tag{27}$$

---

[34] Suppose instead that two projects had the same R^f but different R^s: then a higher R^s could either imply the same p, and the expected return will be rising (D-W), or a lower p, and the expected return will be the same (S-W).

[35] Here the word *signal* refers to an observable that *carries news* and is not to be counfounded to the *signalling* by agents of their quality type.

that is,

$$\frac{g(\tau_1|\chi)}{g(\tau_2|\chi)} > \frac{g(\tau_1|y)}{g(\tau_2|y)} \tag{28}$$

Recall that $G(\tau\,|\,x)$ dominates $G(\tau\,|\,y)$ is the sense of FOSD if and only if for every τ, $G(\tau\,|\,x) \le G(\tau\,|\,y)$, with strict inequality for some value of τ. Now, as $\tau_1 > \tau_2$, $G(\tau\,|\,x)$ dominates $G(\tau\,|\,y)$ is the sense of FOSD if $g(\tau_1\,|\,x) < g(\tau_1\,|\,y)$ or $g(\tau_2\,|\,x) < g(\tau_2\,|\,y)$ or both. This implies that:

$$\int_{\tau \le \tau_1} f(\chi|\tau)dG(\tau) < \int_{\tau \le \tau_1} f(y|\tau)dG(\tau) \tag{29a}$$

which, in turn, implies that

$$g(\tau_1\,|\,x) < g(\tau_1\,|\,y), \tag{30a}$$

or:

$$\int_{\tau \le \tau_2} f(\chi|\tau)dG(\tau) < \int_{\tau \le \tau_2} f(y|\tau)dG(\tau) \tag{29b}$$

which, in turn, implies that:

$$g(\tau_2\,|\,x) < g(\tau_2\,|\,y) \tag{30b}$$

Also, since $\tau_1 > \tau_2$ obviously implies that $g(\tau_1\,|\,x) > g(\tau_2\,|\,x)$ and $g(\tau_1\,|\,y) < g(\tau_2\,|\,y)$, the inequality in equation (26) is easily established. Hence, the MLRP implies FOSD. Q.E.D.

Proposition 8 implies that for every increasing function $U(\tau)$, if the family of densities $\{f(\cdot\,|\,\tau)\}$ has the MLRP, then

$$\int U(\tau)dG(\tau|\chi) > \int U(\tau)dG(\tau|y)$$

PROPOSITION 9. If the densities $\{f(\cdot\,|\,\tau)\}$ have the MLRP for every $x > y$ and $\tau_1 > \tau_2$, so that equation (26) and (28) hold, then $G(\tau\,|\,x)$ dominates $G(\tau\,|\,y)$ in the sense of SOSD.

PROOF. Recall that $G(\tau\,|\,x)$ dominates $G(\tau\,|\,y)$ is the sense of FOSD if and only if, for every τ,

$$\int_{\tau \le \tau^*} [G(\tau|\chi) - G(\tau|y)]d\tau \equiv \Delta(\tau^*) \le 0$$

for all τ^*, with strict inequality for some value of τ. Now, $G(\tau\,|\,x)$ dominates

175

$G(\tau \mid y)$ in the sense of SOSD if:

$$\int_{\tau \leq \tau_1} G(\tau \mid \chi) d\tau < \int_{\tau \leq \tau_1} G(\tau \mid y) d\tau \tag{31a}$$

or

$$\int_{\tau \leq \tau_2} G(\tau \mid \chi) d\tau < \int_{\tau \leq \tau_2} G(\tau \mid y) d\tau \tag{31b}$$

or both. As before, this implies that either equation (29a) or (29b) holds (and hence (30a) or (30b)) (see above). Also, since $\tau_1 > \tau_2$ implies that $g(\tau_1 \mid x) > g(\tau_2 \mid x)$ and $g(\tau_1 \mid y) < g(\tau_2 \mid y)$, the inequalities in (28) and (26) are easily established. Hence, the MLRP implies SOSD.[36] Q.E.D.

Proposition 9, like Proposition 8, also implies that for every increasing concave function $U(\tau)$, if the family of densities $\{f(\cdot \mid \tau)\}$ has the MLRP, then:

$$\int U(\tau) dG(\tau \mid \chi) > \int U(\tau) dG(\tau \mid y)$$

PROPOSITION 10. If the densities $\{f(\cdot \mid \tau)\}$ have the MLRP for every $x > y$ and $\tau_1 > \tau_2$, so that equation (26) and (28) hold, τ_i is a risk parameter such that a higher i denotes smaller risk, and $f(x \mid \tau_1)$ is a MPS of $f(x \mid \tau_2)$ such that $E(\tau \mid x) = E(\tau \mid y)$, then $G(\tau \mid x)$ dominates $G(\tau \mid y)$ in the sense that $G(\tau \mid y)$ is a MPS of $G(\tau \mid x)$. That is, $G(\tau \mid x)$ and $G(\tau \mid y)$ have the same mean but the latter is riskier (has fatter tails) than the former.

PROOF. Recall that $G(\tau \mid x)$ dominates $G(\tau \mid y)$ is the sense of MPS if and only if, for every τ, we have that:

$$\int_{\tau} [G(\tau \mid \chi) - G(\tau \mid y)] d\tau = 0 \tag{32}$$

$$\int_{\tau \leq \tau} [G(\tau \mid \chi) - G(\tau \mid y)] d\tau = 0 \Delta(\tau^*) \leq 0 \tag{33}$$

for all τ^*, with strict inequality for some value of τ. Condition (32) is a mean-preserving condition. Condition (33) implies that $G(\tau \mid x)$ dominates $G(\tau \mid y)$ in the sense of SOSD (as we know, in fact, MPS implies SOSD) and it has been proved above. Since condition (32) is a mean preserving property, it implies that:

---

[36] As Milgrom (1981) points out, the inequality in (26) is necessary and sufficient to conclude that x is more favorable than y in the sense of both first-order and second-order stochastic dominance. As we know, in fact, FOSD implies SOSD (but not the other way around).

$$G(-\infty \,|\, x) = G(-\infty \,|\, y) \qquad (34a)$$

and

$$G(+\infty \,|\, x) = G(+\infty \,|\, y) \qquad (34b)$$

Now, the equality in mean implies that $E(\tau \,|\, y) = E[(\tau \,|\, (x+\varepsilon)]$, where ε has a zero-mean density $g(\tau \,|\, \varepsilon)$ such that $E[\tau \,|\, \varepsilon] = 0$. Then, it must be that:

$$\int \tau g(\tau \,|\, y)\, d\tau = \int \tau g(\tau \,|\, x+\varepsilon)\, d\tau = \int \tau \big[g(r \,|\, x)+g(r \,|\, \varepsilon)\big]\, d\tau = \int \tau g(\tau \,|\, x)\, d\tau, \quad (35)$$

which implies that

$$\int \tau G\,(\tau \,|\, y)\, d\tau = \int \tau G\,(\tau \,|\, x)\, d\tau. \qquad (36)$$

Integrating by parts we have:

$$\tau G(\tau|y)\Big|_{-\infty}^{+\infty} - \int G(\tau|y)d\tau = \tau G(\tau|x)\Big|_{-\infty}^{+\infty} - \int G(\tau|x)d\tau \qquad (37)$$

from which we get

$$\int G(\tau|y)d\tau = \int G(\tau|x)d\tau \qquad (38)$$

so that

$$\int_\tau \big[G(\tau|x)-G(\tau|y)\big]d\tau = 0 \qquad (39)$$

Q.E.D.

Therefore, $g(\tau_1 \,|\, y)$ is a MPS of $g(\tau_1 \,|\, x)$, and $g(\tau_2 \,|\, y)$ is a MPS of $g(\tau_2 \,|\, x)$. Furthermore, since $\tau_1 > \tau_2$ implies increase in risk (greater dispersion or fatter tails), we have that $g(\tau_1 \,|\, x)$ is a MPS of $g(\tau_2 \,|\, x)$, and $g(\tau_1 \,|\, y)$ is a MPS of $g(\tau_2 \,|\, y)$. Now, the MLRP implies that the likelihood ratio $f(x \,|\, \tau_1)/f(x \,|\, \tau_2)$ is monotone in x and increasing if $\tau_1 > \tau_2$. Also, as the proof of condition (32) above has shown, the mean-preservation property is independent of the inequality in (33), which implies SOSD. Hence, the MPS in the conditional densities is maintained in the posterior distributions, while, since the MLRP implies SOSD, it will do so no matter whether the equality of the posterior means holds or not (in other words, the MLRP implies SOSD in all cases, and if the MPS holds for the conditional densities, the MLRP will hold even more so). If the likelihood ratio $f(x \,|\, \tau_1)/f(x \,|\, \tau_2)$ is monotone in x, increasing in risk, and $f(x \,|\, \tau_1)$ is a MPS of $f(x \,|\, \tau_2)$, then $G(\tau \,|\, x)$ dominates $G(\tau \,|\, y)$ in the sense that $G(\tau \,|\, y)$ is a MPS of $G(\tau \,|\, x)$. That is, $G(\tau \,|\, x)$ and $G(\tau \,|\, y)$ have the same mean but the latter is riskier than the former. Q.E.D.

Again, Proposition 10, like Propositions 8 and 9, implies that for every concave function $U(\tau)$, if the family of densities $\{f(\cdot \mid \tau)\}$ has the MLRP *and* the MPS property, then

$$\int U(\tau)dG(\tau|x) > \int U(\tau)dG(\tau|y).$$

Furthermore, the converse of Proposition 10 is also true, at least in the case of two-point distributions. Milgrom (1981) already showed that both FOSD and SOSD imply MLRP, provided a signal x is more favorable than another signal y in either senses. Now, as a signal x can still be more favourable than another signal y in either senses even if the latter is a MPS of the former, then MPS also implies MLRP, provided that, of two signals, one is comparably more favorable than the other (but only for two-point distributions).

Thus, we have a tool to generalize the settings of the D-W and S-W models to continuous distributions, provided that we have signals that are comparable. The MLRP is obviously a stronger condition, as it implies concavity and a family of densities which is increasing in the observables (the signals). Nevertheless, it is a property which nests both FOSD and MPS under the suitable conditions described above. Thanks to the MLRP, lenders could be able to infer the quality type by looking at projects returns for equal levels of the loan sizes.

4.3. The MLRP with loans of variable sizes

The above conclusions concerning models with fixed loan sizes, like the S-W and the D-W ones, can be extended to the case of loans of variable sizes, all the more so. In this sense, the M-R model offers a generalization of both S-W and the D-W models. However, whereas M-R treats the loan size as a choice variable which always allows for complete separation of projects of different quality, we have proposed a different generalization allowing for both separation and pooling of different quality types. To compare Milde and Riley's generalization of the S-W and D-W models with ours, which we have discussed above in section 4.1, let us consider once more the two-point distribution example of these models. Two different projects could have the same R^s and different p's, whereby the higher is p the 'better' will be the project. Conversely, two different projects could have different R^s and equal p, in which case they will be equally risky for the lender. Thus, what really matters is the probability of success: if two projects have different R^s and different p, the correpondent loci of indifference between interest rate and size of the loan will differ in such a way that a higher p will imply a different (steeper) indifference curve. This is so because a higher p implies, *coeteris paribus*, a higher expected return. There will be a point at which the relation between expected return and repayment schedule is 'optimal', and this will differ according to the probability of success, or, in terms of the M-R model,

178

to the threshold level of repayment.

The key point, which gives rise to different 'cases' in M-R, is the relation between quality and loan size, that is, between quality and return of a project. If such a relation is positive (higher quality implies a higher p, which implies a higher return, and a larger loan size can signal such better quality) there will be one type of separating equilibrium, whereby high-quality agents signal their type by accepting larger loans. If such a relation is negative, high-quality agents signal their type by accepting smaller loans. Notice that all this keeps holding even if the size of the loan is fixed: in the former case, high-quality agents will accept a higher interest rate, whereas in the latter they will accept a smaller rate of interest.[37] Hence, letting the loan size vary, adds one dimension to the problem, allowing different pairs of interest rate and loan size for different applicants.

5. SUMMARY AND CONCLUSIONS

In this paper we have analysed the different equilibria that emerge in a competitive credit market. Optimizing risk-neutral firms' demand loans to finance production projects whose quality is not observable from the outside, while banks face an adverse selection problem due to their lack of information and costly monitoring concerning the quality of firm projects: thus, firms and banks sign debt contracts contingent on realized firm output and a given interest rate. Since *ex-ante* unpredictability of the realized output of each project makes actual returns stochastic, firms' actual returns, and thus their ability to repay the loans to banks, are uncertain. Moreover, as a result of costly monitoring, banks cannot enforce contracts specifying the quality of a project, so that contracts are made contingent on realized returns. In addition, firms are assumed to have limited liability with respect to the signed debt contracts with banks, which thus take the form of *standard debt contracts*. Limited liability and unobservability of project quality yield an asymmetric information problem which induces adverse selection on the side of the lenders. However, as both the size of the loan and the loan interest rate are allowed to vary, self-selection on the side of the borrowers is made possible, whereby high-quality firms can elicit better credit conditions than low-quality ones, avoiding negative expected returns for the banks on each contract. Assuming a contracting game of a Wilson (1977) type, we have shown that both separating (that is where self-selection by borrowers of different quality is possible) and pooling equilibria can emerge, where the latter entail the possibility of credit rationing

---

[37] This can be seen in the M-R pictures (see Milde and Riley, 1988, Figure II, p. 108, and Figure III, p. 112) by fixing L on the horizontal axis and plotting the families of indifference curves for the two types of applicants. The resulting interest rates for the two types will correspond to the two points where the indifference curves have the same slope at the given level of L.

for some quality types.

Three main results of this paper are worth summarizing. In the first place, our approach encompasses the main features of the previous models such as S-W and D-W, which can be considered as particular cases (loans have fixed size) of a more general model (loans can vary in size). In the second place, by referring to an observable parameter of *organizational complexity* (or 'technology') characterizing the borrowing firm, our model allows for a more general framework of analysis than M-R's one. In particular, we can replace M-R's three different and unrelated 'cases' with a unifying framework. In the third place, differently from M-R, by adopting a Wilson construction of the contracting game we are able to obtain both credit rationing pooling equilibria and separating equilibria whereby firms of different quality are able to elicit different debt contracts. Therefore, we have strengthened the possibility of obtaining equilibrium credit rationing.

The core of our model construction can be subsumed in the firm *technological* parameter and in the Wilson construction of the contracting game. The technological/organizational parameter has been defined on the basis of a comparison between two extreme types of economies of scale (internal or external), and/or between two kinds of costs (transactional costs or organizational costs). We have stated that, when internal economies of scale and/or transaction costs prevail, a larger size of the loan will signal a higher project quality, while when external economies of scale and/or organizational costs prevail, a larger size of the loan will signal a lower project quality. These results are actually quite close to those reached by M-R in their various cases; however, differently from M-R, in our model they have not been based on some arbitrary assumption of the functional form of the firm production function. This means that, in our model, the relation between project quality and project return which is actually signalled by the size of the loan depends ultimately on the technological/organizational parameter, which is observable, and is independent of the functional form of the production function.

On the other hand, the Wilson construction of the contracting game, characterized by uninformed lenders moving first in a three-stage pure-strategy game which designs a standard debt contract between lenders and borrowers, has allowed us to prove that our model generates a pooling equilibrium under suitable conditions on the indifference curves of different quality types. Thus, having the possibility of getting both pooling and separating equilibria, we are able to offer a richer and more robust framework for type-I credit rationing than M-R's one. In this paper we have proved that, in the case of prevailing internal economies of scale and/or transaction costs: (i) the feasible separating equilibria are suboptimal, since low-quality projects (entrepreneurs) get their first-best contract while the high-quality projects get an amount of loans greater than the size they would have liked to; (ii) the feasible pooling equilibrium is suboptimal, too, since low-quality projects get a larger amount of loans while high-quality projects get a lower amount of loans than their respective first-best levels. We have also proved that, in the case of prevailing external economies of scale and/or organizational costs: (iii) the feasible separating equilibria are suboptimal, since low-quality projects (entrepreneurs) get their first-best contract while high-quality projects get an amount of loans smaller than the amount they would have liked to; (iv) the feasible pooling equilibrium is suboptimal, too, since low-quality projects get a smaller amount of loans while high-quality projects get a higher amount of loans than their respective first-best levels.

Hence, both (ii) and (iii) imply type-I credit rationing for high-quality firms, while (iv) implies type-I credit rationing for low-quality firms. Moreover, (ii) and (iv) emphasize the possibility of type-I credit rationing with pooling equilibria, while (iii) points out the possibility of type-I credit rationing with separating equilibria. As mentioned above, the debt contracts which lead to such a rich menu of possible credit-rationing equilibria have the standard form. Yet, differently from S-W and M-R, which take this form of contract as given, our approach allows us to refer to Innes's results, whereby the optimality of the form of the debt contract is endogenized. For Innes (1993) has proved that, under asymmetric information and variable loan sizes, the monotonicity of the lender's payoff function implies that the standard debt contract is the optimal contract. Hence, a further element strengthening our treatment of credit rationing is that this analysis is not based on the arbitrary assumption of an optimal form of debt contract taken as given.

Despite these achievements, this paper is still constrained by several simplifications, the main being that firms demand loans to finance the working capital needed to activate the production process. No role is left for fixed capital accumulation (but this is a drawback of the whole literature on the topic, for that matter), as there is no fixed capital as such in our model. Moreover, no debt accumulation is allowed, given the strict one-period horizon of the borrowing problem faced by the firm. Further research is called for at this stage, to analyze the problems relating to capital accumulation through debt (and equity) financing under asymmetric information in the capital markets. This will certainly be the next step in our research agenda. By and large, the appraisals of fixed capital financing and of debt financing appear to be the necessary steps toward a more comprehensive analysis of the importance of credit with respect to other financial instruments in market economies.

REFERENCES

Besanko, D., and A. Thakor (1987), 'Collateral and Rationing: Sorting Equilibria in Monopolistic and Competitive Credit Markets', *International Economic Review*, 28: 671-79.

Bester, H. (1985), 'Screening Versus Rationing in Credit Markets with Imperfect Information', *American Economic Review*, 75: 850-5.

Bester, H. (1987), 'The Role of Collateral in Credit Markets with Imperfect Information', *European Economic Review*, 31: 887-99.

Chan, Y., and G. Kanatas (1985), 'Asymmetric Valuation and the Role of Collateral in Loan Agreements', *Journal of Money, Credit, and Banking*, 17:84-95.

Cho, I., and D. Kreps (1987), 'Signalling Games and Stable Equilibria', *Quarterly Journal of Economics*, 102: 179-222.

Coase, R. (1937), 'The Nature of the Firm', *Economica*, 4: 233-61.

De Meza, D., and D. Webb, (1987), 'Too Much Investment: A Problem of Asymmetric Information', *Quarterly Journal of Economics*, 102: 281-92.

De Meza, D., and D. Webb, (1989), 'Efficient Credit Rationing', *European Economic Review*, 36: 1277-90.

Grossman, S., and O. Hart (1986), 'The Costs and Benefits of Ownership: A Theory of Vertical and Lateral Integration', *Journal of Political Economy*, 94: 691-719.

Hellwig, M. (1987), 'Some Recent Developments in the Theory of Competition in Markets with Adverse Selection', *European Economic Review*, 31:319-25.

Innes, R. (1990), 'Limited Liability and Incentive Contracting with Ex-ante Action Choices', *Journal of Economic Theory*, 52: 45-67.

Innes, R. (1991), 'Investment and Government Intervention in Credit Markets when there is Asymmetric Information', *Journal of Public Economics*, 46: 347-81.

Innes, R. (1992), 'Adverse Selection, Investment, and Profit Taxation', *European Economic Review*, 36: 1427-52.

Innes, R. (1993), 'Financial Contracting under Risk Neutrality, Limited Liability and *Ex Ante* Asymmetric Information', *Economica*, 60: 27-40.

Jaffee, D.M., and T. Russell, (1976), 'Imperfect Information, Uncertainty, and Credit Rationing', *Quarterly Journal of Economics*, 90: 651-66.

Kreps, D., and R. Wilson (1982), 'Sequential Equilibria', *Econometrica*, 50: 863-94.

Leland, H., and D. Pyle, (1977), 'Informational Asymmetries, Financial Structure and Financial Intermediation', *Journal of Finance*, 32: 371-87.

Milde, H., and J. Riley (1988), 'Signalling in Credit Markets', *Quarterly Journal of Economics*, 103: 101-29.

Milgrom, P. (1981), 'Good News and Bad News: Representation Theorems and Applications', *Bell Journal of Economics*, 12: 380-91.

Milgrom, P., and J. Roberts (1988), 'An Economic Approach to Influence Activities and Organizational Responses', *American Journal of Sociology*, April.

Miyazaki, H. (1977), 'The Rat Race and Internal Labor Markets', *Bell Journal of Economics*, 8: 394-416.

Riley, J. (1979), 'Informational Equilibrium', *Econometrica*, 47: 331-59.

Rothschild, M., and J.E. Stiglitz (1970), 'Increasing Risk: I. A Definition', *Journal of Economic Theory*, 2: 225-43.

Rothschild, M., and J.E. Stiglitz (1976), 'Equilibrium in Competitive Insurance Markets: An Essay on the Economics of Imperfect Information', *Quarterly Journal of Economics*, 90: 628-49.

Shavell, S. (1979), 'Risk Sharing and Incentives in the Principal and Agent Relationship', *Bell Journal of Economics*, 10: 55-73.

Stiglitz, J.E., and A. Weiss (1981), 'Credit Rationing in Markets with Imperfect Information', *American Economic Review*, 71: 393-410.

Stiglitz, J.E., and A. Weiss (1986), 'Credit Rationing and Collateral', in: J. Edwards, J. Franks, C. Mayer, and S. Schaefer (eds.), *Recent Developments in Corporate Finance*, Cambridge: Cambridge University Press.

Stiglitz, J.E., and A. Weiss (1992). 'Asymmetric Information in Credit Markets and its Implications for Macro-Economics', *Oxford Economic Papers*, 44: 694-724.

Wilson, C. (1977), 'A Model of Insurance Markets with Incomplete Information', *Journal of Economic Theory*, 16: 167-87.

5. Market Imperfections, Unemployment Equilibria and Nominal Rigidities

Andrea Boitani

Mirella Damiani*

1. INTRODUCTION

In current debates it is argued with increasing insistence that the high unemployment rates registered in the European countries in recent years are due to a significant extent to the scant 'flexibility' of their labour markets; a lack of flexibility understood both in the sense of the excessive rigidity of the 'rules' that regulate hirings, dismissals, working hours, and so on, and (now as always) in the sense of excessive wage rigidity.

In this paper we shall not address issues concerning the rules governing the labour market. We shall instead examine the other question - namely that of wage 'rigidity' - in order to show that it provides only a partial and to some extent distorted explanation of unemployment. It would be much more correct, in fact, to point to the institutional arrangements of all markets in accounting for the phenomenon. The modern theories of efficiency wages and of wage bargaining have shown that in neither case can one properly speak of wage 'rigidity'. The problem is not that the market functions poorly but that the subjects which operate within it (both trade unions and firms) are able to exert a powerful influence on macroeconomic outcomes, and that the market institutions alter the rules with respect to the Walrasian ideal of perfect flexibility.[1] Hence modern theories of the labour market combine well with the

* We wish to thank Elettra Agliardi, Roberto Tamborini, Piero Tedeschi and especially Domenico Delli Gatti and Marcello Messori for their comments on a previous draft of this paper. Responsibility for any errors or omissions, however, rests entirely with ourselves. Both authors have benefited from financial support by MURST (60%) and CNR.

[1] For useful surveys of the theory of trade union bargaining see Oswald (1982, 1985) and Ulph and Ulph (1990). As for efficiency wages see Akerlof and Yellen (1986), which contains the main contributions to the subject, Weiss (1991) for a comprehensive survey, and Pisauro (1991) for an analysis of the possible effects of different forms of labour taxation in the presence of efficiency wages.

New Keynesian approach, which emphasises goods market failures due to imperfect competition and macroeconomic externalities.[2]

Broadly speaking, efficiency wages are regarded as an explanation for involuntary unemployment which stands as an alternative to those based on the market power of workers organized into trade unions.[3] This paper examines the interacting effects of trade unions power and efficiency wages considerations on wages and employment. As we shall assume imperfect competion in the goods market we will be able to broaden the analysis to the interactions among failures and imperfections of both markets.

We shall focus in particular on a model in which firms operate in conditions of monopolistic competition, bargain over wages with the trade unions, but are also aware that the work effort of their employees depends on their remuneration, according to the efficiency wage hypothesis. In sections 2 and 3 it is formally proved that each imperfection helps in raising the bargained wage and the 'natural' rate of unemployment above the ideal level of perfectly competitive labour and goods markets. Moreover it is shown that the various imperfections mutually reinforce each other in wage determination, that is the *marginal* effects on equilibrium wages of each labour market imperfection is enhanced with the simultaneous increase of the other imperfection. Conversely, numerical simulations suggest that an increase in one of the imperfections does not reinforce the *marginal* effect of another imperfection on the macroeconomic level of employment.

The same theoretical framework will then be used to show that the sole presence of partly-indexed unemployment benefits renders equilibrium employment sensitive to monetary shocks (section 4). This is a typically Keynesian result which could not be obtained if a perfectly competitive goods market were assumed. If, therefore, the 'imperfection' of the goods market is a prerequisite for monetary shocks to be effective, the *degree* of effectiveness is negatively correlated with the *degree* of real 'rigidity'. On the other hand, it can be shown that as this 'rigidity' grows, increases in unemployment benefits have increasingly marked depressive effects on the level of unemployment.

The economic policy implication of this analysis (section 5) is that it is

---

[2]   The relations between new labour market theories and imperfect competition in the goods market is surveyed in Boitani and Damiani (1995). A survey of the New Keynesian Economics is Ardeni, Boitani, Delli Gatti and Gallegati (Chapter 1 in this volume). See also Dixon, Rankin (1994); Silvestre (1993). A comparison between the New Keynesian Economics and the various Post-Keynesian approaches is conducted, from a methodological point of view, in Boitani and Salanti (1994) while the main contributions to the New Keynesian Economics have been collected in the two volumes edited by Mankiw and Romer (1991).

[3]   A partial attempt at integrating the two theories can be found in Layard, Nickell and Jackman (1991), Annex III.

necessary to intervene on the structure of both the labour and the goods markets in order to achieve higher levels of equilibrium employment. Also to be stressed is the importance of anti-monopolistic policies, even in the presence of partly-indexed unemployment benefits, in order to enhance the effectiveness of 'demand side' anti-cyclical policies.

2. PARTIAL EQUILIBRIUM ANALYSIS

The demand function faced by the i-th firm y_i under monopolistic competition is, as by now standard in the New Keynesian literature:[4]

$$y_i = \frac{y}{z}\left(\frac{P_i}{P}\right)^{-\vartheta}$$

where: $y = \dfrac{M}{P}\,\dfrac{\sigma}{1-\sigma}$; hence:

$$y_i = \frac{\mu}{z}\frac{M}{P}\left(\frac{P_i}{P}\right)^{-\vartheta} \tag{1'}$$

$$\tag{1}$$

where y is overall output, z is the number of firms (= number of goods produced), P_i is the price charged by the i-th firm, P the general price level, M

---

[4] This demand function can be derived from the maximization of a utility function of the representative household,

$$U = \left(z^{\frac{1}{1-\vartheta}}C\right)^{\sigma}\cdot\left(\frac{M}{P}\right)^{1-\sigma}$$

where M is money. Implicit in this utility function, which comprises real money balances, is the hypothesis that expectations about future prices are unit elastic. This hypothesis introduces money neutrality into the model 'by construction'. C is a consumption index (CES) defined as:

$$C = \left(\frac{1}{z}\sum_{i=1}^{z} c_i \frac{\vartheta-1}{\vartheta}\right)^{\frac{\vartheta}{\vartheta-1}}$$

and P is the general price level, defined in turn as:

$$P\left(\frac{1}{z}\sum_{i=1}^{z} P_i^{1-\vartheta}\right)^{\frac{1}{1-\vartheta}}$$

the money supply, and σ can be interpreted as the 'propensity to spend' of households; $\left(\mu = \dfrac{\phi \, \sigma}{1 - \sigma} \right)$.

Assuming the simplest Solow hypothesis about efficiency wages, with z identical firms, one can write the production function, in which the only input is labour, as:

$$q_i = \left(e n_i \right)^{\alpha}^{\phi} \tag{2}$$

where $e = e(w_i)$ is the effort function, with $e' > 0$; $e' < 0$; $\alpha \leq 1$; $(i=1....z)$; w_i is the real wage and n_i employment in firm i.

Suppose that bargaining takes place between a firm operating in a monopolistically competitive goods market with a trade union which represents $\overline{n}$ identical workers. The aim of the firm, which is risk-neutral, is to maximize profit. Assume also, as proposed by Oswald (1982, 1985), that the trade union seeks to maximize the utility of its members and is not interested in increasing the employment of workers extraneous to the organization. One thus has a quasi-concave utility function which generates indifference curves with a kink for a value of employment equal to the number of trade union members $(n_i = \overline{n})$:

$$V_i \left(w_i, n_i \right) = n_i \left(v(w_i) - v(r) \right) \qquad \text{for } n_i \leq \overline{n}$$

$$V_i \left(w_i, \overline{n} \right) = \left(v(w_i) - v(r) \right) \qquad \text{for } n_i \leq \overline{n}$$

where V_i is the trade union's utility function, r is the reservation wage and $v(r)$ is the reservation utility of union members.

Assuming that s stands for the bargaining power of eac $>$ union, the generalized Nash solution to the above problem is achieved by choosing the nominal wage W_i in order to solve the following maximization program:[5]

$$max. \ \Omega = \{ n_i \left[v(w_i) - v(r) \right] \}^s \cdot \pi_i^{(1-s)} \tag{3}$$

$$s.t. \ \pi_{in} = e(w_i) R' \left[e(w_i) n_i \right] - w_i = 0$$
$$n_i \leq n$$

---

[5] The generalized Nash solution may be seen as an approximation of the result obtained, using a non-cooperative approach, with sequential bargaining for which it is supposed that the players' speed of reaction to each others' proposals tends towards infinity. See Binmore, Rubinstein and Wolinski (1986).

where $R_i^{'} = \dfrac{\partial R_i}{\partial (en_i)}$ is the marginal revenue product of labour in efficiency

units, π_i is the profit of firm i and π_{in} is the first derivative with respect to n_i.

If the constraint on employment is not binding, $n_i \leq \bar{n}$, from the first-order conditions for the solution of program (3) one obtains:

$$sw_i \frac{v^{'}}{v(w_i)-v(r)} = (1-s)\frac{n_i w_i}{\pi_i}\left(1-e^{'}R_i^{'}\right)+s\varepsilon\left(1-\frac{\partial\left[eR_i^{'}\right]}{\partial w_i}\right) \qquad (4)$$

where $v^{'} = \dfrac{\partial v}{\partial w}; \varepsilon = \dfrac{1}{1-\beta}; \beta = \dfrac{\alpha(\vartheta-1)}{\vartheta} \leq 1$. ε is the elasticity of the individual

firm's labour demand to the real wage.)

Equation (4) expresses the balance of gains and losses for each party: the percentage marginal benefit for the workers deriving from a wage increase, as expressed by the term on the left-hand side, must be equal to the cost that derives from it both for the firm in terms of reduced profits, and for the workers in terms of reduced employment, as results from the two terms on the right-hand side. Obviously, gains and losses are to be weighted with the bargaining power of each party.

The wage/employment combination obtained depicts a departure from the efficient allocation of resources that would come about in a competitive setting because of the combined effect of the degree of firms' monopoly in the goods market and the unions' market power in determining wages, and of the information asymmetry captured by the effort function. Assuming that the trade unions are risk-neutral and that their utility function is of the type $V_i = n_i(w_i - r)$, the production function (2) and an effort function with constant elasticity of the type $e = w_i^{\eta}$ can be used, with $\eta < 1$ to simplify (4), which can be written as:[6]

$$sw_i \frac{1}{w_i - r} = (1-s)\frac{\beta}{1-\beta}(1-\eta)+s\frac{1}{1-\beta}(1-\beta\eta) \qquad (5)$$

from which the bargained wage can be calculated:

---

[6] The constant elasticity effort function is also used by Lindbeck and Snower (1991). Note that, contrary to the standard assumption of Solow's model, here e(0)=0.

$$w_i = \frac{\beta(1-\eta)+s(1-\beta)}{\beta(1-\eta)}r \qquad (6)$$

Assuming $\eta<1$, which is necessary to obtain $w_i>0$, is justified because the presence of the unions induces firms to pay higher wages than they would otherwise wish to pay on the basis of efficiency considerations alone[7]. Moreover, without efficiency considerations (with $\eta=0$), (6) would reduce to:

$$w_i = \frac{\beta+s(1-\beta)}{\beta}r \qquad (6')$$

which is the standard result of right-to-manage models.

The following table shows all the cases obtainable from the various combinations of hypotheses concerning trade union power and the effort function.

	$e=1(\eta=0)$	$e\neq1(\eta>0)$
$s=0$	PERFECT COMPETITION	EFFICIENCY WAGE
$0<s<1$	RIGHT TO MANAGE	RIGHT TO MANAGE *CUM* EFFICIENCY WAGE
$s=1$	MONOPOLY UNION	MONOPOLY UNION *CUM* EFFICIENCY WAGE

Both (6) and (6') show the bargained wage as a mark-up on the reservation wage, but it is evident that the bargained wage obtainable from (6) is higher than that obtainable from (6'), and that efficiency considerations therefore push up the bargained wage.

It is possible to assess the influence of the various relevant parameters and their interaction on the bargained wage. For this purpose expression (6) can be rewritten simply as:

$$w_i = \gamma r \qquad (6'')$$

---

[7] The 'Solow condition' for efficiency wage models without bargaining is that, in equilibrium, the elasticity of the effort function is one. A less than unit elastic effort function is assumed by Layard, Nickell and Jackman (1991), Annex 3.1, where an analysis of efficiency wages combined with union bargaining is sketched.

where $\gamma = \dfrac{\beta(1-\eta)+s(1-\beta)}{\beta(1-\eta)}$. It is therefore sufficient to assess the sign of

the partial derivatives of γ with respect to the parameters. It can easily be checked that:

$$\frac{\partial \gamma}{\partial \alpha} = -\frac{s}{\alpha^2(1-m)(1-\eta)} < 0 \tag{7}$$

where $m = \dfrac{1}{\vartheta}$, $\beta = \alpha(1-m)$, with m expressing the firm's degree of monopoly.
As α represents the inverse of the elasticity of employment to output, a higher α implies a lower real wage because the elasticity of labour demand increases, rendering the trade-off between wage and employment more unfavourable to the trade union.

Vice-versa, obviously, the greater the trade union's power, the higher the wage that it is able to win for its members:

$$\frac{\partial \gamma}{\partial s} = \frac{(1-\beta)}{\beta(1-\eta)} > 0 \tag{8}$$

Moreover, the presence of trade-union power reverses the traditional (Kaleckian) inverse relation between the firm's monopoly power and the real wage, in that the trade union manages to appropriate part of the firm's rent. Hence the higher this rent, the higher the bargained wage:

$$\frac{\partial \gamma}{\partial m} = \frac{s}{\alpha(1-m)^2(1-\eta)} > 0 \tag{9}$$

The more pressing the reasons that induce firms to pay wages higher than competitive ones, independently of trade-union power, the higher the wage, which will therefore vary positively with an increase in the elasticity of the effort function:

$$\frac{\partial \gamma}{\partial \eta} = \frac{s(1-\beta)}{\beta(1-\eta)^2} > 0 \tag{10}$$

By computing the second mixed derivatives it can be shown that the various imperfections of both the labour and the goods markets *marginally* reinforce each other in determining a bargained wage higher than the 'Walrasian' one:

$$\frac{\partial^2 \gamma}{\partial m \, \partial s} = \frac{1}{\alpha(1-m)^2(1-\eta)} > 0 \tag{11}$$

$$\frac{\partial^2 \gamma}{\partial m \, \partial \eta} = \frac{s}{\alpha(1-m)^2(1-\eta)^2} > 0 \tag{12}$$

$$\frac{\partial^2 \gamma}{\partial \eta \, \partial s} = \frac{(1-\beta)}{\beta(1-\eta)^2} > 0$$

(13)

Expression (13) is of special interest. Greater bargaining power enables the trade union to obtain higher wages the greater the elasticity of the effort function, because firms are more willing to accept trade-union demands the more sensitive effort is to the real wage. In other words, the ability of firms to curb wages is weakened by the information asymmetry from which they suffer in their dealings with the workers.

This result conflicts with the findings of Lindbeck and Snower (1991) and Lindbeck (1993) concerning the interactions between efficiency wages and insiders-outsiders. Lindbeck and Snower argue that it is easy to show that the two market imperfections examined reciprocally weaken each other: 'the greater the market power of unions is, the smaller is the need for the firm to raise the wage rate for efficiency wage reasons, and vice versa' (Lindbeck, 1993, p. 45). However, Lindbeck and Snower do not provide a convincing proof of their conclusion, which can actually be disproved by means of numerical simulations using parameter values within the range of acceptability assumed by the two authors (Boitani and Damiani, 1995a).

3. GENERAL EQUILIBRIUM

In order to check the results set out above, and also to assess the effects of the various imperfections on the overall employment level, it is necessary to take the further step of identifying the outcomes obtainable in a general economic equilibrium context. First, the reservation wage, which is given for each individual operator, should be considered as an endogenous variable. For example, it can be specified as a weighted average of the unemployment benefit fixed in real terms, weighted with the probability of not finding a job, and of the real pay obtainable from other firms weighted with the probability of being employed:

$$r = u \, b + (1 - u)w$$

(14)

where b is the real benefit paid to the unemployed and u is the unemployment rate, w is the wage earned in other firms, n is total employment, and l total

labour force $\left(u = \dfrac{l-n}{l} \right)$.[8] Thus the strategy of each trade union can be defined as an optimal replay function to the other wage strategies.

---

[8]   For the sake of simplicity, it is assumed that unemployment benefits are entirely financed out of lump-sum taxes (t) on all workers including the unemployed: tl=(l-n)b. Given the homotheticity of preferences, the distribution of these taxes has no influence on aggregate demand. The balanced budget hypothesis entails: $t = \left[(l-n)/l\right]b = ub$.

The symmetrical Nash equilibrium is obtained when, consequent on bargaining between individual firms and trade unions, the same pay $w_i = w$ is established in each of the z firms. By imposing this condition and substituting r in equation (6) one obtains in the (w, n) space a positive sloping curve which represents the combinations between bargained wages and employment levels achievable in the labour market. This relation cannot be interpreted as a labour supply function in the usual sense of the term because it is not derived from the maximizing choices of each worker. It can instead be considered as the outcome of the collective bargaining between firms and trade unions which establishes the symmetrical equilibrium $w_i = w$. It is the well known 'wage rule':

$$w = \frac{\gamma(l-n)}{l-\gamma n}b \tag{15}$$

$$\frac{\partial w}{\partial n} = \frac{\gamma(\gamma-1)l}{(l-\gamma n)^2}b > 0 \tag{16}$$

since $\gamma > 1$. The wage equation (15), which comprises all the contractual arrangements available in the labour market, can be straightforwardly transformed into a relation between real wage and unemployment rate:

$$w = \frac{\gamma u}{1-\gamma(1-u)}b \tag{17}$$

which enables determining a minimum unemployment rate, other than 0 and equal to $(\gamma-1)/\gamma$, in correspondence to which the real wage tends towards infinity, so that the wage rule in the (w, u) plane becomes vertical. Moreover, as the unemployment rate rises, the wage tends towards a minimum value equal to the unemployment benefit. The wage/employment combination that comes about and is compatible with equilibrium in the goods market will therefore not be able to generate full employment levels of production.

It is interesting to note that the effects of variations in the parameters already analysed at a partial equilibrium level keep the same sign as far as the wage rule is considered. In fact, using expression (15), by simple derivation one obtains:

$$\frac{\partial w}{\partial \gamma} = \frac{l(l-n)}{(l-\gamma n)^2}b > 0 \tag{18}$$

However, the global effects of variations in the parameters on equilibrium wages and employment depend on the impact of these same parameters on the so-called price rule, that is on the relation between wages and employment obtained from the maximization of firms' profit under monopolistic competition and from the hypothesis of symmetric equilibrium ($P_i = P$ as well as $w_i = w$).

Utilizing the demand function (1) - under the simplifying hypothesis that $\sigma = 0.5$ - and the production function (2), together with the constant elasticity effort function, one obtains the price rule:

$$w = \left(\frac{n}{z}\right)^{\frac{1-\alpha}{\eta\alpha-1}} \cdot \beta \frac{1}{1-\eta\alpha} \tag{19}$$

In the (w, n) space, the price rule (PP) is a negatively sloping curve,[9] its derivative depends on the same parameters that enter the wage rule (ww) except for trade union power. As firms' degree of monopoly increases, the (PP) schedule shifts downwards, because the wage that firms are willing to pay for each given level of employment is lower:

$$\left.\frac{\partial w}{\partial m}\right|_{PP} = \left(\frac{n}{z}\right)^{\alpha-1} \cdot \frac{\alpha}{1-\eta\alpha} \cdot w^{\eta\alpha} < 0 \tag{20}$$

Given that with an increase in m the (ww) schedule shifts upwards, as already shown above, there is an inevitable negative effect on employment, while, at this level of analysis, the effect on the equilibrium wage remains indeterminate. Conversely, greater elasticity of the effort function increases the wage that firms are willing to pay for each given level of employment, and hence the (PP) schedule shifts upwards. Since increases in η also shift the (ww) schedule upwards, in this case there is a positive total effect on wages, while the effect on employment is ambiguous:

$$\left.\frac{\partial w}{\partial \eta}\right|_{PP} = \frac{\alpha}{1-\eta\alpha} \log w \cdot w > 0 \tag{21}$$

In order to assess the variations in the equilibrium levels of both wages and employment, given the difficulty of identifying explicit solutions for the model under examination, a number of numerical simulations were used which employed values for the parameters within the acceptability range of each of them.

As Figure 5.1 shows, as the degree of monopoly (m) increases, equilibrium employment diminishes monotonically (an old Kaleckian finding), whilst wages increase monotonically, as explained above. The upward shift of the (ww) curve more than off-sets the downward shift of the (PP) curve.

---

[9] In fact $\dfrac{\partial w}{\partial n} = \dfrac{1-\alpha}{\eta\alpha-1} z^{\frac{\alpha-1}{\eta\alpha-1}} \cdot \beta^{\frac{1}{1-\eta\alpha}} \cdot n^{\frac{2-\alpha(1+\eta)}{\eta\alpha-1}} < 0$, because $\eta\alpha < 1$.

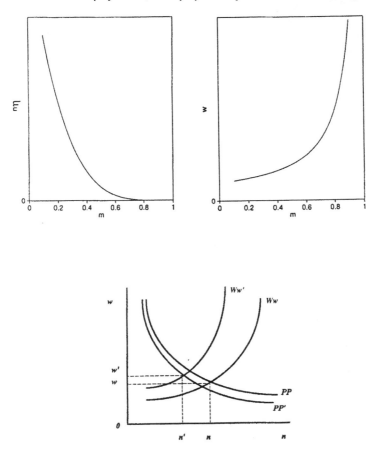

Figure 5.1 Changes in the equilibrium values of w and n as m increases.

The same happens when increases in the elasticity of the effort function (η) occur, although the negative effect on employment is weaker than that caused by increases in the degree of monopoly, as shown in Figure 5.2.

Increases in trade union power causes shift only in the (*ww*) schedule (Figure 5.3): hence one has unambiguously higher equilibrium wages and lower equilibrium employment levels.

More complex are things when considering increases in the coefficient α, which expresses the inverse of employment elasticity to output. In this case, while the real wage diminishes monotonically, the level of employment rises up to intermediate values of α and then falls (Figure 5. 4). Whereas increases in α push the wage rule downwards - as revealed by joint examination of (7) and (18) - the price rule shifts first upwards and then downwards. After

195

a certain point, the indirect positive effect on 'labour demand' exerted by a lower real wage associated with higher values of α is more than off-set by the direct negative effect of employment's lesser elasticity to output.

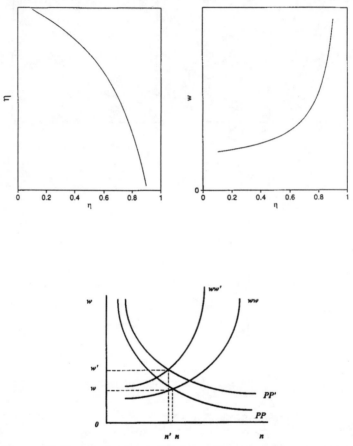

Figure 5.2 Changes in the equilibrium values of w and n as η increases.

It is also possible to show, again using simple simulations, that the combined effects on the equilibrium values of n and w exerted by simultaneous changes in the parameters expressing the degree of market imperfection (s, m, η) reinforce each other in the case of wages.

More controversial are the combined effects of union bargaining power and efficiency wages on the determination of employment levels. A higher value of the union bargaining power shifts upwards only the wage rule with

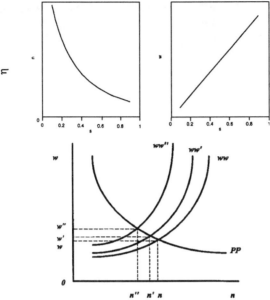

Figure 5.3 Changes in the equilibrium values of w *and* n *as* s *increases.*

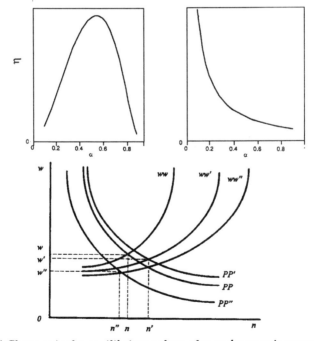

Figure 5.4 Changes in the equilibrium values of w *and* n *as* α *increases.*

unequivocal negative effects on employment. On the other hand, a greater elasticity of the effort function shifts upwards also the (PP) schedule, because the wage that the firms are willing to pay for each level of employment increases when η increases. Therefore a greater η has a positive total effect on wages, but has an ambiguous impact on employment. To tackle this analytically untractable issue, some numerical simulations have been performed. The results are shown in table 5.1 and 5.2.

Table 5.1 shows how the wage increases due to higher unions' bargaining power increase monotonically with higher values of the elasticity of the effort function. The numerical values of the first derivative of w with respect to the unions' bargaining power (s) are calculated for the initial values $l = 1, b = 1, z = 10, \alpha = 0.75, m = 0.3, s = 0.1$.[10]

Table 5.1

η	$\partial w / \partial s$
0.1	1.33864
0.2	1.51034
0.3	1.73235
0.4	2.03048
0.5	2.45169
0.6	3.09124
0.7	4.17548
0.8	6.40056
0.9	13.3789

Table 5.2 shows that the unemployment rate increases due to higher unions' bargaining power, calculated for the same initial values of the parameters, are not monotonic. As the elasticity of the effort function approaches unity the unemployment rate increases become smaller and smaller.

Tables 5.1 and 5.2 show that the combined effects on the equilibrium levels of n and w exerted by simultaneous changes of s and η not orly reinforce each other in the case of wages, as already shown in analytical terms, but reinforce or weaken each other in the case of employment. An increase in each imperfection has negative effects on employment, but the marginal effects can fade with simultaneous increases of the other imperfection.

The intuition behind such a result is that a greater elasticity of the effort

---

[10] The qualitative results shown in tables 5.1 and 5.2 are unaffected by the values assumed for the scale variables l and z.

function pushes up wages, while simultaneously reduces the absolute value of the elasticity of employment to wages and therefore reduces the effect of employment shrinkage.

Table 5.2

η	$\partial w / \partial s$
0.1	1.70805
0.2	1.71446
0.3	1.72143
0.4	1.72872
0.5	1.73556
0.6	1.73969
0.7	1.73424
0.8	1.69492
0.9	1.50574

As a conclusion, the overall effect of the combined actions of efficiency wages and union bargaining are positive on wage patterns and negative on employment levels. Moreover, the efficency wages and union power mutually reinforce each other to increase the bargained wage, but the effects of their interaction are ambiguous in the case of employment. The higher the wage elasticity of effort, the lower the reduction in firms' profits due to an increase in the real wage, hence the stronger the impact of unions on bargained wages. At the same time, the negative impact on employment of a higher union bargaining strength is marginally mitigated by the higher responsiveness of productivity to wages.

4.   NOMINAL RIGIDITIES AND MARKET IMPERFECTIONS

In the model analysed above, although the employment level is below full employment, it is entirely determined by real variables, while money is wholly ncutral - as in models of 'classical' derivation. However, it only requires the presence of 'small' nominal rigidities for the Keynesian result of non-neutrality to be obtained.

A plausible hypothesis advanced in justification of nominal rigidities and non-neutrality envisages the presence of unemployment benefits *fixed in*

Financial Constraints and Market Failures

nominal terms. This hypothesis has been analysed by Dixon (1990, 1991) and is examined by Boitani and Damiani (1995b) in a model conforming with the one set out in previous sections - with right-to-manage bargaining in the labour market and monopolistic competition in the goods market - to show that Dixon's results can be obtained in a context more general than the one he examines.[11] In that which follows we shall further generalize the model in order: i) to take account of the efficiency wages hypothesis, again on the assumption that the effort function has constant elasticity; ii) to take account of varying degrees of nominal rigidity, that is of different degrees of benefit indexation.

Suppose that for each of the z price-making firms operating in the system the output demand curve is given by (1') while the production function is, as is customary, a Cobb-Douglas such as (2). The firm-level unions (but under monopolistic competition firm and sector-level unions coincide) assume the general price level as given and take the unemployment benefit to be their minimum reference wage. For the sake of simplicity, assume that unemployment benefit is the only alternative to the wage deriving from employment in any firm; that is that the chances of finding a new job after dismissal are nil. Thus the real reservation wage can be expressed as:

$$r = B / P \tag{22}$$

The Nash solution to right-to-manage wage bargaining is identified by solving the maximization problem:

$$max \quad \Omega = \left[n_i \left(\frac{w_i}{P} - \frac{B}{P} \right) \right]^s \pi_i^{(1-s)} \tag{23}$$

$$\text{s.t.} \quad n_i^d = \left(\frac{Wi}{P} \right)^{-\varepsilon} \cdot \beta^\varepsilon \left(\frac{y}{z} \right)^{\frac{\varepsilon}{\vartheta}} \cdot e^{\varepsilon\beta}$$

The optimal monetary wage is fixed by applying a mark-up to the unemployment benefit: $W_i = \gamma B$, where γ is still equal to: $\dfrac{\beta(1-\eta)+s(1-\beta)}{\beta(1-\eta)}$

In symmetrical equilibrium $W = W_i = \gamma B$, from which one straightforwardly deduces that the wage rule in the (W, n) space is a horizontal straight line whose intercept with the W axis depends on the value of γ and therefore on all the parameters comprised in γ.

---

[11] Dixon's hypothesis is used by Fender and Yip (1993) to study monetary policy in an interesting two-period model. Other hypotheses to microfound the rigidity of nominal wages have been advanced by Bhaskar (1990) - which is also analysed in Boitani and Damiani (1995b) - Akerlof (1980 and 1982) and Holden (1994).

If trade unions and firms lie on their optimal reply function, symmetrical equilibrium in the goods and labour markets allows the following equations to be obtained for the level of employment and aggregate real output:

$$n = \frac{M\beta}{\gamma B} \tag{24}$$

$$y = \left(\frac{M}{\gamma B}\right)^{\frac{\alpha(1-\eta)}{1-\eta\alpha}} \cdot \beta^{\frac{\alpha}{1-\eta\alpha}} \tag{25}$$

Moreover, on the basis of the quantitative relation derivable from the maximization of utility by households, and set out at the beginning of section 2, and assuming once again $\sigma=0.5$ for the sake of simplicity, the general price level can be obtained as:

$$P = M^{\frac{(1-\alpha)}{1-\eta\alpha}} (\gamma B)^{\frac{\alpha(1-\eta)}{1-\eta\alpha}} \beta^{-\frac{\alpha}{1-\eta\alpha}} \tag{26}$$

Suppose now that a monetary shock of magnitude μ occurs such that $M = M_0(1+\mu)$ after the shock, where M_0 is the money supply before the shock, and assume that the nominal benefit is set on the basis of a full indexation rule to the general price level. One then obtains the following results:

$$B = b_0 P_0 (1+\mu) = B_0 (1+\mu) \tag{27}$$

where b_0 and B_0 are respectively the real and nominal benefit before the shock μ on the money supply. It is then straigthforward to derive:

$$P = P_0 (1+\mu) \tag{28}$$

$$n = \frac{M_0(1+\mu)\beta}{\gamma B_0(1+\mu)} = n_0 \tag{29}$$

Expression (29) confirms that real rigidities (such as those caused by monopolistic competition, efficiency wages, and union bargaining power) are not sufficient, in the absence of nominal rigidities, to obtain real effects of monetary shocks. However, the introduction of a small nominal friction, such as a partial indexation for the unemployment benefit, causes the monetary disturbances to have real effects.

One can write the price level after the shock as a function of the former price level P_0, the magnitude of the shock μ, the degree of benefit indexation and the parameter of price adjustment x of the z maximizing firms in symmetric equilibrium:

$$P = P_0(1+\mu)^{kx} \tag{30}$$

where $x = \dfrac{(1-a)}{(1-a)-(k-1)a(1-\eta)} \leq 1$. The nominal benefit can then be written as:

$$B = b_0 P_0 (1+\mu)^{kx} \tag{31}$$

It is easy to verify that $x \leq 1$ for $0 \leq k \leq 1$, with $x=1$ for $k=1$, the full indexation case. In the presence of a nominal rigidity both the general level of prices and wages and real magnitudes depend on the money supply. The equation for the employment level is:

$$n = \frac{M_0(1+\mu)\beta}{\gamma B_0(1+\mu)^{kx}} = n_0(1+\mu)^{(1-kx)} \geq n_0 \tag{32}$$

By acting through the quantitative equation on the price level, an increase in the money supply reduces the real value of the unemployment benefit, thereby expanding, through a reduction of the real reservation wage, the demand for labour.

In order to assess the effectiveness of economic policy measures, expression (32) can be used to derive the multiplier associated with nominal shocks. The results suggest that the real influence of monetary disturbances increases with the degree of nominal rigidity, that is inversely with the degree of benefit indexation. For $k<1$ it holds:

$$\frac{dn}{d\mu} \equiv \phi = (1-kx)n_0(1+\mu)^{-kx} > 0 \tag{33}$$

$$\frac{d\phi}{dk} = -A\phi < 0 \tag{34}$$

where $A = \dfrac{(1-\alpha)(1-\alpha\eta)}{((1-\alpha)-(k-1)\alpha(1-\eta))^2}\left(\dfrac{1}{1-kx}+\log(1+\mu)\right) > 0$

Despite the non-neutrality of the money supply, the equilibrium level of employment is homogeneous of degree 0 in M and B: an increase in nominal money balances, if accompanied by a full indexation rule for benefits, will not cause changes in the real magnitudes. Obviously, given the money supply, by appropriately altering the degree of indexation of the benefits paid to the unemployed, different Pareto-ranked levels of output and employment can be obtained. Hence, for every given mix of policies (M, k) there exists a single macroeconomic equilibrium; but suitable alterations to the mix give rise to a continuum of employment equilibria which Dixon labels as the 'Natural Range of Unemployment'.

It should be stressed that in a Walrasian economy, the presence of nominal frictions alone is not enough to generate Keynesian outcomes. In a competitive labour market, for example, a partly indexed unemployment benefit would not induce the economy to move away from the full employment allocation of labour resources. Only in a world of price-makers, and in which real 'rigidities' are obtained from maximizing behaviour, do possible nominal stickinesses enable the result of the non-neutrality of nominal shocks to be obtained.

It should also be pointed out that it is precisely an instrument acting 'on the supply side' (namely the degree of indexation of the unemployment benefit) which makes it possible for measures designed to boost demand - such as increasing the money supply - to have effects on the real variables. A policy intended to achieve more efficient equilibria therefore entails the coordinated use of different instruments in order to ensure that they do not neutralize each other. In the presence of a partial indexation rule for benefits, an expansionary monetary policy - which pushes up the general price level - will reduce the subsidy in real terms, thereby cutting back the real wage and increasing employment.

However, when the nominal rigidity is accompanied by growing imperfections in the goods and labour markets, monetary policy becomes less effective; as can be seen by calculating the variations in the money multiplier (ϕ) with respect to the elasticity of the effort function, to trade union power and to firms' degree of monopoly:

$$\frac{\partial \phi}{\partial \eta} = -F\phi < 0$$

where
$$F = \frac{k(1-\alpha)(1-k)\alpha}{((1-\alpha)-(k-1)\alpha(1-\eta))^2} + \frac{1}{\gamma}\frac{s(1\beta)}{\beta(1-\eta)^2} > 0. \qquad (35)$$

$$\frac{\partial \phi}{\partial s} = -(1-kx)(1+\mu)^{-kx}\frac{n_0}{\gamma} \cdot \frac{(1-\beta)}{\beta(1-\eta)} < 0 \qquad (36)$$

$$\frac{\partial \phi}{\partial m} = -(1-kx)(1+\mu)^{-kx}\frac{n_0}{\gamma} \cdot \frac{s}{\alpha(1-m)^2(1-\eta)} < 0 \qquad (37)$$

These results can be straightforwardly explained in terms of the traditional graphical apparatus of aggregate demand and supply. The partial indexation of the benefit renders the aggregate supply curve elastic instead of vertical (as in the case examined in section 3). As real rigidities increase, however, the elasticity of the aggregate supply curve diminishes, with consequently lower real effects of the shifts in the aggregate demand curve generated by monetary shocks.

An increase in real 'rigidities', therefore, reduces the possibility of increasing employment by means of traditional expansionary monetary policies. Measures which intervene to reduce the market power and the information asymmetries of agents involved in bargaining may help not only to reduce equilibrium unemployment but also to enhance the effectiveness of 'demand side' anti-cyclical policies.

5. CONCLUSIONS

The analysis conducted in previous sections has shown the interactions among the various 'imperfections' of both the labour and goods markets in the determination of wages and equilibrium employment and in the effectiveness of monetary policy when nominal rigidities are present. Although it is not claimed that the subject has been exhaustively dealt with, it emerges that explaining unemployment with wage 'rigidities' is not correct. When wages are determined optimally, given the informational asymmetries and the institutional arrangements of the labour market, it makes little more sense talking of the 'rigidity' of the real wage than it does talking of the 'rigidity' of the prices fixed by oligopolistic or monopolistic firms in order to maximize their profits (Hahn, 1987).

The fact that each market imperfection helps to raise the unemployment rate above the ideal of perfect competition is intuitive. We have shown that, first, these various 'imperfections' reinforce each other in generating equilibrium results distant from the social optimum and, second, that they combine with nominal rigidities to push down the equilibrium employment level and to reduce the anti-cyclical effectiveness of the monetary instrument. And we have highlighted a number of interesting interactions between the 'supply side' and the 'demand side' of a macroeconomic model.

The economic policy implications to be drawn, with all the caution necessary when working with simplified models, seem quite clear. Reducing involuntary equilibrium unemployment requires pro-competitive policies in *both* the labour market *and* the goods market. The flexibility of the labour market obtained by curbing trade union power is not sufficient in the presence of high levels of firms' monopoly power. Moreover, curbing trade union power is of limited effectiveness in the absence of measures designed to reduce information asymmetries in the labour market. As we have seen, a high elasticity of the effort function to the wage - which is a measure, albeit approximate, of such asymmetries - strengthens the unions' bargaining power by rendering firms more willing to negotiate higher real wages, with negative effects on employment.

Measures designed to reduce market imperfections also seem necessary to cushion the negative impact of possible nominal wage rigidities due to the presence, for instance, of partly-indexed unemployment benefits. Moreover, such 'supply side' policies would give greater effectiveness to counter-cyclical demand policies, like monetary policies. Hence, in a structurally imperfect economy (macroeconomic) demand and (microeconomic) supply policies have to be used together in order to pursue higher employment levels.

REFERENCES

Akerlof, G.A. (1980), 'A Theory of Social Custom of which Unemployment May Be one Consequence', in Akerlof (1984), 69-100.

Akerlof, G.A. (1982), 'Labour Contracts as Partial Gift Exchange', in Akerlof (1984), 145-174.

Akerlof, G.A. (1984), *An Economic Theorist's Book of Tales*, Cambridge, Cambridge University Press.

Akerlof, G.A. and J.L. Yellen (eds.) (1986), *Efficiency Wage Models of the Labor Market*, Cambridge, Cambridge University Press.

Ardeni, P.G., A. Boitani and D. Delli Gatti and M. Gallegati (1995), 'The New Keynesian Economics: A Survey', Chapter 1 of this volume.

Bhaskar, V. (1990), 'Wage Relativities and the Natural Range of Unemployment', *Economic Journal*, 100, supplement, 60-66.

Binmore, K.A., A. Rubinstein and A. Wolinski (1986), 'The Nash Bargaining Solution in Economic Modelling', *Rand Journal of Economics*, 17, 176-188.

Boitani, A. and M. Damiani (1995a), 'Interactions between Efficiency Wages and Bargaining Theories', *University of Perugia Working Paper*, n. 1.

Boitani, A. and M. Damiani (1995b), 'Mercato del lavoro e Nuova Macroeconomia Keynesiana', in Amendola A. (ed.) (1995), *Disoccupazione e mercato del lavoro*, Napoli, ESI.

Boitani, A., D. Delli Gatti and L. Mezzomo (1992), 'Concorrenza imperfetta, esternalità e spiegazioni delle rigidità nella Nuova Economia Keynesiana', *Economia Politica*, 9, 299-361.

Boitani, A. and A. Salanti (1994), 'The Multifarious Role of Theories in Economics: The Case of Different Keynesianisms', in Klein P. (ed.) (1994), *The Role of Theories in Economics*, Boston, Kluwer, 121-158.

Dixon, H. (1990), 'Imperfect Competition, Unemployment Benefit and the Non-Neutrality of Money: an Example', *Oxford Economic Papers*, 42, 402-413.

Dixon, H. (1991), 'Macroeconomic Policy in a Large Unionised Economy', *European Economic Review*, 35, 1427-1448.

Dixon, H. and N. Rankin (1994), 'Imperfect Competition and Macroeconomics: A Survey', *Oxford Economic Papers*, 46, 171-195.

Fender, J. and C.K. Yip (1993), 'Monetary Policies in an Intertemporal Macroeconomic Model with Imperfect Competition', *Journal of Macroeconomics*, 15, 439-453.

Hahn, F.H. (1987), 'On Involuntary Unemployment', *Economic Journal*, 97, supp., 1-16.

Holden, S. (1994), Wage Bargaining and Nominal Rigidities', *European Economic Review*, 38, 1021-1039.

Layard, R., S. Nickell and R. Jackman (1991), *Unemployment: Macroeconomic Performance and the Labour Market*, Oxford, Oxford University Press.

Lindbeck, A. (1993), *Unemployment and Macroeconomics*, Cambridge Mass., MIT Press.

Lindbeck, A. and D.J. Snower (1991), 'Interactions between the Efficiency Wage and Insider-Outsider Theories', *Economics Letters*, 37, 193-196.

Mankiw, N.G. and D. Romer (eds.) (1991), *The New Keynesian Economics*, 2 voll., Cambridge Mass., MIT Press.

Oswald, A. J. (1982), 'The Microeconomic Theory of the Trade Union', *Economic Journal*, 92, 576-595.

Oswald, A. J. (1985), 'The Economic Theory of Trade Unions: an Introductory Survey', *Scandinavian Journal of Economics*, 87, 160-193.

Pisauro, G. (1991) 'The effect of Taxes on Labour in Efficiency Wage Models', *Journal of Public Economics*, 46, 329-345.

Silvestre, J. (1993) 'The Market Power Foundations of Macroeconomic Policy', *Journal of Economic Literature*, 31, 105-141.

Ulph, A. and D. Ulph (1990), 'Union Bargaining: A Survey of Recent Work', in D. Sapsford and T. Tzannatos (eds.) (1990), *Current Issues in Labour Economics*, Macmillan, London, 86-125.

Weiss, A. (1991), *Efficiency Wages*, Clarendon Press, Oxford.

6. Nominal Shocks, Net Worth and Economic Activity: A New Keynesian View of the Monetary Transmission Mechanism*

Domenico Delli Gatti

Mauro Gallegati

1. INTRODUCTION

The New Keynesian (NK) Economics has provided plenty of different and sometimes contrasting explanations of the impact of a nominal shock on economic activity. This *embarras* de *richesses* (Blanchard and Fischer, 1989) is certainly a sign of vitality however it may also be a source of confusion and misunderstanding. The implications of different types of 'imperfections' have been studied for each and every market (labour, goods and financial markets) on the simplifying assumption that developments in the rest of the economy were irrelevant. Thorough attempts to build a complete macromodel are most needed, in order to take into account the complex relations among different markets and different types of market imperfections. Unfortunately, research in this direction is still in its infancy.

Of course, there are some notable exceptions, especially for that body of NK literature which stresses the macroeconomic role of market power on the goods and labour markets. A case in point is the model of Blanchard and Kiyotaki (1987), who reject the neutrality of money and the policy ineffectiveness proposition relying upon some form of (nominal) rigidity.

*   We thank, for their most insightful comments and criticisms C. Goodhart, E. Baltensperger, P. Bacchetta, C. Favero and participants to the conference of the Confederation of European Economic Association held in Gerzensee (Bern) on April, 27 1994; E. Agliardi, A. Boitani, C. Lucifora, M. Marconi, M. Messori, G. Rodano, E. Saltari, R. Tamborini, G. Weinrich, and participants to the seminars held at the universities of Macerata, Roma and Milan (Catholic University). Of course the usual disclaimer applies.
The present paper is a much extended and modified version of a paper published by the Manchester School, Delli Gatti and Gallegati (1997).

Until the late 80s, a similar attempt was still lacking for that strand of NK literature which emphasizes informational imperfections on capital markets. In a series of recent papers, B.Greenwald and J.Stiglitz (G-S hereafter) have tried to fill the gap laying the microfoundation of a NK macromodel on the assumption of incomplete and asymmetric information (see, for instance, Greenwald and Stiglitz,1988, 1990, 1993). Contrary to Blanchard and Kiyotaki, they reject neutrality and the policy ineffectiveness proposition in a flex-price framework.

In their most recent contribution (Greenwald and Stiglitz,1993) monetary policy affects real output by means of 'price shocks' - which hit the equity base of the corporate sector and influence firms' production decisions, that is aggregate supply. G-S admit that this result has not much to do with Keynes, since aggregate demand does not affect real output[1]. In our opinion, however, this is not the main reason of dissatisfaction. There is more to worry from a NK point of view: G-S' result is not inconsistent with the basic tenet of New Classical Macroeconomics, that is the policy ineffectiveness proposition. In fact G-S' price shock is basically the same as Lucas's 'price surprise', so that their claim that monetary policy affects real output through price shocks is tantamount to saying that changes in monetary policy are effective only if not anticipated. Robert Lucas would certainly agree.

In this chapter, we identify the conditions upon which a NK non-neutrality proposition can be established in a theoretical framework similar to the one proposed by G-S.

In section 2, we present and discuss the stylized features of the economy under scrutiny. Some of the basic assumptions are borrowed from G-S, but we discard that of perfect foresight on the part of lenders. G-S assume, in fact, that banks predict inflation correctly and modify the nominal (contractual) interest rate accordingly in order to keep constant the real return to lending. The implications of this assumption are far reaching. Since the real interest rate is given and constant, output will not respond to monetary policy measures. Policy ineffectiveness is re-established through the Fisher effect,[2] which G-S share with monetarists of all sorts and generations. For instance, if the central bank switch to an expansionary policy stance, the inflation prospects worsen in the eyes of bank managers, who will charge a higher nominal interest rate on loans extended to corporate clients in order to keep the real interest rate constant. The long run aggregate supply, therefore, will not be affected. Only in the short run will output respond to the policy move inasmuch as firms are

---

[1] 'To traditional Keynesians the model of this paper may appear strange: it seems to attribute all the sources of output variability to the supply rather than the demand side' (Greenwald and Stiglitz, 1993, p.103)

[2] As a matter of fact, the empirical literature on the Fisher effect has not reached a consensus yet. Most of the times, however, the empirical evidence does not support the hypothesis (Summers,1983; Mishkin, 1984, 1991).

caught by surprise. By ruling out perfect foresight on the part of banks, we dismiss the hypothesis of a given and constant real interest rate, which is the root of the policy ineffectiveness proposition in GS' framework.

Section 3 is devoted to the analysis of firms' production decisions when information is incomplete on the goods market and asymmetric on the Stock market, so that equity rationing occurs and firms have to rely on bank loans in order to fill their financing gap. Therefore, they run the risk of default. Assuming that bankruptcy is costly, firms behave as if they were risk averse. Firms' production decisions and aggregate supply, therefore, are influenced by the amount of net worth or equity base.

In section 4 we present and discuss the relations between cash flow and corporate debt when firms face a financing constraint, showing that both net worth and corporate debt are increasing linear functions of the level of economic activity. In section 5 we open the 'black box' of the market for bank loans and analyze the monetary transmission mechanism. G-S assume unlimited (endogenous) supply of bank loans however the nature and functions of the credit market and the relations between monetary authorities and the banking system are only touched upon. In a regime of endogenous credit supply, the Central Bank pegs the *nominal* interest rate and the banking system accommodates the demand for bank loans. Credit supply, therefore, is demand-determined at the given (nominal) interest rate. In a sense, we replace Fisher's conjecture according to which the *real* interest rate is exogenous with the hypothesis that the *nominal* interest rate is exogenous and under the control of the central bank. This assumption, of course, does not imply money illusion on the part of firms. In fact both the nominal interest rate and the price level play a role in determining the real burden of debt, which in turn affects real output.

The most important result of the model in a regime of accommodating lending policy is the rejection of the policy ineffectiveness proposition even if policy moves are anticipated. In a sense this is a straightforward result since the nominal interest rate is a target of monetary policy and an argument of the aggregate supply equation. If the central bank switch to an expansionary policy stance, pushing down the interest rate, firms' debt burden becomes lighter and they expand production. In the short run, the output response to a policy move is magnified by the price surprise.

In section 6, we assess the macroeconomic implications of a regime of exogenous credit supply in which the Central Bank controls monetary aggregates through the stock of high powered money and the required reserve ratio. The interest rate on bank loans plays the role of the equilibrating mechanism on the credit market. In this case, a change in the stock of (high powered) money is neutral if perfectly anticipated.

Monetary policy, however, can exert a non-transitory influence on real output through the required reserve ratio. The root of this result is the fact that aggregate supply depends on credit availability, while aggregate demand depends on money balances. Since a change in the reserve ratio leads to changes of credit and money of the same sign but different magnitudes, the policy move exerts a non-negligible impact on output. In fact, if the central bank switch to an expansionary policy stance, pushing down the required reserve ratio given the stock of high powered money, the credit multiplier (the supply of bank loans) increases more than the money multiplier (the money supply) and the output response is positive.

We draw some conclusions and trace the lines of future research in section 7.

2. THE BACKGROUND

In order to keep the argument as simple as possible, we start from the model of a closed economic system without public sector. Three types of agents, that is, firms, households and banks, interact on the markets for labour, credit, (consumption) goods and money. Households supply labour services and demand goods and money in order to carry on transactions. Firms supply goods and demand labour services and bank loans. Banks supply deposits and loans. For the sake of simplicity, in the following we will assume that agents do not hold currency in their portfolio, that is all the transactions are carried out by means of checks drawn on demand deposits. In this case money coincides with deposits at banks and base money coincides with banks' reserves. Following G-S we adopt the following assumptions:

(**A.1**) *Technology and market structure.* Each firm carries on production in a world of perfect competition by means of a constant returns to scale (CRS) technology which uses only labour as an input. The CRS production function is:

$$y = n$$

where y is output and n employment. In the following, therefore, output and employment will be synonymous.

(A.1) is a convenient simplifying assumption but the qualitative results are robust to different assumptions concerning technology. A decreasing returns to scale technology, for instance, would yield basically the same results.

(**A.2**) *Uncertainty.* The market environment is 'noisy', that is information over the selling price is limited and incomplete: each firm is not sure at which price it will sell its goods. In other words competition is perfect but not pure due to informational imperfections in the goods market.[3] Price uncertainty is captured by assuming that the price charged by each firm p is a random variable with expected value equal to the average price level P - that is $E(p)=P$ - and finite variance. As a consequence, also the *relative price* $u=p/P$ is a random variable with $E(u)=1$ and finite variance.

(A.3) *Financing.* Standard labour contracts imply a commitment on the part of firms: once hired, workers must be paid the wage agreed upon, whatever the selling price happens to be. Therefore firms must anticipate the wage bill.[4] In a sense, this assumption rules out the possibility for the firms to share the risk of a loss with their workers by means of a wage cut.

(A.4) *Equity rationing* . We rule out the issue of new equities as a viable way of raising funds, due to *equity rationing* (Myers and Majluf, 1984; Greenwald, Stiglitz and Weiss, 1984) which in turn is a consequence of asymmetric information on the Stock market.

Due to equity rationing, firms can finance the wage bill either by depleting their net worth or 'equity base' *(A)* - to be defined precisely later - or by borrowing from banks *(B)*. The demand for bank loans therefore is equal to the wage bill *(Wy)* less the equity base:

$$B = Wy - A$$

where W is nominal wage. Therefore, debt in real terms is:

$$b = wy - a$$

where $b=B/P$, $w=W/P$ and $a=A/P$.

Agents' net assets (assets less liabilities) in this simplyfied economy are shown in table 6.1.

---

[3]   In G-S' framework, uncertainty over the selling price is due to the time structure of production and sale: since production takes time and must be carried out before output is sold, commodities produced today can be sold only tomorrow and future market conditions are not known with certainty.

   Of course a time-lag is the simplest and most common source of market uncertainty but it is not the only one. Even if firms carry on production and sale at the same time, they may not be able to perceive changes in market conditions if they are unable to pierce the veil of informational imperfections.

[4]   In G-S' framework, due to the time structure of production and sale mentioned above workers must be hired and paid before earning sales proceeds. In a sense, in G-S' world, capital is a wage fund which firms must anticipate to their workers. This notion of 'capital' has a classical flavour.

Table 6.1 Agents and net assets (assets - liabilities)

Agents (net) assets	Households	Firms	Banks	Total
Money	M		- M	0
Reserves			H	H
Loans		- B	B	0
Equity base		-A		-A
Capital		Wy		Wy
Total	M	0	0	M=H+Wy-A

Key: M = money (deposits), B = bank loans (corporate debt), A = equity base, W=nominal wage, y =employment, H =base money (banks' reserves).

(**A.5**) *Debt* .In the short run the burden of debt coincides with debt servicing. The burden of debt in each period, therefore, is iB where i is the gross nominal interest rate $(0<i<1)$.[5]

Therefore, for each firm nominal profit is:

$$\Pi = py - iB$$

while real profit is:

$$\pi = uy - ib \tag{2.1}$$

The expression ib represents the cost that the firm incurs in order to carry on production (production costs) which coincides with the *actual burden of debt in real terms*.

Since $E(u)=1$ (see (A.2) above), expected real profit is:

$$E(\pi) = y - ib$$

(**A.6**) *Bankruptcy*. Bankruptcy occurs if real profit becomes negative $(\pi<0)$. Rearranging terms in equation (2.1), this *bankruptcy condition* boils down to:

$$u < i\frac{b}{y} = i\left(w - \frac{a}{y} \right) \equiv \overline{u} \tag{2.2}$$

---

[5]   We do not take into account the impact of the accumulation of debt, which is crucial in explaining business fluctuations. This is the basic tenet of the financial instability hypothesis (Minsky, 1975, 1982, 1986). Eckstein and Sinai (1986) present and discuss the empirical evidence supporting this view. An attempt to put a formal structure on this idea can be found in Delli Gatti, Gallegati and Gardini (1993).

that is: bankruptcy occurs if the relative price is lower than a *critical threshold* ($\overline{u}$) which turns out to be the *average production cost* (see section 3, below). Quite reasonably, in fact, the firm avoids default if it succeeds in recovering at least the average production cost.

(A.7)*Bankruptcy costs*. Bankruptcy is costly. First of all, there are the direct legal and administrative costs of default (Gordon and Malkiel, 1981; Altman,1984; White, 1989). Second, bankruptcy may bring about indirect costs which surface as changes in the stream of cash flows. Third, managers and directors may suffer a loss of reputation, since in the eyes of the public bankruptcy cannot always be attributed to bad luck instead of mismanagement (Gilson, 1990; Kaplan and Reishus, 1990). It is reasonable to assume that the cost of bankruptcy is an increasing function of the firm's size as measured by the level of output. For the sake of modelling convenience, we assume that the cost of bankruptcy (CB) in real terms is a quadratic function, that is:

$$CB = cy^2 \tag{2.3}$$

The parameter c is strictly positive and will be referred to hereafter as the 'bankruptcy coefficient'.

(A.8) *Imperfect information*. Neither borrowers nor lenders can foresee inflation correctly. In other words we rule out perfect foresight for both firms and banks. Therefore they both can be caught by surprise by policy moves.

The lender could 'insure' against prospective losses due to inflation charging a nominal interest rate which incorporates expected inflation. GS assume that lenders are perfectly informed and able to predict inflation correctly. In other words lenders (and only lenders) have perfect foresight. According to G-S, the real interest rate is given and known to banks who adjust the contractual interest rate for inflation in order to keep constant the real return to lending activity.[6] This procedure must be abandoned if uncertainty is pervasive. There is no reason why lenders should be better equipped and smarter than borrowers in forecasting inflation.

The list of assumptions above aims essentially at providing a link between financial variables (the equity base) and aggregate supply as will become clear in the following section. Uncertainty over the selling price (A.2) is a necessary condition for bankruptcy to occur.In an uncertain environment, in fact, the realization of the selling price can be lower than the average production cost, that is realized profits can be negative. If the selling price were known with certainty, the firm would decide in advance whether to start

---

[6]   From the intertemporal utility maximization program, G-S conclude that the real interest rate is equal to the time preference rate of the representative consumer.

production or not according to the profit prospects. Actual profit would never be negative: if sales revenue were smaller than production costs, the entrepeneur would not start production.

A loss *per se* would not lead to bankruptcy if the firm could share it either with its workers (by means of a wage cut) or with other investors, by raising funds on the Stock exchange. Standard labour contracts (A.3) and equity rationing (A.4) rule out this possibility. This is the reason why the firm must rely entirely upon bank loans in order to fill the financing gap. By doing so, the firm runs the risk of going bankrupt (A.6).

Finally, bankruptcy would not impinge on production and employment if it did not imply additional costs. Bankruptcy costs (A.7) lead to *de facto* risk averse behaviour, which provides a crucial link between the financial conditions of the corporate sector and aggregate supply.

3. FINANCIAL CONSTRAINTS AND AGGREGATE SUPPLY: THE OUTPUT-EQUITY LINE

The firm's objective function (say V) is the difference between expected real profit $(E(\pi))$ and the real cost of bankruptcy (CB) in case bankruptcy occurs. We denote the probability of bankruptcy by F. Therefore, the firm's problem is:

$$\underset{y}{Max}\ V = E(\pi) - CB \bullet F = y - i(wy - a) - cy^2 F \qquad (3.1)$$

In order to solve the problem in the simplest way, we assume that the distribution of the random variable u is *uniform* with expected value equal to one[7].

We assume that $u \in [0,2]$. The p.d.f. therefore will be $f = 1/2$. The expected value is $E(u) = 1$ and the variance $\sigma^2 = 1/3$.

The probability of bankruptcy, in this case, is:

$$F = \Pr(u < \overline{u}) = \int_0^{\overline{u}} f(u)du = \frac{\overline{u}}{2} \qquad (3.2)$$

The probability of bankruptcy, therefore, is an increasing linear function of the threshold price $\overline{u}$. Substituting (2.2), (2.3) and (3.2) into (3.1) and rearranging, we end up with the following expression:

---

[7] This is not the procedure followed by G-S, which is much more complicated. They define the expected real return to lending - without imposing any restriction on the density function of the relative price - which turns out to be a function of the threshold price level. Assuming that lenders aim at keeping the real return to lending constant (equal to the given rate of time preference of the representative consumer), they evaluate the probability of bankruptcy as a function of output and the equity base.

$$Max_{y} \quad V = y - i(wy - a) - \frac{cy}{2}i(wy - a) = y - i(wy - a)\left(1 + \frac{c}{2}y\right) \quad (3.1')$$

From the expression above, it is clear that - due to the risk of bankruptcy - total cost is a multiple of the cost of production *(i(wy-a))*, the 'mark up' being an increasing function of the level of economic activity (output) and of the bankruptcy coefficient.

The conditions for a maximum of *V* are:

$$FOC: \quad 1 - iw - ciwy + \frac{cia}{2} = 0$$

$$SOC: \quad -ciw < 0$$

FOC can be interpreted as follows: the *real expected marginal revenue (EMR)*, which is equal to the expected relative price which in turn is equal to one, must be equal to the *real marginal cost (MC)*, which consists of two components: the *marginal production cost (MPC=iw)* and the *marginal bankruptcy cost* $MBC = ci\left(wy - \frac{a}{2}\right)$. The former is independent of output and the equity base[8], while the latter is an increasing function of output and a decreasing function of the equity base. In Figure 6.1, *MBC* is the vertical distance between *MC* and *MPC*.

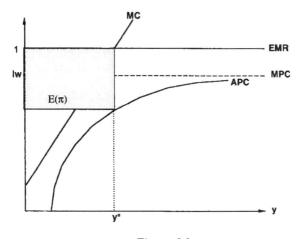

Figure 6.1

---

[8]   This follows from assumption (A.1). In fact if the technology is CRS, the marginal product of labour is always equal to one.

The average cost *(AC)* is the sum of the average production cost, which coincides with the threshold relative price: $APC = i\left(w - \dfrac{a}{y}\right) = \bar{u}$ and the average bankruptcy cost $ABC = \dfrac{cy}{2}(wy - a)$. In Figure 6.1 ABC is simply the vertical distance between AC and APC [9].

In Figure 6.1, y^* is optimal output. Therefore the shaded area represents maximum expected profits. If the realization of the selling price turns out to be much lower than expected, that is if the relative price is much lower than unity, average production costs incurred in producing y^* will be higher than sales proceeds and the firm will go bankrupt. In this case the firm incurs addditional (bankruptcy) costs.

FOC can be thought of as a *labour demand* equation in implicit form. It is easy to verify that the demand for labour is a decreasing function of the real wage and the interest rate and an increasing function of the equity base. An increase of the real wage and/or the interest rate pushes up the marginal cost and leads to a reduction of output. An increase of the equity base reduces the probability of default and the marginal bankruptcy cost (without affecting the marginal production cost) and leads to an increase of output. In order to simplify the argument, we assume:

(A.9) *The real wage is given* that is $w = \bar{w}$.

(A.9) can be interpreted as an infinitely elastic *labour supply* curve. In this case equilibrium on the labour market rules out involuntary unemployment. It represents, however, equally well an instance of *real* wage rigidity: in this case there can be involuntary unemployment. It is worth noting that real wage rigidity *per se* does not imply the non-neutrality of money. A sufficient condition for non neutrality in NK models is, in fact, *nominal* price or wage rigidity (due, for instance, to staggered wage contracts or small menu costs, as shown in Blanchard and Kiyotaki, (1987), section 3). We do not impose any kind of nominal rigidity. The non neutrality results of the present paper, therefore, cannot be attributed to (A.9), which is put forward only for the sake of modelling convenience.

In order to simplify the argument, we normalize the real wage to one: $\bar{w} = 1$. This implies: $b = y - a$.

Solving *FOC* for y and taking (A.9) into account we end up with the

---

[9]   Note that if $wy < a$, the firm can finance the wage bill entirely by means of the accumulated cash flow. No debts (and no costs) are incurred so that profits coincide with revenues. Of course bankruptcy is ruled out in this case.

following:

$$(YA) \qquad y = \frac{1-i}{ci} + \frac{1}{2}a$$

(YA) is the equation of the upward sloping *output-equity line* on the *(y,a)* plane: the volume of output supplied by firms is an increasing linear function of the equity base. The reason for this fact has already been hinted at above: an increase of the equity base reduces the probability of default and the marginal bankruptcy cost allowing for an increase of output.

The interest rate is a shift parameter for the *YA* line: for each level of the equity base an increase of the interest rate reduces output.

4. NET WORTH AND ECONOMIC ACTIVITY: THE EQUITY-OUTPUT LINE

The equity base in nominal terms is a random variable *(Z)* defined as revenues less debt commitments and dividends. We assume that:

(A.10) The flow of dividends is proportional to the equity base: $D=mZ$ where $0<m<1$ is the dividend-payout ratio.

Therefore, we can write:

$$Z = py - i(Py - Z) - mZ$$

Rearranging we get:

$$Z = \theta y(p - iP) \qquad where \quad \theta = \frac{1}{1+m-i}$$

In the following we will assume that:

(A.11) $m=i$ so that $\theta=1$

This assumption is tantamount to saying that shareholders are remunerated at the same rate as debtholders.

Denoting by A the expected value of the random variable Z we can write:

$$A = E(Z) = y[E(p) - iP^e] = y(P - iP^e)$$

Finally, dividing by P we get:

$$(AY) \qquad a = (1 - ih)y \qquad where \qquad h = \frac{P^e}{P}$$

where $h=P^e/P$ is the *price surprise*. If the current average price level increases relative to the expected price (a *positive* price surprise), that is if h goes *down*, the real burden of debt becomes lighter and the equity base increases. The opposite is true, of course, if a negative price surprise occurs.

In order to assure that the equity base is positive, in the following we will assume that:

(A.12) $ih < 1$

(AY) is the equation of the upward sloping *equity-output line* : the volume of net worth that firms build up is an increasing linear function of the level of economic activity as measured by output. The reason for this is simple. Other things being equal, an increase of output pushes up both total revenue and total cost: thanks to (A.12), however, the former increases more rapidly than the latter allowing for an increase in the equity base.

The interest rate and the price surprise are shift parameters for the *AY* line: for each level of output, an increase of the interest rate or a negative price surprise reduces net worth.

We are now ready to discuss the demand and supply of credit. The demand for credit is:

$$b^d = y - a \tag{4.1}$$

Equilibrium on the credit market is brought about by:

$$b^d = b^s = b \tag{4.2}$$

Substituting (4.2) into (4.1) we obtain:

$$b = y - a \tag{4.3}$$

Solving (4.1)(4.3) and taking *(AY)* into account we get:

$$b = ihy \tag{4.4}$$

Both corporate debt and the equity base are increasing linear functions of output. Both the debt-output ratio and the equity base-output ratio are polynomials of the interest rate and the price surprise. The debt-equity ratio, that is the *degree of leverage* is:

$$\frac{b}{a} = \frac{ih}{1 - ih} \tag{4.5}$$

From (4.5) it is clear that the degree of leverage is independent of the level of economic activity and is an increasing function of the interest rate and the price surprise.

5. ENDOGENOUS SUPPLY OF BANK LOANS

We can envisage two polar credit regimes. The first one, which is dealt with in this section, can be characterized as

(A.13) *Accommodating lending policy.* Banks accommodate the demand for loans at the given nominal interest rate, that is the interest rate is exogenous (and somehow under the control of the central bank) while the supply of credit is endogenously determined by demand.
Alternatively we can think of the credit supply process as controlled by the central bank while the interest rate plays the role of the adjustment mechanism on the credit market. In other words the credit supply is exogenous while the interest rate is endogenous. The macroeconomic implications of this alternative credit regime will be dealt with in the next section.

5.1. Aggregate Supply

Solving *(YA)(AY)* for *y* and *a* we obtain the following reduced form:

$$y = \frac{2(1-i)}{ci(1+ih)} \tag{5.1}$$

$$a = \frac{2(1-i)(1-ih)}{ci(1+ih)} \tag{5.2}$$

Since both the *(YA)* and the *(AY)* line slope up, stability is assured if the latter is steeper than the former (see AP.1 in the appendix to this chapter), which is certainly true (Figure 6.2).

A decrease of *h* (a positive price surprise, that is an increase of the current price relative to the expected price) makes the *AY* line rotate downward: the resulting new macroeconomic equilibrium is characterized by a higher level of output and the equity base (Figure 6.3).

An increase of the interest rate makes the AY curve rotate upward and the YA curve shift downward and yields a lower level of output and the equity base (Figure 6.4).

219

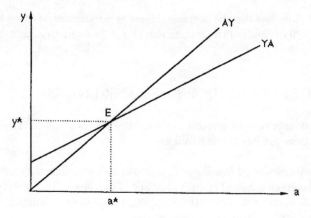

Figure 6.2

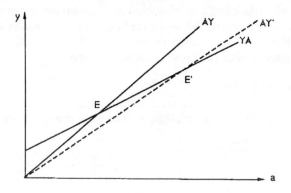

Figure 6.3

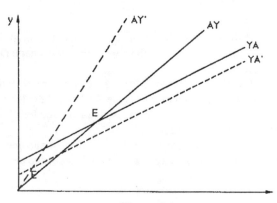

Figure 6.4

Moreover, taking into account (4.4), we get:

$$b = \frac{2h(1-i)}{c(1+ih)}$$

For the sake of simplicity, in the following we adopt a *log-linear approximation* of (5.1). Denoting by '^' the logarithm of a variable, we can write:

$$(AS.I) \quad \hat{y} = y_0 - y_1\hat{i} + y_2(\hat{P} - \hat{P}^e) \qquad \text{where} \quad y_0 > 0, y_1 > 0, y_2 > 0$$

(AS.I) is the *aggregate supply function*. When agents are not caught by surprise, $P=P^e$, so that aggregate supply boils down to:

$$(AS.I') \quad \hat{y} = y_0 - y_1\hat{i}$$

Adopting a convenient - even if not appropriate - label, we will refer to (AS.I') as the *long-run aggregate supply function* (LAS), which is a vertical line on the $(\hat{P}, \hat{y})$ plane. Therefore (AS.I) represents the *short-run aggregate supply function* (SAS), which is an upward sloping straight line on the same plane. The (log of the) interest rate is a shift parameter for both lines.

The aggregate supply function in our framework is clearly and closely related to the Lucas-Sargent aggregate supply function but this striking resemblance is misleading. While the latter is derived from equilibrium in the labour market alone, the former is derived from analysis of the interaction of the labour and the credit markets. This is the reason why the interest rate shows up in the function. Moreover, while the price surprise in the Lucas-Sargent framework represents a *monetary misperception* on the part of workers-producers, that is the incorrect evaluation of the nature of the shock they are facing - mistakenly interpreted as a real shock instead of a nominal one - which affects directly labour supply and production decisions, in the present framework the price shock affects firms' production decisions only indirectly through its impact on the perceived equity base and the probability of bankruptcy.

5.2 Aggregate demand

In order to close the model we need an aggregate demand function. We want to keep the argument as simple as possible and as close as possible to the standard New Classical macromodel. Therefore we adopt the following assumption:

(A.14) *Aggregate demand.* Aggregate demand is derived from a simple quantity equation. Assuming, for the sake of simplicity, that velocity is equal to one, we can write:

$$M = Py \qquad \text{or} \qquad \frac{M}{P} = y \qquad\qquad (5.3)$$

that is output is equal to real money balances.

Money is the sum of corporate debt and high powered money[10], hence: $H+B=Py$. Dividing by P we get: $H/P=y-b=a$. Hence:

$$\frac{H}{P} = (1 - ih)y \qquad\qquad (5.4)$$

Moreover, in the following we will assume that

(A.15) *High powered money* is a decreasing function of the interest rate, that is:

$$H = H(i) \qquad H_i < 0$$

In this credit regime, therefore, the stock of money is endogenous (given the interest rate) since both base money and credit are endogenous. This monetary regime is by no means too peculiar and abstract. As a matter of fact the issue of endogeneity/exogeneity runs through the whole history of monetary thought, with prominent figures in the profession holding opinions on either side. Leaving aside the classical monetary controversies, the assumption of exogeneity has been challenged at least since the Radcliffe report. In the Keynesian camp, Tobin (1970) has sometimes embraced and Kaldor has always strongly endorsed the endogeneity hypothesis. The endogenous view of money creation has been heralded thereafter by Post Keynesian monetary theorists (see Moore, 1988, for a survey in this vein). Also in the Real Business Cycle literature, however, money has been considered endogenous ('reversed causation' hypothesis; King and Plosser, 1984).

Well known and influential theorists, which by no means can be considered unorthodox, still hold the endogenous view even if the mainstream in contemporary monetary theory has always been biased towards exogeneity. Goodhart, for instance, has forcefully argued against the exogenous view. According to Goodhart (1989), the multiplier analysis is a mere tautology: the

---

[10] This is also the conclusion which can be drawn from table 6.1: M=H+Wy-A.

process of money creation runs from a change in interest rate - whether endogenously determined by market forces or governed by the central bank - to a readjustment of monetary aggregates and not the other way round.

Equation (5.4) can be rewritten as follows:

$$P = \frac{H(i)}{(1 - ih)y} \tag{5.5}$$

(5.5) is the equation of the *price level*, which is equal to the ratio of base money to the proportion *(1-ih)* of nominal income. The reaction of the price level to changes in the interest rate is *a priori* undecided. In fact an increase (decrease) of the interest rate brings about a decrease (increase) of both base money and the parameter (1-ih). In the following we will assume:

(A.16) *Price response.* The price level decreases with an increase of the interest rate and viceversa: $P_i < 0$.

It is easy to see that this is the case if (the absolute value of) the interest elasticity of H is greater than (the absolute value of) the interest elasticity of *1-ih*.

We adopt a log-linear approximation of (5.5). The price equation in logs, therefore, can be written as follows:

(AD.I) $\hat{P} = p_0 - p_1\hat{i} - p_2(\hat{P} - \hat{P}^e) - \hat{y}$ *where* $p_0 > 0$, $p_1 > 0$, $p_2 > 0$

When agents are not caught by surprise, the price level equation is:

(AD.I′) $\hat{P} = p_0 - p_1\hat{i}$

(AD.I') is the *long-run aggregate demand function* (LAD), which is a downward sloping straight line on the $(\hat{P}, \hat{y})$ plane.
(AD.I) represents the *short-run aggregate demand function* (SAD), which is a downward sloping straight line on the same plane. From a quick inspection at the equations we can conclude that LAD is steeper than SAD.

In this framework aggregate demand and supply are clearly *interdependent* following a nominal shock, that is a change of the interest rate. Moreover, this interdependence concerns both the long run and the short run curves. An increase of the interest rate engineered by the central bank, in fact, leads to an inward shift of both the AD and AS curves.

5.3 Rational expectations equilibrium

The AD-AS system can be solved for the rational expectations equilibrium

Financial Constraints and Market Failures

values of $\hat{P}$ and $\hat{y}$ *given* $\hat{i}$. The solutions are:

$(RE.I.1)$ $\hat{y}^* = y_0 - y_1\hat{i} + \dfrac{y_2(p_1 - y_1)}{1 + p_2 + y_2}(\hat{Ei} - \hat{i})$

$(RE.I.2)$ $\hat{P}^* = (p_0 - y_0) - \dfrac{p_1 - y_1}{1 + p_2 + y_2}[\hat{i} + (p_2 + y_2)\hat{Ei}]$

where $\hat{Ei}$ is the expected value of the (log of the) interest rate conditional on information available at the moment expectations are formed.

From the RE solution of the AD-AS system we derive the following proposition:

(P.1) *Long run policy effectiveness* Even if changes of the interest rate are perfectly anticipated, monetary policy affects real output.In fact long run income is a decreasing function of the interest rate.

Proof: If $\hat{Ei} = \hat{i}$, (RE.I.1) boils down to:

$(RE.I.1')$ $\hat{y}_l^* = y_0 - y_1\hat{i}$

The effect of changes in the interest rate on the price level is undecided *a priori*. If changes in the interest rate yield a relatively weak income response $(p_1 > y_1)$ the price level is a decreasing function of the interest rate and viceversa. In fact, if $\hat{Ei} = \hat{i}$, (RE.I.2) boils down to:

$(RE.I.2')$ $\hat{P}_l^* = (p_0 - y_0) - (p_1 - y_1)\hat{i}$

Therefore the long run interest elasticities of income and the price level are as follows:

$\varepsilon_l^y = -y_1$

$\varepsilon_l^p = -(p_1 - y_1)$

In Figure 6.5 we show the long run impact of an increase in the interest rate when the income response is weak.In this case the correlation of output and the price level following the interest rate increase is negative, while in the latter case it is positive. Interdependence between supply and demand - which has been stressed above - is the root of this result. In traditional Keynesian macromodels demand shocks can explain only a positive correlation. Nominal shocks, in fact, affect only the AD curve, which shifts along an upward sloping

224

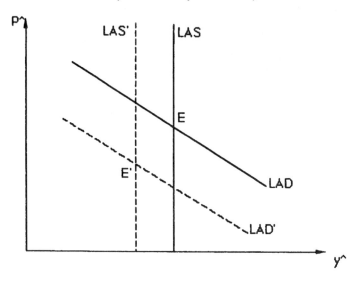

Figure 6.5

AS curve. A negative correlation between price and quantity can be explained only by a real (supply) shock. Here the nominal shock can produce either a positive or a negative correlation.

If firms are caught by surprise by changes of the interest rate (that is if there is a price shock):

• the (absolute value of the) short run interest elasticity of income is smaller than the long run elasticity if the long run interest elasticity of the price level is negative (weak income response: $p_1 > y_1$) .

• the short run interest elasticity of the price level is smaller than in the long run.
   In fact, it is easy to verify that:

$$\varepsilon_y^s = \varepsilon_y^l + \frac{y_2 \varepsilon_p^l}{1 + p_2 + y_2}$$

$$\varepsilon_p^s = \frac{\varepsilon_p^l}{1 + p_2 + y_2}$$

In Figure 6.6 we represent the unanticipated impact of an increase of the interest rate in the case of a weak income response.

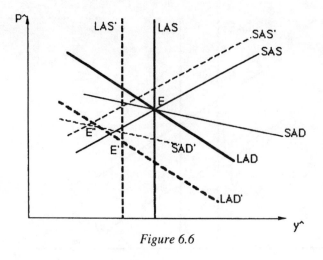

Figure 6.6

6. EXOGENOUS SUPPLY OF BANK LOANS

In this section, we explore the consequences of a credit regime characterized by:

(**A.17**) *Non accommodating lending policy.* Banks extend a given and constant amount of loans $(\overline{B})$: in this case the interest rate is endogenously determined by equilibrium on the credit market. In this new framework, we can write:

$$\frac{\overline{B}}{P} = \frac{2h(1-i)}{c(1+ih)} \tag{6.1}$$

Rewriting (6.1) as an interest rate equation, we get:

$$i = \frac{2h - \dfrac{\overline{B}}{P}c}{h\left(2 + \dfrac{\overline{B}}{P}c\right)} \tag{6.2}$$

That is the interest rate is a decreasing function of the real supply of bank loans and of the price surprise (a decrease of h - that is a positive price surprise - has a negative impact on the interest rate). Substituting equation (6.2) into equation (5.1), we obtain:

$$y = \frac{\dfrac{\overline{B}}{P}\left(2 + c\dfrac{\overline{B}}{P}\right)}{2h - c\dfrac{\overline{B}}{P}} \qquad (6.3)$$

From (6.3) it is clear that aggregate supply is function of the real supply of bank loans and of the price surprise.

Taking a log-linear approximation of (6.3), we can write:

$$(AS.II) \quad \hat{y} = y_0(\hat{\overline{B}} - \hat{P}) + y_1(\hat{P} - \hat{P}^e) + y_2$$

(AS.II) is the aggregate supply function in a regime of exogenous credit. When agents are not caught by surprise, aggregate supply boils down to:

$$(AS.II') \quad \hat{y} = y_0(\hat{\overline{B}} - \hat{P}) + y_2$$

(AS.II') is the equation of LAS which is a downward sloping straight line. In other words, long run aggregate supply is a decreasing function of the price level. This apparently counterintuitive result is due to the fact that an increase in the price level makes the stock of credit in real terms shrink, pushes up the interest rate and depresses economic activity because it increase the marginal production and bankruptcy costs.

(AS.II) is the equation of SAS: a straight line which can be either upward sloping (if $y_0 < y_1$) or downward sloping (if $y_0 > y_1$). A change in the price level, in fact, affects the price surprise and the real supply of credit in opposite directions. For example an unexpected increase of the price level makes the real burden of debt lighter, but the supply of bank loans shrinks in real terms, pushing up the interest rate. If the former (positive) effect prevails, SAS slopes upward. If the opposite is true, it slopes downward. The level of debt is a shift parameter for both LAS and SAS.

As to aggregate demand, we assume a standard quantity theory equation, in which logs can be written as follows :

$$(AD.II) \quad \hat{P} = \hat{\overline{M}} - \hat{y}$$

The RE equilibrium solutions are:

$$(RE.II.1) \quad \hat{y} = \frac{y_2 - y_0(\hat{\overline{M}} - \hat{\overline{B}})}{1 - y_0} + \frac{y_1}{(1 - y_0)(1 - y_0 + y_1)}[(\hat{\overline{M}} - E\hat{\overline{M}}) - y_0(\hat{\overline{B}} - E\hat{\overline{B}})]$$

(*RE.II.*1) $\hat{P} = \dfrac{\hat{\bar{M}} - y_0\hat{\bar{B}} - y_2}{1 - y_0} - \dfrac{y_1}{(1-y_0)(1-y_0+y_1)}[(\hat{\bar{M}} - E\hat{\bar{M}}) - y_0(\hat{\bar{B}} - E\hat{\bar{B}})]$

where $E\hat{\bar{M}}$ and $E\hat{\bar{B}}$ are the expected values of (the logs of) money and credit conditional on information available at the moment expectations are formed.

From the RE equilibrium solutions we derive the following proposition:

(**P.2**) *Long run policy effectiveness.* Even if perfectly anticipated, monetary policy affects real output if and only if it modifies the ratio of money to credit.

Proof. If $E\hat{\bar{M}} = \hat{\bar{M}}$ and $E\hat{\bar{B}} = \hat{\bar{B}}$, (RE.II.1) boils down to:

(RE.II.1') $\hat{y}_l^* = \dfrac{y_2 - y_0(\hat{\bar{M}} - \hat{\bar{B}})}{1 - y_0}$

According to (RE.II.1') long run output is a decreasing function of the ratio of money to credit.

The long run price level is:

(RE.II.2') $\hat{P}_l^* = \dfrac{\hat{\bar{M}} - y_0\hat{\bar{B}} - y_2}{1 - y_0}$

Even if it is perfectly anticipated, a specific shock (which hits either credit or money) affects long run output. A *general* shock (which hits *both* aggregates), on the contrary, affects long run output only if the reactions of credit and money are different. If the impact is the same on both aggregates, there will be no output response.

We can clarify the transmission mechanism of a nominal shock with the help of Figure 6.7 (in which we have assumed

$y_2 - y_0(\hat{\bar{M}} - \hat{\bar{B}}) > 0$ and $\hat{\bar{M}} - y_0\hat{\bar{B}} - y_2 > 0$).

Let's start from a long run equilibrium such as point A. A *specific* shock to *credit* - for instance an increase in the volume of loans that banks are willing to extend - pushes the interest rate down and stimulates production. If the money supply is unaffected, as it is the case since the shock is specific to credit, the price level is bound to fall: the LAS line shifts up along the negatively sloped AD line (see point B). A specific shock to credit is a *supply* shock which yields a negative correlation between output and the price level.

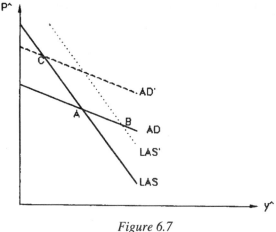

Figure 6.7

A *specific* shock to *money* - for instance an increase in liquidity made available to the public - boosts demand and pushes up the price level. If the volume of loans is unaffected, as it is the case when the shock is specific to money, the real supply of credit shrinks, the interest rate goes up and production falls: the AD line shifts up along the negatively sloped LAS curve (see point C). The output and price responses to a specific shock to money are of opposite sign with respect to the output and price responses to a specific shock to credit. Output and the price level, however, are negatively correlated. A specific shock to money is a demand shock which yields a negative correlation between output and the price level.

A *general* shock which hits *both* credit and money affects long run output only if the two aggregates respond in opposite directions or - in case the direction of the reaction to the shock is the same - if the magnitude of the impact is different.

In order to evaluate policy moves in the light of (P.2) we have to probe further into the process of credit and money supply determination. So far we have not been explicit on the determinants of money and credit: we have simply and crudely assumed that they are exogenous. We can assume that both aggregates are somehow under the control of the central bank.

First of all, the central bank decides the level of high powered money (banks' reserves). Moreover, since the money multiplier is equal to the reciprocal of the reserve ratio (say ρ)[11] and the credit multiplier is equal to the money multiplier minus 1, the central bank controls also the money and credit multipliers. In other words, the central bank can control both credit and money through base money and the required reserve ratio.

---

[11] In our framework, in fact, money coincides with deposits at banks.

229

The ratio of money to credit, in a log-linear specification, is equal to:

$$\overline{M} - \overline{B} = (\overline{H} + \chi_m) - (\overline{H} + \chi_b) = \chi_m - \chi_b$$

The difference is the log of the ratio of the credit multiplier to the money multiplier. The ratio being smaller than unity, the logarithm will be negative:

$$\chi_b - \chi_m = \log\left(\frac{1}{\rho} - 1\right) - \log\left(\frac{1}{\rho}\right) = \log(1-\rho) < 0$$

If a change in monetary policy is engineered by means of a change in base money and if this is perfectly anticipated, monetary policy does not affect output. In fact in this case the policy move is a *general* shock which has the same impact on both credit and money so that the difference between the two aggregates does not change.

The transmission mechanism of the monetary impulse in this case can be described as follows. The increase in liquidity made available to the public boosts demand and pushes up the price level. If the supply of bank loans were constant, the real supply of credit would shrink and production would fall (as in Figure 6.7, point C). This is not the case, however, because the supply of bank loans increases alongside liquidity. The real supply of credit (and of money) does not change and the same is true for the interest rate and aggregate output: the nominal shock is absorbed by a proportional change in the price level. In fact, taking into account the definitions of credit and money in terms of base money and the multipliers, (RE.II.1') and (RE.II.2') can be rewritten as:

(RE.II.1") $\quad \hat{y}_l^* = \dfrac{y_2 - y_0(\chi_m - \chi_b)}{1 - y_0}$

(RE.II.2") $\quad \hat{P}_l^* = \dfrac{\chi_m - y_0\chi_b - y_2}{1 - y_0} + \hat{\overline{H}}$

From the expression above it is clear that an increase of base money does not affect output while it translates into an identical increase of the price level: the elasticity of the price level to base money is one. Diagrammatically, this outcome is due to a simultaneous identical upward shift of the AD and LAS lines (Figure 6.8).

If a change in monetary policy is engineered by means of a reduction of the required reserve ratio, even if perfectly anticipated, monetary policy affects output: in this case the policy move is a general shock whose impact on credit is different from the impact on money. In order to evaluate the impact on long run equilibrium of a change of the required reserve ratio, first of all we

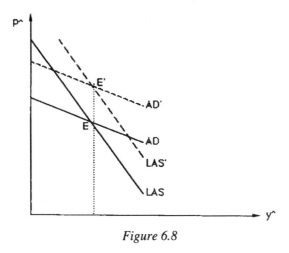

Figure 6.8

take the derivatives of the log of the credit and money multiplier with respect to the reserve ratio:

$$\frac{\partial \chi_b}{\partial \rho} = \frac{1}{(1-\rho)}\frac{\partial \chi_m}{\partial \rho} \qquad \text{where} \qquad \frac{\partial \chi_m}{\partial \rho} = -\frac{1}{\rho}$$

In other words, the reaction of the (log of the) credit multiplier to a given change in the required reserve ratio is a multiple of the reaction of the log of the money multiplier. This implies that a decrease in the reserve ratio leads to an upward shift of the AS curve greater than the shift of the AD curve. The new long run equilibrium will be characterized by a higher level of income while the reaction of the price level is a priori undecided.

The transmission mechanism of such a policy move as above can be described as follows. The volume of loans extended to firms increases and the interest rate goes down, stimulating output. If the supply of money were constant, the real supply of money would shrink and the price level would fall (as in Figure 6.7, point B). This is not necessarily true in this case, however, because liquidity also increases, boosting aggregate demand and supporting the price level. The sign of the long run price reaction to a given change of the policy parameter is *a priori* undecided: a quick inspection at equation (RE.II.2") confirms this intuition. If the increase in liquidity is smaller than the increase in bank loans, however, even if the price level increases, the real supply of credit increases leading to a positive output response. The nominal shock is absorbed partly by a change in the price level and partly by a change in output. Diagrammatically, this outcome is due to a simultaneous but *not identical* upward shift of the AD and LAS lines (Figure 6.9).

231

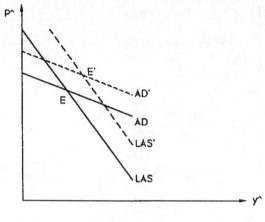

Figure 6.9

It is worth noting that a monetary policy move is a demand and supply shock at the same time because both demand and supply are influenced by monetary and financial factors. In the case of a change in base money output and the price level are incorrelated. In the case of a change of the policy parameter, output and the price level can be either positively or negatively correlated as we have shown above.

7. CONCLUSIONS

In this paper, we have presented and discuss ed some extensions of the basic framework put forward by G-S in 1993. We borrow from G-S some of the assumptions concerning the economy under scrutiny, but we discard one of their conjectures, namely that the real interest rate is given and constant. The implications of this assumption are far reaching: since changes in the stock of money are offset by changes of the nominal interest rate charged by banks to corporate clients, policy ineffectiveness is re-established through the Fisher hypothesis. Only in the short run will there be an output response insomuch as firms-borrowers are caught by surprise by the policy move. We dismiss the hypothesis of a given and constant *real* interest rate.

The most important result of the model in a regime of accommodating lending policy is the rejection of the policy ineffectiveness proposition even if rational expectations are fulfilled. In a sense this is a straightforward result since the nominal interest rate is a target of monetary policy and an argument of long run aggregate supply. If the central bank switch to an expansionary policy stance, pushing down the interest rate, firms' debt burden becomes lighter and they expand production.

The macroeconomic implications of a regime of exogenous credit supply are much more complicated. In this case the central bank controls monetary aggregates through the stock of high powered money and the required reserve ratio however, not the interest rate on bank loans, which is endogenously determined in the credit market equilibrium. A change in the stock of (high powered) money is neutral if anticipated but monetary policy can influence real output through the required reserve ratio. In fact, if the central bank pushes down the required reserve ratio given the stock of high powered money, the credit multiplier (the supply of bank loans) increases more than the money multiplier (the money supply), the real credit supply increases and firms expand production.

REFERENCES

Aaron, H.A. and Pechman, J.A. (eds.) (1981), *How Taxes Affect Economic Behaviour*, Washington D.C., Brookings Institution.

Altman, E.I. (1984), 'A Further Empirical Investigation of the Bankruptcy Cost Question', *Journal of Finance*, 39, 1067-1089

Blanchard, O. and S. Fischer, (1989), *Lectures on Macroeconomics*, MIT Press, Cambridge (Mass.).

Blanchard, O. and Kiyotaki, N. (1987), 'Monopolistic Competition and the Effects of Aggregate Demand', *American Economic Review*, 77, 647-66.

Delli Gatti, D. and M. Gallegati, (1997) 'Financial Constraints, Aggregate Supply and the Monetary Transmission mechanism', *Manchester School*.

Delli Gatti D., M.Gallegati, and L.Gardini, (1993), 'Investment Confidence, Corporate Debt and Income Fluctuations', *Journal of Economic Behaviour and Organization*.

Eckstein, O.and A. Sinai, (1986), 'The Mechanism of the Business Cycle in the post War Era', in R. Gordon (ed.).

Gilson, S.C. (1990), 'Bankruptcy, Boards, Banks and Blockholder: Evidence on Changes in Corporate Ownership and Control when Firms Default', *Journal of Financial Economics*, 27, 355-388.

Goodhart, C. (1989), *Money, Information and Uncertainty*, Cambridge (Mass.), MIT Press.

Gordon, R.H. (ed.) (1986), *The American Business Cycle*, Chicago, Chicago University Press

Gordon, R.H. and B.G. Malkiel, (1981), 'Corporation Finance' in H.A. Aaron and J.A. Pechman (eds.) (1981)

Greenwald, B. and J. Stiglitz, (1988), 'Imperfect Information, Finance Constraints and Business Fluctuations', in Kohn, M. and Tsiang, S.C. (eds.) (1988), 103-140.

Greenwald, B. and J. Stiglitz, (1990), 'Macroeconomic Models with Equity and Credit Rationing', in R. G. Hubbard, (ed.) (1990), 15-42.

Greenwald, B. and J. Stiglitz, (1993), 'Financial Market Imperfections and Business Cycles', *Quarterly Journal of Economics*, 108, pp. 77-114.

Greenwald, B., J. Stiglitz, and A. Weiss, (1984), 'Informational Imperfections in the Capital Markets and Macroeconomic Fluctuations', *American Economic Review*, 74, 194-200.

Hubbard, G.R. (ed.) (1990), *Financial Markets and Financial Crises*, NBER, Chicago.

Kaplan, S. and D. Reishus, (1990), 'Outside Directorship and Corporate Performance', *Journal of Financial Economics*, 27, 389-410.

King, R. and C. Plosser, (1984), 'Money, Credit and Prices in a Real Business Cycle', *American Economic Review*

Kohn, M. and S.C. Tsiang, (1988), *Finance Constraints, Expectations and Macroeconomics*, Oxford, Oxford University Press.

Mankiw G. and D. Romer (eds.) (1991), *New Keynesian Economics*, MIT Cambridge Press. (Mass).

Mishkin, F.S. (1984), 'The Real Interest Rate: A Multi-country Empirical Study', *Canadian Journal of Economics*, 2, pp.283-311.

Mishkin, F.S, (1991), 'Is the Fisher Effect for Real?' Graduate School of Business, Columbia University.

Minsky, H.P. (1975), *John Maynard Keynes*, New York, Columbia University Press

Minsky, H.P. (1982), *Can 'It' Happen Again? Essays on Instability and Finance*, Armonk N.Y., M.E. Sharpe.

Minsky, H.P. (1986), *Stabilizing an Unstable Economy*, New Haven, Yale University Press.

Moore, B. (1988), *Horizontalists Vs.Verticalists*, Cambridge, Cambridge University Press

Myers, S.C. and N.S. Majluf, (1984), 'Corporate Financing and Investment Decisions when Firms Have Information that Investors Do Not Have', *Journal of Financial Economics*, 13, 187-221.

Summers, L. (1983), 'The Nonadjustment of Nominal Interest Rates: A Study of the Fisher Effect', in J. Tobin (ed.) (1983)

Tobin, J. (1970), 'Post Hoc, Ergo Propter Hoc', *Quarterly Journal of Economics*

Tobin, J. (ed.) (1983), *Macroeconomics: Prices and Quantities*, Oxford, Basil Blackwell.

White, M.J. (1989), 'The Corporate Bankruptcy Decision', *Journal of Economic Perspectives*, 3, 129-151.

APPENDIX

(A.1) Properties of the *YA-AY equilibrium.* We assume the following adjustment mechanism:

$$dy = \frac{1-i}{ci} + \frac{1}{2}a - y$$
$$da = (1 - ih)y - a$$

The jacobian matrix of the system is:

$$J = \begin{pmatrix} -1 & \frac{1}{2} \\ 1 - ih & -1 \end{pmatrix}$$

$$\mathrm{tr}(J) = -2 < 0$$

Therefore

$$\det(J) = \frac{1}{2}(1 - ih) > 0$$

According to the Routh-Hurwicz conditions, in this case equilibrium is stable.

(A.2) *Properties of the AD-AS equilibrium. Endogenous credit supply.* We assume the following adjustment mechanism:

$$(A.2.1) \quad d\hat{y} = y_0 - y_1\hat{i} + y_2(\hat{P} - \hat{P}^e)$$
$$(A.2.2) \quad d\hat{P} = p_0 - p_1\hat{i} - p_2(\hat{P} - \hat{P}^e)$$

The Jacobian matrix of the system above is:

$$J = \begin{pmatrix} -1 & y_2 \\ -1 & -(p_2 + 1) \end{pmatrix}$$

$$\mathrm{tr}(J) = -(p_2 + 2) < 0$$
$$\det(J) = p_2 + y_2 + 1 > 0$$

According to the Routh-Hurwicz conditions, in this case equilibrium is stable.

In the long run $p_2 = y_2 = 0$. The stability of equilibrium is preserved under this restriction of the parameters.

(A.3) *Properties of the AD-AS equilibrium. Exogenous credit supply.*
We assume the following adjustment mechanism:

$$(A.3.1) \quad d\hat{y} = y_0(\hat{\bar{B}} - \hat{P}) + y_1(\hat{P} - \hat{P}^e) + y_2 - y$$

$$(A.3.2) \quad d\hat{P} = \hat{\bar{M}} - \hat{P} - \hat{y}$$

The Jacobian matrix is:

$$J = \begin{pmatrix} -1 & -y_0 + y_1 \\ -1 & -1 \end{pmatrix}$$

$$\mathrm{tr}(J) = -2 < 0$$
$$\det(J) = 1 + y_0 - y_1$$

It is easy to verify that:

$$\det(J) > 0 \quad \text{if} \quad y_1 - y_0 > -1$$

The determinant is positive if the SAS line is upward sloping or if - being downward sloping - it is steeper than the AD line (on the $(P, \hat{y})$ plane). According to the Routh-Hurwicz conditions, in this case equilibrium is stable. If $\det(J) < 0$ equilibrium is a saddle point.

In the long run. The determinant is positive (equilibrium is stable) if LAS is steeper than AD. If $\det(J) < 0$ equilibrium is a saddle point.

Index

game theory, in models 117, 118
Gardini, L. 45, 54
Garretsen, H. 28
GDP 62
Geanakopolos, J.D. 28
general equilibrium 192-9
  new model 126
  temporary general equilibrium 91-8
Gertler, M. 33, 39, 86
Gilchrist, S. 86
Gilson, S.C. 213
Gintis, H. 117
Goodhart, C. 222
goods markets 129
Goodwin, R.M. 55
Gordon, R.H. 213
Gordon, R.J. 2, 20, 58, 61, 110, 112
Grandmont, J.M. 55, 83, 91
Graziani, A. 43, 121
Greenwald, B. 18, 35, 43, 45, 49, 51,
  54, 56, 58, 60, 61, 64, 81, 82, 85,
  87, 89, 91, 93, 95, 97, 116, 119,
  120, 121, 124, 126, 130, 131, 132,
  208
Greenwald-Stiglitz models 96, 98, 101,
  232
Grossman, H. 4
Grossman, S. 5, 146

Hahn, F.H. 27, 85, 109, 112, 204
Hall, R.E. 57
Haltiwanger, J. 31, 59
Hargreaves Heap, S. 20, 116
Hart, O. 14, 40, 118, 120, 146
Heller, W.P. 14, 30
Hellwig, M. 42, 87, 148
Hicks, J.R. 4, 83, 85, 91, 107, 108, 120,
  121, 132
Hicks-Modigliani-Klein formula 1
hierarchical relations 146
Hodgman, D.R. 41
Holden, S. 200
Holmstrom, B. 40, 120
Hubbard, R.G. 33, 38, 60, 62, 125
hysteresis 27, 61

imperfect competition, and nominal
  rigidities 9-32
imperfect information 213-14
impulse-propagation methodology 54

incentive compatability 149
income fluctuations, and deterministic
  cycles 54-7
index-linking, in New Keynesian
  Economics 59
inflationary expectations, and money
  growth 95-6
information economics 5
information theory 118
Innes, R. 131, 142, 143, 145, 148, 149,
  150, 154, 181
insider-outsider models 25, 27, 117, 192
interest rates 45, 52, 107, 108-9, 209
  effect on output and price 98
investment
  in model 131
  theory 61
investment theory, of New Keynesian
  Economics, West Coast stream
  (NKEiai) 131
involuntary unemployment 50, 106,
  107, 111, 113, 116, 186
  and labour market imperfections
  21-8
IS-LM model 1, 2, 82
  revision 3

Jackman, R. 24, 186, 190
Jacobian matrix 235
Jaffee, D. 39, 41, 120, 142
Jensen, M.C. 35, 120
John, A. 14, 30

Kahneman, D. 30
Kaldor, N. 9, 222
Kaldor-Hicks-Goodwin methodology 54
Kanatas, G. 143
Kaplan, S. 213
Keeton, W.R. 40, 123
'Keynes effect' 107-8
Keynes, J.M. 64, 119
  General Theory 8, 91, 95, 106, 107,
  109, 111, 132
  limits of macroeconomic legacy
  106-12
  see also New Keynesian Economics
Keynesian economics 3
'Keynesianism' 111
Kindleberger, C.P. 33
King, R. 222